*Fly/Ride*
# Europe
## 1987

# *Fly/Ride* Europe 1987

**Ed Perkins**
and
the Editors of
Consumer Reports Books

Consumers Union
Mount Vernon, New York

Special thanks to Dennis P. Barker of Consumers Union, Mount Vernon, New York, and Margaret Heraty in London for providing updates and original research for this 1987 edition.

Copyright © 1987 by Consumers Union of United States, Inc.
Mount Vernon, New York 10553
All rights reserved including the right of reproduction
in whole or in part in any form
First printing, March 1987
ISBN: 0-89043-070-5
ISSN: 0883-0649
Manufactured in the United States of America

*Fly/Ride Europe 1987* is a Consumer Reports Book published by Consumers Union, the nonprofit organization that publishes *Consumer Reports*, the monthly magazine of test reports, product Ratings, and buying guidance. Established in 1936, Consumers Union is chartered under the Not-For-Profit Corporation Law of the State of New York.

The purposes of Consumers Union, as stated in its charter, are to provide consumers with information and counsel on consumer goods and services, to give information on all matters relating to the expenditure of the family income, and to initiate and to cooperate with individual and group efforts seeking to create and maintain decent living standards.

Consumers Union derives its income solely from the sale of *Consumer Reports* and other publications. In addition, expenses of occasional public service efforts may be met, in part, by nonrestrictive, noncommercial contributions, grants, and fees. Consumers Union accepts no advertising or product samples and is not beholden in any way to any commercial interest. Its Ratings and reports are solely for the use of the readers of its publications. Neither the Ratings nor the reports may be used in advertising or for any commercial purpose. Consumers Union will take all steps open to it to prevent such uses of its material, its name, or the name of *Consumer Reports*.

# Contents

Preface to the 1987 Edition     vii
Introduction     1

**Part I: Guide to North Atlantic Air Fares**
1. Transatlantic Overview     7
2. Major Airlines     31
3. Low-Fare Airlines     45
4. Charters     50
5. Bulk Fares     64
6. Flexible-Schedule Travel     70
7. Discount Tickets     79
8. Quality Air Travel     91
9. Other Possibilities     95
10. Stopovers and Connections     104
11. Projected 1987 Transatlantic Air Fares     108

**Part II: Getting Around Europe**
12. Internal European Transportation Options     137
13. Rail Travel     149
14. Rental and Lease Cars     180
15. Flying Around Europe     199
16. Buses and Ferries     213
17. Urban Transportation     230
18. Hotels and Tour Packages     265
19. Airport and Airline Security     280

Bon Voyage!     283

Index     285

# Preface to the 1987 Edition

The European countries and the transatlantic airlines survived last summer's severe decline in tourism, the "terrorism slump," and are looking to 1987 as a year to recoup. Their expectations for 1987 may be well founded. Unless some new disaster strikes, all the signs point toward a good year for European travel.

If any prediction can be made at all, it's a familiar one. Costs of travel to Europe and within Europe will probably be up a little. Some of the increase will be due to continued inflation in European countries. Some could be due to further decline in the U.S. dollar—a decline abetted by the U.S. government feeling increased pressure to lower the U.S. balance-of-payments deficits and letting the value of the dollar against foreign currencies slide. We've also probably seen the end of declining fuel prices. Changes in price this year are more likely to be in the upward direction, putting pressure on the airlines to raise their fares and possibly boosting the expenses of those who choose to tour Europe by car.

Despite European Common Market (E.E.C.) actions, airfares within Europe probably will not drop much. Don't hold your breath waiting until U.S.-style airfare wars break out on the Continent. While several governments there have adopted policies designed to foster more competitive inter-European air transportation, progress toward real competition—and the lower fares it can bring—is glacially slow.

Just as we were completing this book, People Express and New York Air were absorbed into Continental. Ultimately, the three lines will operate as a single system. Continental promises this system will be "the biggest low-fare airline in the country," but fully integrating three airlines this large will take some time. In absorbing People Express's international routes, Continental will probably start to make some changes. Fare cuts would be surprising, a few new fare routes would not.

But a lot could happen by summer. If a low-fare line looks like a good alternative for you, be sure to check with Continental.

In sum, 1987 is shaping up as a fairly uneventful year. Airfares and other travel costs will be somewhat higher than they were last year and don't look for any spectacular price cuts or highly innovative service ideas. After the recent ups and downs of oil crises, terrorist attacks, and airline bankruptcies, an uneventful year may not be such a bad thing. Those bound for Europe can set aside their concern about the more drastic contingencies and concentrate on having a good time.

—Ed Perkins
*January 1987*

# Introduction

*Why a European Guidebook
Only for Transportation?*

Why do you need a guidebook that covers only transportation to Europe and within Europe? With all those general guides to Europe, that's a good question. And the answer is simple: This book can save you hundreds of dollars. For example, it tells you how to:

- Save as much as $200 on your air ticket to Europe—compared with what the airlines tell you is their cheapest fare.
- Save up to $100 a week on a European automobile rental, by knowing which rental companies have the best deals in each country.
- Pay as much as $100 less than Eurailpass for just as many miles of rail travel—by using individual tickets or the much-cheaper passes from individual countries.

Even good, professional travel agents aren't always aware of all the pros and cons of the available transportation options. It's easy—maybe a little too easy—for them simply to call up the cheapest fare or rental in the computer and book it for you on the spot.

But most of the cheaper options aren't in the computers—and even the best agents can't always keep up with all the fare options that keep coming into the marketplace. While it's usually a good idea to buy through a travel agent, you, the traveler, should be in charge of the transaction. That means know what you want!

Many agents may be unaware of the important quality differences among the various major low-fare and charter lines.

Even the best of Economy-Class air service is at the margin of unacceptable comfort and service; avoiding the very worst services in the market can make a big difference in your travel enjoyment.

Other guidebooks do a very limited job. Most guides focus mainly on sightseeing, accommodations, and restaurants—they often oversimplify the complicated transatlantic air-fares questions. Many don't mention fares from cities other than New York. The travel industry also seems bent on selling Eurailpass as the universal solution to local transportation, which it is not, rather than as just one of several options.

The first part of this book deals with the various types of air service available across the Atlantic. It covers air fares in much greater detail than you'll find anywhere else—the officially published fares plus some surprising ways to buy air services for less than the published fares. It also covers the more important quality aspects of transatlantic air travel.

The second part deals with travel within Europe, by all the major modes: air, rail, automobile, bus, and ferry. Emphasis is on showing you how to travel the way you prefer at minimum cost.

The book does not cover complete tour packages in great detail. After all, it's not difficult to compare published prices for complete holiday packages. However, chapters 6 and 18 list some ways to save money by buying complete package tours in a normal fashion or on a last-minute basis. And, of course, the information on airline convenience, comfort, and contingencies applies equally to independent travelers as to those on package tours.

Finally, this guide does not cover the absolute minimum-cost travel mode characterized by hitchhiking, bicycling, backpacking, "gypsy" bus service, and special student flights and fares. This mode of travel is the almost exclusive province of young people and is extensively covered in a specialized body of guidebooks geared to the student/youth market.

But if you're part of the "mainstream" of travelers—of any age—interested in obtaining mainstream comfort, quality, and convenience at minimum cost, this transportation guidebook should help you. It will unscramble what's going on with the air fares; what the total range of local travel options is. It's a key to possibly big-dollar savings and a substantially more enjoyable travel experience.

This book can help you both before and during your trip—whether vacation or business. It's useful during the earliest planning stages to help you find the best way to get to Europe. And you can take it along to help you with your travels once you're there. Use whichever series of destination guidebooks appeals to you—this guide goes well with all of them.

# Part I

## Guide to North Atlantic Air Fares

# 1

# Transatlantic Overview

*A Framework for Comparing Transatlantic Air Travel Options*

Getting there may well have been "half the fun" in the days of leisurely steamship travel, but in these days of mass-market jet travel, getting there involves, more often than not, a lot of hassle, especially if you travel during the busiest seasons. So, when it comes to transportation, plan defensively! Good planning and research can ease most of the worst travel problems.

Objectives

As the first step in transportation planning, you should clarify for yourself—and for your travel agent, if you're dealing with one—exactly what you want for your transportation dollars. While it's impossible for anyone else to identify your own detailed personal objectives, chances are that your major concerns will stack up something like the following list:

1. to minimize travel costs—either absolutely or in relation to the standards of quality you require
2. to minimize your total en route travel time and the inevitable hassles of travel
3. to maximize the levels of service and comfort you'll experience during your transatlantic crossing, within the constraints of the fares you're willing to pay
4. to minimize avoidable travel risks—those unhappy surprises that cost you either time or money

> Shelley Berman's classic definition of air travel, "hours of boredom interspersed with moments of stark terror," obviously overstates the apprehensions of flight. But if "boring" is the worst thing you can say about your flight—you've had a good one.

For most people, setting objectives means accepting some tradeoffs. You can't expect the same option to give both top-quality service and low prices. You may opt for the absolute rock-bottom price, regardless of convenience and comfort. Or, you may prefer slightly higher-cost options that provide baseline convenience and comfort levels. Perhaps you'll go for considerably higher quality, if you can get it for a good price.

But, wherever you stand, don't start to do any planning, undertake any research, or make any other decisions about any aspect of your trip until you've identified your objectives.

## Transportation Options

Since low costs of some kind are probably an important objective for you, it's a safe bet that you're among the huge majority of people who will use one of the three most popular, best-established approaches to minimizing air fare:

1. an Economy-Class promotional fare on one of the major airlines
2. one of the specialized low-fare airlines
3. a charter

But three other, newer approaches to low air fares will be promoted and sold much more widely in 1987 than in prior years, and you may well find one or the other to offer substantial reductions below the lowest of the better-known alternatives:

1. **bulk** or **net fares,** on either major or low-fare airlines, purchased from a consolidator or tour operator rather than directly from the airline

2. **discounted tickets,** on either major or low-fare airlines, obtained through a discounter or a broker of "last-minute" travel bargains
3. **unconventional ticket sources,** especially frequent-traveler coupons

You may be a member of the minority more concerned with comfort and service than with rock-bottom price; you'll use one of the higher-quality options:

1. **Business Class** on a major airline
2. **First Class** on a major or low-fare airline
3. a **Business-Class** or **First-Class charter**

If you're thinking about going a long way into the Eastern Mediterranean—or if you have to make lots of stops along the way—you may find it cheaper to use one of the special **round-the-world excursion fares** than to take the ordinary round trip.

Finally, if you can't comply with the various restrictions and uncertainties that accompany most low-fare deals—or if you haven't done your homework—you'll end up paying full-fare Economy Class.

Your key planning question, of course, is how to select your best bet in transatlantic transportation. Given the proper facts, it's relatively easy. Those four basic travel planning objectives translate directly into the "four c's" of evaluating transatlantic transportation: **cost, convenience, comfort, and contingencies.** For just about any traveler, the final selection requires a balance of these four factors, weighed and adjusted in accordance with each traveler's individual needs, attitudes, and priorities.

---

In their sales materials, airlines usually use full-fare Economy Class as the standard of comparison. The reason is obvious: when compared to full-fare Economy, APEX and similarly priced fares can be touted as fabulous bargains. But full-fare Economy is really an artificial standard, since no cost-conscious vacation or business travelers should actually have to use it.

## Comparing Costs

You should use the cost of an advance-purchase Economy-Class Excursion on a major airline (see page 31 for a definition of major airline) as the norm against which to measure all others. This type of fare is usually called APEX or Super APEX for transatlantic flights (domestic Super Savers are essentially the same). It's the best standard for three reasons:

1. it's the most widely used type of ticket for transatlantic vacation travel
2. it's available for virtually all U.S.-to-Europe routes
3. unless you opt for a high-quality service, it represents the ceiling on what you should pay—the more interesting low-fare options are all cheaper than Super APEX

**General Price Levels**

Here's approximately how these major options will stack up for 1987, with APEX or Super APEX as the standard of comparison pegged at an index of 100 percent.

| | |
|---|---|
| APEX | 100% |
| Full-Fare Economy | 150–250% |
| Business Class | 150–350% |
| First Class | 300–600% |
| Low-Fare Airline | 65–85% |
| Charter/Bulk Fare | 60–80% |
| First-Class Charter | 90–120% |

Specific 1986 price levels for individual routes are shown in chapter 11; 1987 fares, while not available at press time, are expected to be in this range. New this year are user fees totalling $13 added to the price of each ticket from the United States to Europe and back.

On some routes, you'll even find minor differences in fare levels among various airlines for the same fare options. But you'll find substantially greater differences in service quality, comfort, and convenience factors. Most fares will be competitive: quality factors will usually dictate your final airline/schedule choice once you've zeroed in on your preferred fare option.

## Geographical Variation Within the United States

At one time, all U.S.-to-Europe fares were "constructed" by combining a standard fare from New York to the European city with a domestic add-on from each U.S. city to New York. While that system still applies to some types of fares, it is no longer universal, especially for the cheapest tickets. New nonstop services between Europe and cities across the United States to the West Coast have given rise to special direct fares that are substantially lower than those determined by the earlier add-on system. However, an airline that offers connecting service through New York, for example, could construct its fare this way because it's the easiest method. Get more than one fare quote.

It would be ideal to show fare comparisons for all major U.S. cities. Instead, specific fare comparisons are presented for four geographically representative U.S. gateways: New York, Chicago, Texas (either Dallas or Houston, depending on specific direct routes), and the West Coast (with fares that, in most cases, apply to both Los Angeles and San Francisco).

## Seasonal Variations

Demand for transatlantic air travel is quite seasonal. The main peak period is in midsummer—mid-June through mid-September. There's a secondary peak over the year-end holiday season. For years, airlines and tour operators have used seasonal pricing as a way to fill planes during the rest of the year.

At least three distinct seasonal pricing levels will be used on most transatlantic routes during 1987. Most people will be traveling in midsummer, so peak-season fare levels—specifically peak-season APEX or Super APEX—are the most realistic bases for comparison. Again, with peak-season APEX as the norm, at an index of 100 percent, the seasons and their associated fare levels will probably vary as follows:

| | | |
|---|---|---|
| Peak | May through September* | 100% |
| Shoulder | Spring, Fall, Dec. 10–24 | 80%–90% |
| Basic | Rest of year | 60%–85% |

*Depending on your destination.

Specific seasonal dates vary by route. In addition, some routes call for a special top-price "peak of peaks" mini-season in midsummer; others include both "low-basic" and "high-basic" variants. Finally, supply/demand balances are fine-tuned on some routes with differential pricing for midweek trips (lower) and weekend trips (higher). Specific dates—which vary among specific routes—are shown in chapter 11.

**Restrictions**

Obviously, a very large share of the total vacation travel market is price-sensitive: the higher the prices, the fewer the travelers. So the airlines have to offer low fares to the vacation market. On the other hand, airlines don't want all their passengers—especially business travelers—to pay bottom dollar if they can be charged much higher fares.

The answer? Simple—airlines have addressed the vacation market by placing various restrictions on the vacation-market fares that make them less appealing or useful to business travelers: advance purchase; round-trip purchase requirements; minimum/maximum length-of-stay; prohibitions on stopovers,

---

**At the risk of restating the obvious—virtually everything about your European trip will be better if you can travel off-season. Lower air fares are just the beginning. Off-season flights are sometimes less crowded, therefore more comfortable; service is better. Everything else is less crowded, too—museums, churches, the great natural wonders. Europe's real cultural programs are in full swing—the ones put on for the Europeans rather than the tourists. Hotels—especially in the countryside—are much less crowded; you seldom need reservations. The weather is usually better, and you can save lots of money in the warmer-climate countries because you won't have to stay in top-price hotels in order to find air-conditioned rooms. If you're planning a trip to Europe for July or August, the first thing you should do is to consider rescheduling it for May, June, September, or October!**

standby status, and the like. Business travelers generally find these restrictions too inconvenient or too uncertain for their needs. However, in most cases, only the restrictions and fares are different—all Economy-Class passengers, regardless of the type of fares they pay, fly in the same cabins and (usually) receive the same in-flight amenities.

Restrictions are most stringent on the major airlines—the lines that have the most to lose if business travelers switch to low-fare services. Still, even low-fare airlines and charters have some restrictions—more often than not imposed by governments to "protect" the major airlines from full open-market competition.

Many of the lowest-price options—especially on the major airlines—are **excursion fares.** That term simply means that a round-trip ticket is required. In most cases, an **open-jaw route** is also acceptable. An open-jaw itinerary also requires purchase of two transatlantic flight segments, but with a difference: you can either fly from a U.S. city to one city in Europe and return to the same U.S. city from another city in Europe, or you can fly from one U.S. city to Europe and return from the same European city to a different U.S. City.

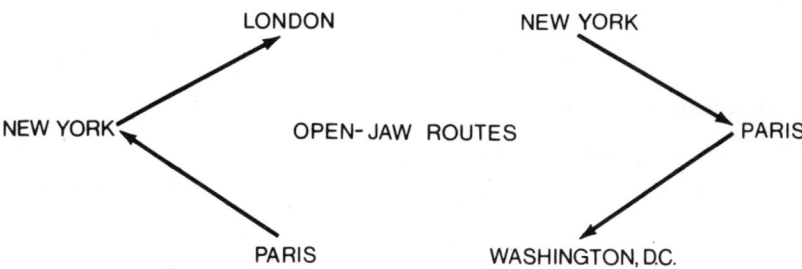

In an open jaw, transportation between the two European or U.S. gateways can be either by surface transportation or by airline, with a separate ticket.

### Status Fares

Some types of air fares include special lower-cost provisions for travelers of special status. They most usually apply to children and youth/student categories. On occasion, some lines have also offered special consideration for seniors, the military, and the clergy. The availability of these special-status deals varies by type of fare and, in some cases, by country of destination.

Families including special-status individuals therefore face even greater complexities of choice. For example, some types of low-cost fares provide special fares for children (e.g., APEX), others do not (e.g., most charters). Thus, the total transportation bill for a family of two adults and two children might be less with APEX than with a charter, despite the fact that the individual adult charter fares are substantially below APEX.

Comparing Convenience

The two main air-travel convenience factors are routes and schedules. While you can't calculate a numerical convenience index, you're obviously better off with nonstop or minimum-stop flights and convenient arrival and departure times. You might think it would be easy to evaluate these convenience factors, but even the terms used by the travel industry to describe the nature of a particular flight may not convey the realities you encounter.

**Route Factors**

For starters, a person might assume that a flight advertised as "nonstop" doesn't stop anywhere between the departure and arrival cities. But some airlines and tour operators may neglect to tell you that some supposedly nonstop flights from the West Coast can't make it to Europe without stopping for fuel at Bangor, for example. This problem is most prevalent with charters. Only under extremely rare conditions are major-airline flights unable to keep to planned truly nonstop schedules.

Most people might assume that a "direct" or "through" flight connects two cities without change of plane. Again, a reasonable assumption isn't always correct. Airlines—even the best of the major carriers—frequently apply a single flight number to what is actually a connection involving a change of planes. Where you have a choice, a genuine "through" or "direct" flight is clearly a better bet than one requiring you to gather up all your carry-on belongings, get off, go to another gate, line up, get reseated and finally resettled.

Not much can be misconstrued about "connecting flights," and airlines tend to promote them accurately. Again, however, there are connections that are more or less tolerable. Most airlines try to minimize walking distance within gateway airports for connections with their own flights. For that reason, single-airline connections can be much more convenient than connections between two airlines, especially at such monster airports as Kennedy or O'Hare. On the other hand, some charter programs involve a domestic flight within the United States on a scheduled airline to New York combined with a charter between New York and Europe; these "connections" often entail long distances between arrival and departure gates or terminals at Kennedy and layovers that can stretch out for many benumbing hours.

**Schedule Factors**

Schedule convenience is more subjective than some of the other convenience factors. Most travelers don't like to leave or arrive in the wee hours of the morning; many find it inconvenient to have to leave or arrive during local rush hours. Beyond these obvious factors, however, traveler opinion seems to vary—some travelers like to leave or arrive early in the day, others in the afternoon; some travelers prefer day flying, others prefer to save vacation time by flying at night.

In any event, transatlantic travelers don't have much flexibility when it comes to schedules. Because of the combination of distance, flight time, and time-zone differences, most transatlantic schedules follow the same pattern:

- eastbound flights leave the United States in late afternoon or early evening and arrive in Europe the following morning
- westbound flights leave Europe late morning or early afternoon and arrive in the United States the same afternoon or early evening—thanks to a five- to eight-hour time-zone change

Virtually all the airlines—major, low-fare, and charter—conform to this general pattern. It's convenient and efficient for the airlines. It's not so convenient for travelers: every day, planeloads of tourists arrive in European cities, often early in the morning, and sometimes hours before the departing tourists have checked out of their hotels. What veteran traveler can ever forget those hotel lobbies in London or Paris filled with red-eyed, rumpled arrivals, sitting with (or often on) their luggage, catatonically waiting for their rooms to be prepared?

Comparing Comfort

Comfort depends mainly on two factors: how full your flight is, and how roomy your seat is—width and legroom.

You might, at first, assume that neither of these comfort factors is subject to your control. Fortunately, you can do something about ensuring a relatively comfortable flight.

**Load Factors**

Frequent travelers know that there's nothing like an empty seat next to them to ensure a comfortable flight. Even a plane with the most overstuffed high-density seating is endurable when you can spread a few of your articles—and a few parts of your anatomy—into the adjoining seat. Personal service is also much better on flights with light loads. In fact, whenever you hear a frequent traveler proclaim that he or she had a "good flight," chances are ten to one that it wasn't more than about 60 percent full.

At least some of the time, you can do something to increase your odds of an uncrowded flight. You can choose to travel on a day when you'll be relatively sure of lighter than average loads. Midweek days are typically lighter than weekend days. Off-season is a better bet than peak-season. In some cases—especially if you're booking near your departure date—your travel agent can check with the airline to determine which of several alternative flights will be the most lightly loaded. Don't hesitate to ask for this information, either—remember that the airline would rather have you fly on a slow day than when it's booked solid.

**Cabin Comfort**

Infrequent travelers are often surprised to learn that all Economy-Class airline seats don't provide the same amount of room.

Certainly, you'd seldom find out from the airlines—their promotion would lead you to believe that they all offer fabulous luxury in seating, and almost no carriers are really open and accurate about their seating standards.

In fact, there are substantial differences among various airlines in the width of seats and in the legroom they provide—it's strictly a matter of individual airline policy. By selecting one of the airlines that offers above-average comfort—or, at least, avoiding those that fly the worst cattle cars—you can do a lot to make your flight more pleasant.

Airlines' seat-width options are limited by the cabin dimensions of the airplanes they fly. In general, the number of Economy-Class seats per row in a wide-body airplane can be only one of two alternatives; in a narrow-body airplane, the number of seats per row is usually the same for all airlines.

The maximum Economy-Class seat widths for the types of airplanes used across the Atlantic fall into four width groups, as indicated in Table 1. Widths shown in the table are measured between armrest centers—indicative of the maximum side-to-side space available. Some airlines, however, use narrower seats in some or all locations, either to allow middle seats to be wider than outside seats, to provide wider aisles, or to standardize seating among different airplane types.

Do width differences of a half inch or so seem trivial? Don't believe it! When even the best Economy-Class seating is very tight, only a half inch less space for each nine or ten passengers in a row noticeably crowds everybody.

Front-to-rear space is important at two levels—literally. Legroom is obviously important. So, too, is chest-level room for reading, eating, and working. Front-to-rear space is measured

**Table 1  Maximum Aircraft Seat Widths**

| Aircraft type | Average number of seats per row | Maximum width (inches) |
|---|---|---|
| DC-10 | 9 | 20 |
| L-1011 | 9 | 20 |
| 767 | 7 | 20 |
| 747 | 10 | 19.5 |
| DC-8 | 6 | 19 |
| DC-10 | 10 | 18.5 |
| L-1011 | 10 | 18.5 |

> In most airplanes, a small number of seats provide substantially greater legroom than average or typical seats. Experienced travelers often ask for seats in rows by doors and emergency exits, for example, which normally have greater pitch than those in the rest of the plane. Some travelers prefer bulkhead seats (the front row in a cabin)—many provide extra space, and even when they don't, there's nobody right in front of you to lean his or her seat back into your lap. On the other hand, you often can't see the movie from some of these exit-row seats, and many are right opposite noisy galleys; travelers with babies are often assigned to the bulkhead rows. In any event, there aren't enough of these especially roomy seats to go around. Your best bet is to choose a flight where seating throughout the plane is reasonably comfortable.

by **pitch,** which is the interval at which seat rows are installed. Pitch is not governed by airplane type; all modern commercial airplanes have seat tracks that allow airlines to adjust pitch in increments of 1 inch or less to suit individual policies.

The effective difference between the roomiest (36-inch) and tightest (30- and 31-inch) pitch is moderated through use of thin-back seats in the tighter installations. Compared with seats built, say, fifteen years ago, modern thin-back seats provide an effective legroom improvement of 3 to 4 inches. But airlines usually neglect to mention that their new thin-back seats do almost nothing to improve chest-level room. Moreover, most of their competitors with 33- or 34-inch pitch are also likely to be using thin-back seats if the seating is fairly new. While you'll probably find a new thin-back installation at 33 inches to be every bit as comfortable as the average normal Economy-Class seating at 34 inches, you'll find 31- and 32-inch pitch, even with the thin-back seats, to be noticeably more crowded.

Seat arrangement also affects comfort. Being wedged into a middle seat between two other travelers is extremely uncomfortable, and some arrangements result in a higher percentage of wedged-in passengers than others. Table 2 shows the max-

**Table 2  Wedged-In Passengers**

| Seats per row | Arrangement | Maximum load with no wedged-in passengers | Percent of wedged-in passengers at 90% load |
|---|---|---|---|
| 9 | 2–5–2 | 89% | 3% |
| 7 | 2–3–2 | 86 | 4 |
| 10 | 3–4–3 | 70 | 20 |
| 6 | 3–3 | 67 | 23 |

imum load factor (in percent) that can be accommodated in each commonly used Economy-Class seating arrangement without wedging anyone in between two others, as well as the percent of passengers who are wedged in when the airplane is 90 percent full.

When airplanes run 80 to 100 percent full, as is often the case during the peak season, the nine-across (most scheduled-airline DC-10s and L-1011s) and seven-across (scheduled-airline 767s) arrangements give you a better chance to avoid being wedged in than the ten-across (747s and many charter DC-10s and L-1011s) or six-across (DC-8s) arrangements—or of sitting next to someone else who is wedged in, which is almost as bad.

---

**IATA (International Air Transport Association) is the airline/government cartel that has diligently worked for high fares and restrictions and against meaningful competition. Although it makes occasional gestures in the consumer interest, its actions are almost always anti-consumer.**

**Take, for example, the question of seating. Several years ago, IATA decreed that airlines should provide Economy-Class passengers with no more than 34-inch pitch legroom, and seats no wider than those cited above. IATA actually described this limit-the-quality dictum as serving the public interest. There were no minimum levels of allowable comfort; the decree gave IATA members the freedom to pack you in as tightly as they like.**

*Consumer Reports Travel Letter* developed a composite seat-comfort index that combines the effects of seat width, pitch, and arrangement into a single measure. Table 3 shows seating data, including the *CRTL* Comfort Index, for all of the airplanes expected to fly between the United States and Europe this summer.

**Table 3   Transatlantic Airline Seating**

| Airline | Aircraft | Seat pitch (inches) | Seats across | CRTL Comfort Index |
|---|---|---|---|---|
| Aer Lingus | 747 | 33 | 10 | 81 |
| Air France | 747 | 34 | 10 | 85 |
| Air India | 747 | 34 | 10 | 85 |
| Air New Zealand | 747 | 34 | 10 | 85 |
| Alia | 747 | 34 | 10 | 85 |
|  | L-1011 | 33 | 9 | 88 |
| Alitalia | 747 | 32 | 10 | 77 |
| American | DC-10 | 33 | 9 | 88 |
| Balair[a] | DC-10 | 32 | 9 | 81 |
| Br. Airways | 747[b] | 36 | 9 | 100 |
|  | 747[c] | 33 | 10 | 81 |
| Br. Caledonian | 747 | 34 | 10 | 85 |
|  | DC-10 | 34 | 9 | 92 |
| Condor[a] | DC-10 | 32 | 10 | 69 |
| Continental | DC-10 | 32 | 9 | 84 |
| Delta | L-1011 | 32 | 9 | 84 |
| Eastern | DC-10 | 34 | 9 | 92 |
| Egyptair | 747 | 34 | 10 | 85 |
| El Al | 747 | 34 | 10 | 85 |
| Finnair | DC-10 | 34 | 9 | 92 |
| Hawaiian[d] | L-1011 | 32 | 10 | 69 |
| Iberia | 747 | 34 | 10 | 85 |
|  | DC-10 | 34 | 9 | 92 |
| Icelandair | DC-8 | 32 | 6 | 72 |
| JAT | DC-10 | 33 | 9 | 88 |
| KLM | 747 | 34 | 10 | 85 |
| Kuwait | 747 | 32 | 10 | 77 |
| LTU[a] | L-1011 | 34 | 10 | 77 |
| Lufthansa | 747 | 34 | 10 | 85 |
|  | DC-10 | 34 | 9 | 92 |
| Martinair[a] | DC-10 | 32 | 10 | 69 |
| Northwest | 747 | 34 | 10 | 85 |
| Olympic | 747 | 34 | 10 | 85 |

| | | | | |
|---|---|---|---|---|
| Pakistan | DC-10 | 33 | 9 | 88 |
| Pan American | 747 | 33 | 10 | 81 |
| SAS | 747 | 34 | 10 | 85 |
| | DC-10 | 34 | 9 | 92 |
| Sabena | 747 | 34 | 10 | 85 |
| | DC-10 | 34 | 9 | 92 |
| Spantax[a] | DC-10 | 31 | 10 | 65 |
| Swissair | 747 | 34 | 10 | 85 |
| | DC-10 | 34 | 9 | 92 |
| TAP | L-1011 | 33 | 9 | 88 |
| Tower[d] | 747 | 34 | 10 | 85 |
| Total Air[a] | L-1011 | 32 | 9 | 84 |
| TWA | 747 | 34 | 10 | 85 |
| | L-1011 | 34 | 9 | 92 |
| | 767 | 32 | 7 | 84 |
| Virgin Atlantic | 747 | 31 | 10 | 73 |

[a] Charter airline
[b] Convertible Business-Economy cabins
[c] Economy cabins
[d] Scheduled airline with extensive transatlantic charter service

**The Comfort Index**

Seat-pitch and configuration data were obtained from the airlines. However, because measuring methods among airlines are inconsistent, and because width measurements between outside and inside seats vary in many installations, seat-width measurements are based on technical information supplied by aircraft manufacturers.

The number of seats per row (as discussed in the text and used in the configuration calculations) refers to typical rows in the center portions of the aircraft cabin. While there are fewer seats per row in the tapered cabin sections at the front and in the rear, the size of individual seats usually remains constant throughout the entire Coach cabin.

The Comfort Index is derived according to the formula $I = 8(P/2 + W - C/40) - 203$, where $I$ = the Comfort Index; $P$ = seat pitch in inches; $W$ = seat width in inches; and $C$ = the percent of occupied middle seats at 90 percent load.

The constant divisor of 2 for the pitch measurement accounts for use of thin-back seats in short-pitch installations: The overall effect on comfort of any given pitch reduction is only half the measured reduction, due to the greater space efficiency of newer seats. The configuration percentage is divided by 40 to keep its overall influence on the index to a realistic level. The constant multiplier 8 provides a reasonable range of index values, and the constant 203 is subtracted to set the index of the highest-ranked conventional Coach-Class airplane (the United DC-10) at a value of 100.

Although no conventional Economy-Class seating can truthfully be described as "comfortable" when the plane is close to full, you'll generally find that seating with *CRTL* Comfort Indices of 81 or more will meet reasonable expectations for seat room. When you get down into the 70s, you'll feel noticeably crowded, and you should avoid planes with indices in the 60s, if you can, as flying sardine cans of the worst sort.

**Other Comfort and Service Factors**

Beyond seating standards, the other cabin-service elements that contribute to your overall flight comfort tend to be fairly subjective. While full, hot-meal airline food service at 40,000 feet may be a fantastic technological accomplishment, the results seldom justify the efforts, at least in Economy Class.

There are travelers, of course, who comment on the food as a key element of airline service quality. In reality, there's probably never been an Economy-Class airline meal as good as what $6 will buy at your local diner or fast-food restaurant. Obviously, then, the difference between the best and worst airline meals is, at most, a $2-to-$3 question—hardly a figure on which to base a $1,000 ticket purchase. Maybe food looms important to many travelers because there's so little else to do but eat on a flight. Whatever the reason, it's better to base your airline choice on more important convenience and comfort factors and forget about the food.

Beverage and entertainment pricing is a more substantial item in choosing among airlines than food. When airline drinks sell for $3.00 or so and movie headset rentals are about $3.50, free drinks and/or entertainment are a substantially better reason than food quality differences for favoring one carrier over another. For 1987 travelers, quite a few of the major transatlantic airlines will have a free-drink, free-headset policy in Economy Class.

Airline in-flight surveys almost always show very high ratings for intangible service factors that reflect personal attention from ground and air staff—responses such as "friendly people" and "lots of personal attention" keep cropping up. That's easily understandable in such a people-oriented business. It's also such an intangible—and variable—factor that no consumer-research analysis can treat it. And, in most cases, load factor is the most important determinant of cabin-service quality: when the plane's not full, you get lots of friendly attention; when it's loaded, you're given minimal treatment. What happens to you is so totally dependent on which particular cabin staff is assigned to your flight that there's simply no way to make an accurate prediction. If you insist on using some kind of service factor in your choice, you might as well go by your personal set of nationalistic stereotypes—it's as good a rationale as any other.

## Comparing Contingencies

Finally, you'll want to make some sort of assessment of your risk—what happens when there's a major foul-up, and how easy is it to recover? Although you could draw up an almost endless list of potential difficulties, five problems are the most likely:

1. flight cancellations—missed connections or missed return flights
2. overbooking
3. lost baggage
4. personal illness or other emergency requiring predeparture trip cancellation or unscheduled early return after you're in Europe
5. being stranded due to operator failure

It's clear that some transportation options are more responsive to these problems than others. For example, at the top end of the scale, a First-, Business-, or full-fare Economy-Class ticket on a major airline provides almost as much flexibility as having the price of the ticket as cash in your pocket. You can transfer these tickets among airlines, essentially at will, at any time.

At the opposite end, some of the cheaper options lock you

into very inflexible positions. Specific differences are described in subsequent chapters.

### Determine Your Personal Benchmarks

As you explore the various low-fare flight possibilities, it's important to have your own benchmarks against which to measure the options available to you. Thus, no matter what form of ticket you ultimately decide to use or how you decide to buy it, you should use an APEX (or equivalent) trip on one of the major airlines as the standard of comparison. To develop these benchmarks, simply find out from your travel agent or directly from one or more airlines:

- The APEX (or similar) fare for your preferred route, during the time of year you intend to fly, on the days you want to travel. In comparing APEX fares, use as your benchmark the fare quoted by an airline that offers direct service between your city of origin and your European gateway. If you're traveling with children or others eligible for special-status fares, determine the total family cost for APEX, including any children's or youth fares that might apply.
- The best available schedule on a major airline—minimum total flying hours, whether or not nonstop flights are available, layover or connection times, if necessary, and arrival and departure times.
- The comfort standards offered on the major airline(s) you're considering—in most cases, the majors will all offer standard seating.
- Your assessment of any contingencies you might face with an APEX trip on a major airline. Normally, risks of airline or operator failure will be minimal with this option, but the restrictions may pose a potential risk if you're likely to encounter last-minute changes in your travel plans.

This APEX trip will be your benchmark. It will clearly show you what you have to beat with any alternative you might consider. And, if you can't beat the price, it's undoubtedly the way you'll finally travel.

### Using This Guide

Obviously, this guide—updated for spring 1987—can't offer truly up-to-date air-fare information for summer and fall 1987.

The airlines usually don't know what the complex interactions of market forces, exchange rates, fuel prices, and government policies will bring six weeks in advance, let alone six months.

The fare data in this guide can still be very useful to travelers planning 1987 European trips because:

- Estimated fare levels will be close to final figures, barring some major pricing upheavals.
- Relative fare levels—for the different types of service, to different European countries, from different parts of the United States, over different seasons—should probably be quite accurate, within a few percentage points. Any major changes should escalate or reduce most fare levels in about the same relationship.
- The trade-offs between costs and the other important factors—convenience, comfort, and contingencies—should change little, if at all, from the data presented.

Travelers are urged to use this guide for general exploration of available options and to identify the specific questions that need to be asked. Then call or visit a travel agent as early as possible to get precise answers to the questions you know to be important and exact costs that should confirm the projections you've been able to make by using this book. To ensure that you have the greatest likelihood of getting the best prices on fares as well as your first choices on dates and other specific arrangements, you should begin this process at least two months ahead of your departure date, if possible.

### Using and Selecting a Travel Agent

Despite occasional warnings in this book about travel agents' potential shortcomings, most travelers to Europe are probably better off buying their air tickets and tour packages from a travel agent rather than directly from an airline.

- Travel agents generally avoid the obvious biases of airline ticket offices in any questions that deal with airline choice.
- Many travel agents typically can provide far more personal guidance about travel in general, and especially details about the various destination countries in Europe, than airline ticket counter personnel.

- Some of the more interesting air-fare alternatives are available only through travel agents—you simply can't buy them directly from any airline.
- Travel agents provide convenient "one-stop" shopping for all your travel arrangements, including air tickets, rail passes, rental cars, and hotel accommodations.
- Now that most agents have reservation computers, they are no longer at a disadvantage, compared with airline offices, in terms of immediate access to information and immediate confirmation of space.

Those computerized reservations systems have done wonders for travel agents' efficiency. They permit virtually instant schedule information, space availability, and confirmation—not just for airline seats, but also for rooms in thousands of hotels, rental cars, and all sorts of other travel services. But there's a down side to the computer story. Some agents may rely on the computers to such an extent that they are not prepared to deal with services not listed there. And, unfortu-

---

You certainly don't have to deal with a travel agent to get good travel counsel or to take advantage of some attractive rates. If you decide you'd rather deal with an airline than a travel agent, and you still want some personal guidance about your trip, visit one of the airlines' "vacation centers" in a major city. These airline offices are geared to provide much of the same kinds of travel information that you get from a good travel agent; people who staff them are usually far more informative than the often-harried personnel in airline ticket offices or at airport desks.

The company you work for may have an in-house travel department. While these offices are established primarily to arrange for business travel, many take care of employees' personal travel needs, as well. Such travel offices can often arrange for you to enjoy the benefits of corporate rates and corporate discounts on your vacation trips.

nately, some of the very best air-fare deals are not listed—even the relatively popular and well-known charters. Moreover, while this book doesn't deal with hotels in depth, it should be noted that the computer systems tend to include more of the higher-priced European hotels. Budget hotel reservations, more likely than not, are not available through computers here unless the hotels have U.S. representatives or belong to chains with U.S. reservation services.

Travel agents do not charge clients for making the most common and conventional travel arrangements. They earn their pay on commissions from the airlines, hotels, cruise lines, tour operators, and other suppliers. Commissions on most travel services generally run from 8 to 12 percent, but can be as high as 40 percent for some special services such as travel insurance.

You can't save money by-passing travel agents, at least on conventional travel services. Airlines, hotels, car-rental companies, and other suppliers typically will not sell direct to the public at net, "no-commission" prices.

Commissions are normally the agents' only income source. However, unless you're a very good year-round customer, you can expect an agent to ask you to cover any extraordinary costs your trip may entail, especially extensive telecommunications (phone or telex) direct to Europe for last-minute reservations or changes or extra rewriting or reissuing of airline tickets. The agent cannot recover these extraordinary costs from the suppliers, and agencies are therefore within their rights to ask customers to reimburse them. And, of course, you'll be expected to cover any cancellation charges or refund penalties assessed by airlines or hotels.

Agents are not immune to the financial realities of the business world. As in any marketplace where agents' incomes are based on commissions, the more you spend, the more income your travel agent makes. Most professional-minded agents resist trying to upgrade a typical budget-minded traveler from APEX to Business- or First-Class air service—perhaps because the price difference is so great that any such attempt would be absurd. But financial pressures might sometimes prejudice travel agents' advice toward APEX on a major airline and away from cheaper charter and bulk-fare deals, especially since the cheaper air fare not only reduces commission income but also (usually) requires more work and therefore entails higher costs.

So, if you're interested in one or more of these low-price options, and your agent tries to steer you away from them, you should find another agent—one who knows about these deals and is willing to arrange for them.

One other caution: on occasion, an airline might grant "override" commissions that are much higher than usual—perhaps up to 50 percent. The purpose, of course, is to get agents to book travelers on their flights rather than those of competitors. When big overrides are offered, some agents ticket their clients on itineraries that are clearly not in their clients' best interests, often explaining circuitous routings and connection delays as a consequence of "no space available" on more direct services. But if your agent schedules you by what appears to be the "long way around," make sure that either no better connections are available or that the suggested schedule offers some substantial price advantage.

How to select a travel agent? First, you have to recognize that a big shakeout has started to occur among travel agencies. Some are keeping abreast of the rapid changes in the travel marketplace of the late 1980s, while others are trying to turn back the clock and operate by 1970s rules. With airline deregulation have come a number of ways for travelers to minimize the prices they pay for individual travel services—specifically, to pay less than the sellers' official asking prices without any sacrifice in quality, convenience, or reliability. All of these techniques are available to travel agents. You should view them as important items in a modern agent's "toolbox" of travel sources—alternatives that any agent should call upon to help his or her clients get the best value. Specifically, any agent who wants to compete in the 1980s should be prepared to tap any or all of the following resources:

- discount airline tickets, obtained from consolidators, that can be sold to travelers at substantially lower prices than the airlines ask for the same tickets (see chapter 7)
- discount hotel accommodations, obtained through consolidators, tour operators, or consortium volume-buying programs, that can cut hotel costs by at least 20 percent at a large number of locations around the world
- frequent-flier airline coupons, obtained from coupon brokers, that can cut the costs of First-Class and Business-Class air travel by as much as 70 percent (see chapter 9)

- discount cruises and package tours, obtained either directly from the tour and cruise operators or from clearinghouses, that can cut 10 to 20 percent from a large number of cruises and tours—and cut prices even more for bookings made within a few weeks of departure

Agents who want to turn back the clock complain loudly about unethical competition from discount sources, but the fact is that most consolidators, tour operators, coupon brokers, and clearinghouses are happy—even eager—to sell their services through travel agencies. These agents also claim that discounters are unreliable, often citing horror stories about travelers who dealt with discounters. Certainly, some discounters are unethical (and even more are ethical but undercapitalized, which may be worse), and some travelers have encountered trouble and lost substantial amounts of money in discount arrangements. But it's a serious breach of logic to conclude that all discounters are unethical and their discount arrangements risky. The fact is that there are ethical and financially sound suppliers in all the discount groups—consolidators, consortiums, coupon brokers, and clearinghouses. Individual agents can serve their clients best by locating and using reliable discount sources rather than complaining about unreliable ones.

The travel agency market seems to be evolving toward the same sort of stratification that has occurred in the securities market:

- Some inexperienced travelers may need advice and counsel throughout the entire travel planning process, starting with the selection of places they want to visit. Like unsophisticated investors who rely on a stockbroker's research and recommendations, these travelers need a great deal of personal service and attention. This market is big enough to support a large number of travel agents who charge full commission on travel services sold at full retail prices. If you need this kind of help, by all means seek out a good full-service agency—the recommendation of a satisfied friend or business colleague is the best way to find one.
- On the other hand, experienced and knowledgeable travelers, like investors who do their own research, are interested mainly in efficient execution of orders at the best price, not hand-holding. They can logically expect their agents to ob-

tain the very best prices available—including the discount prices that are so widely available for most travel services, most of the time, in most areas. If your friends or colleagues can't recommend such an agency to you, look for the small discount travel ads you find in the Sunday travel sections of most major newspapers, then call around to find out which one seems to offer the combination of services you require.

Exchange Rates

All air fares quoted in this book are officially priced in U.S. dollars, unless otherwise indicated. Some car rentals and rail passes are also officially priced in U.S. dollars, and dollar prices do not change as a result of changes in exchange rates.

Some car-rental rates and many surface-travel rates are officially priced in the local currencies of individual European countries. In this book, these prices have been converted to U.S. dollars, except for local transportation costs in individual European cities, which are reported only in local currency. Dollar conversions were calculated at the rates in Table 4 as of December 1986.

**Table 4    European Currency per Dollar**

| | |
|---|---|
| Austria | 14.2 |
| Belgium | 42.0 |
| Denmark | 7.61 |
| Finland | 4.9 |
| France | 6.6 |
| Greece | 141.0 |
| Holland | 2.28 |
| Ireland | .74 |
| Italy | 1394.7 |
| Luxembourg | 42.0 |
| Norway | 7.60 |
| Portugal | 149.5 |
| Spain | 135.7 |
| Sweden | 7.0 |
| Switzerland | 1.69 |
| West Germany | 2.01 |
| UK ($s per pound) | 1.43 |
| Yugoslavia | 456.8 |

# 2

# Major Airlines

*Popular, Convenient,
and Conventional*

The term **major airline** refers to one of the large group of established, old-line companies that have been flying for decades. Majors based in the United States that provide transatlantic service are American, Delta, Eastern, Northwest Orient, Pan American, and TWA. The European-based transatlantic majors are Aer Lingus (Ireland), Air France, TAP–Air Portugal, Alitalia (Italy), British Airways, British Caledonian, Finnair, Iberia (Spain), KLM (Netherlands), Lufthansa (West Germany), Olympic (Greece), Sabena (Belgium), SAS (Denmark-Norway-Sweden), and Swissair. Their "major" status reflects long-term history and size. It also reflects exclusive membership in the IATA fraternity during precompetitive, preregulation times, and current participation in the various major-airline fare-setting systems. They almost always charge identical fares on the routes they serve jointly.

Although not based in Western Europe, Air India, Alia (Jordan), El Al (Israel), JAT (Yugoslavia), Kuwait, and Pakistan are also majors, and part of the worldwide system. These lines have government authority to fly you from a few U.S. cities to several European gateways—almost always at the same fares as those of the other major lines.

Historically, these major airlines have attempted to offer a price and quality spectrum of air service appealing to virtually all segments of the international travel market. They've certainly come close. For that reason, over the years, these lines have carried the overwhelming majority of transatlantic passengers—and they will again in 1987.

As indicated in chapter 1, the major airlines' primary ap-

> A great deal of confusion about terms exists in the travel marketplace. While *promotional fare* is a term regularly used inside the travel industry, it is not generally used in dealings with customers. Instead, airlines tend to talk—erroneously—about their "discount fares" in ads and other sales materials. This distinction isn't just hair-splitting—real discount fares exist, and they're quite different from promotional fares.
>
> The fares set by airlines at levels below "normal" full fares are (usually) formally filed with the government or industry agencies that deal with such things and are properly called promotional fares. Most promotional fares are lower-priced versions of Economy Class, but, in times past, promotional variations on First Class have occasionally been sold.
>
> The term *discount fare* should be reserved for tickets sold for less than the fare set by the airlines for any particular type of ticket. Again, these true discounts are usually applied to Economy-Class fares, but discounts are also available on some Business- or First-Class fares, as well. True discount fares are described in chapter 7.

proach to low-fare markets is to offer special Economy-Class fares with restrictions that make them unattractive to business travelers. Often marketed as "discount fares" to the public, they are more correctly termed **promotional fares.**

All of the different major airlines' promotional fares are listed in the several computerized reservation systems travel agents use. These systems also specify restrictions and space availability. No travel agent should have any trouble determining the amount of the fare or how it can be applied.

APEX and Super APEX

The most popular, most heavily utilized promotional fares are those known as **advance-purchase** excursions. They're usually advertised as APEX—the obvious acronym—or Super APEX.

Some lines use other names for the same type of fare. Lufthansa calls it "Holiday," for example, and Olympic once came up with the appalling "Luv A Fare."

Incidentally, there are no operational differences between APEX and Super APEX. The latter term was introduced in 1981 to promote some special cuts in the regular APEX fares on direct flights from the main U.S. gateway cities. By and large, this feature remains in effect: single-airline APEX fares from major U.S. gateway cities to Europe are usually lower than connection APEX fares from U.S. cities that do not have direct service.

Typically, APEX fares have up to six main restrictions:

- advance purchase
- minimum/maximum allowable length of stay
- the implicit round-trip requirement
- prohibition against en route stopovers
- cancellation penalties
- and "capacity control," or arbitrary limitation on the number of seats on each flight that are sold at APEX prices

Advance purchase means that you have to make your reservations and purchase your tickets a specified minimum time period in advance of your departure date. Normally there is no maximum limit on advance purchase. In addition, some APEX rules require that tickets be purchased within a specified time period after you make reservations, regardless of how far in advance of departure.

"One-way APEX" fares are available on a few routes and should be investigated if you're planning a lengthy stay abroad.

APEX fares on most routes from the U.S. to Western Europe permit no en route stopovers, either at East Coast U.S. gateways or at intermediate European cities. A few APEX fares to some European points and to several cities in the Middle East do permit limited stopovers in Western Europe, sometimes at extra cost. Only a very few APEX-type fares allow travelers from the interior United States to stop over in New York or some other East Coast U.S. gateway (see chapter 10).

Another restriction is that APEX fares are usually "capacity controlled." This means that airlines can arbitrarily limit the number of seats they sell at APEX prices, on a flight-by-flight basis. The APEX allocation can be very small—it can even be

> Buying your tickets a long time ahead—like so many travel decisions—has both advantages and disadvantages. It's certainly an easy way to make sure that you get seats on the flights and dates you prefer—a real advantage if you plan to travel during peak periods. Early ticket purchase also usually gives you a hedge on fares changing between the time you buy your tickets and your departure date. Although international airlines aren't required to do so, most of them "lock in" your reservation at the rate you paid. If fares are subsequently increased, your ticket price remains unchanged. If fares go down, the airline will refund the difference.
>
> The disadvantages of early purchase are that you increase the chance of incurring a cancellation penalty if you have to change your plans or if you subsequently find a lower fare on some other kind of service (such as a charter) for which you are not entitled to a fare-reduction refund, and you're lending the airline a lot of money at no interest.

zero—during heavy travel times when managements believe those seats can be filled with high-fare passengers. Even during more competitive times, APEX seats may sell out early on particular flights, leaving only higher-priced seats for late bookings.

Finally, most APEX and Super APEX U.S.-to-Europe fares provide reduced fares for children. The most typical formula is that children between ages two and eleven travel at two-thirds of the regular APEX fare. Children under age two go at 10 percent of the adult fare; but if the plane is full, they don't get a separate seat—you have to hold them. Details are listed in chapter 11.

The 1987 APEX Fare Outlook

The tables in chapter 11 show peak-season major-airline APEX fares from four representative U.S. gateways to twenty-five primary-city gateways in Western Europe and the Eastern Mediterranean. Fares shown in the tables are those listed in airline computers (or obtained directly from airlines) as of late 1986. The tables also show effective dates and applicable restrictions.

Obviously, fares finally adopted for the peak season will differ, to some degree, from values early in the year. Even the airlines won't know exactly what they'll be charging for peak season until late spring. But the actual, final figures should probably be fairly close—and the relationships among different classes of fare and fares on different routes should be very similar to those for peak 1986.

A basic assumption in the use of late 1986 fares is that there won't be many cost pressures on fares during the winter and spring of 1987. Clearly, the outbreak of political turmoil anywhere in the Mediterranean Basin or in Eastern Europe would have an impact on fares.

Final 1987 peak-season fares will be a compromise between two offsetting economic forces:

- poor financial performance over the last few years by most major airlines will pressure them to increase revenues, mainly by increasing fares
- increased competition from low-fare alternatives will put an effective lid on the amount of fare increases that travel markets will tolerate

The net result should be a minor inching up of APEX and related major-airline fares this year.

Convenience

The major airlines provide nonstop, direct, and connecting flights to and from far more U.S. and European points than any other class of carrier does. In terms of convenience (and also contingencies, as discussed later) almost any nonstop flight is to be preferred over almost any direct flight or connection, regardless of other advantages and disadvantages.

The majors can't be beaten for schedule convenience, either. Wherever they serve, flights on most routes operate every day.

The most popular routes (like New York to London) may have up to ten daily flights; only a few, such as Seattle to London, may have less-than-daily schedules.

Major U.S. airlines will have direct service to Europe from many more U.S. cities than could possibly be included in any summary tabulation. You'd expect them to run more through-plane services from interior U.S. points than their European competitors, and they do. What you might not expect is that they also run direct flights to as many or more European cities than the European lines—mainly because the U.S. lines typically run the same flight beyond its first European gateway to additional cities farther east, while European lines almost invariably require connections at their first-stop major gateway cities for services to other points.

But don't assume that "through-plane" service on the U.S. lines means that you won't have to change planes at some point. Some airlines station small, short-range planes (727s and 737s) permanently in Europe. The jumbo plane takes you to, say, London or Frankfurt, where you change to the smaller plane for other cities to the east—Munich or Vienna, for example. Or, on a flight operating from interior U.S. points to Europe, you may start off your trip on a 727 or DC-9, and change to a jumbo plane at a U.S. East-Coast gateway. Unfortunately, these connections often carry the same flight number as the transatlantic flight. So if you're considering what appears to be a through flight with one or more intermediate stops, you might check to see if a "change of gauge" is involved—either in the United States, in Europe, or in both—and select another airline if you don't like the idea of changing planes.

## Comfort

All 1987 transatlantic service on scheduled major airlines will feature wide-body jets; 747s will predominate, with quite a few DC-10s, L-1011s, and 767s. Seating data on all aircraft expected to be used for transatlantic service are shown in Table 3, page 20. For the most part, Economy-Class seating will be comparable on most major airlines, with *CRTL* Comfort Indices between 81 and 92.

One airline, however, provides substantially more room in

some Economy-Class seats. Two of the cabins on British Airways 747s contain seats that can be converted on the spot to either Economy or Business Class, depending on the relative number of travelers in each class on any flight. When used for Economy Class, seating is nine across (instead of the normal ten across), and pitch is 36 inches (instead of the typical 33 to 34 inches). Convertible seats in rows 17 through 26 are often allocated to Economy Class, and they provide substantially improved comfort compared with conventional Economy seating. Unfortunately, British Airways normally doesn't preassign these seats to Economy—they are given out, when loads permit, only on the day of departure. So, if you're flying British Airways—and the substantially improved comfort is a good reason to do so—you should check in early to be assigned (or reassigned) seats in the convertible section.

In 1985, several European-based major airlines adopted a free-drink, free-headset policy. Usually, a move such as this is immediately matched by all major competitors, but, for some strange reason, the main U.S. airlines and some other European lines did not. For 1987, Air France, British Airways, British Caledonian, Egyptair, El Al, Icelandair, JAT, KLM, Lufthansa, and Swissair will offer headsets and alcoholic beverages at no charge to all Economy passengers. On the other lines, expect to pay about $3.50 for a headset (to hear the audio programs and movie soundtrack), $3.00 for a drink, $2.50 for wine, and $1.50 for beer. Buying drinks and entertainment on those lines that charge for them could easily add $10 to $20 per person to the cost of a trip—enough to influence your airline choice, and certainly more significant than any real or imagined differences in meal service.

## Contingencies

Traveling with a major airline, even on the cheapest APEX or Super APEX, is probably your best insurance policy against Murphy's Law—"What can go wrong will go wrong"—affecting your trip. When equipment breaks down, or weather across the ocean grounds the plane you were supposed to take, the majors, with their huge fleets and frequent flights, are better able to cope than are the smaller low-fare lines or charters. If your airline can't handle you, it can arrange for a fellow major line to pinch-hit. If you and your baggage go separate ways, the majors—with daily or more frequent flights on most routes—can usually return it to you within a day or two. If you're denied boarding because of overbooking, you have specific—and sometimes very rewarding—recourse.

Of course, your absolutely lowest-risk schedule option is a nonstop trip on a major airline. It's pretty hard to miss a connection or have your baggage put off at the wrong airport on a nonstop. In fact, getting a nonstop flight is probably worth giving up something in the way of comfort or other advantages available only on through or connecting schedules.

If your route doesn't have nonstops, a true direct flight is almost as good. If you have to connect, on-line connections are generally less risky than off-line. All the major airlines are making special efforts to provide smooth on-line connections at their various "hub" centers.

The majors have specific policies that entitle you to meals and accommodations if they have to keep you waiting for a delayed/canceled flight and to allowances for immediate necessities if they lose your baggage. Remember, however, that accommodations are normally not authorized for delays at the airport where your trip originates—the presumption is that you can just go home until things are fixed.

Major lines' APEX fares probably give you the best protection among the low-cost options against the technical and operational vicissitudes of flying. But you pay a price in flexibility. The airlines mean what they say about the restrictions. If you fail to show up for your return flight, you can't just get on the next one—you are no longer eligible for the APEX fare. While your "busted" APEX ticket is still worth its cash value (less any applicable refund penalties), you have to exchange it for a higher-fare ticket to get home—an exchange that can cost you hundreds of dollars. Of course, if failure to make your scheduled APEX return flight is due to a delayed connecting flight, you'll be allowed to get on the next available return flight without penalty. And if you miss your flight due to a medical problem or other documentable emergency, a letter from a qualified physician or government official (depending on circumstances) will normally permit you to reschedule your return without penalty.

Voluntary rerouting and rescheduling rules vary with route.

In most cases, any change (except an upgrade to a higher class of service) entails a penalty of $50, or, occasionally, 10 percent of the ticket value. Normally, you can retain the APEX price level (with penalty) if you change flights within the advance-purchase requirements for new tickets. However, on a few routes, no-minimum-time reroutings and reschedulings are allowed—either free or for a set charge. If you think you'll change your plans after you're in Europe, however, you'll probably be better off with some more flexible low-fare option than APEX, for example, a one-way charter.

A few years ago, a guide such as this would have stated flatly that flying with a major airline is a 100 percent guarantee against getting stranded—a problem that still plagues charters. After the Braniff and Continental bankruptcies, however, such a statement would be rash in the extreme. In this deregulated environment, major-airline failure is a distinct, if distant contingency. You can spot some dire warnings about airline solvency in just about any issue of the *Wall Street Journal*. It's possible—although unlikely—that another of the major U.S. carriers could cease operations in 1987.

You wouldn't be stranded if you were in Europe when the line on which you had a return ticket failed. The other major lines would almost certainly offer to bring you home without extra charge. But if this unhappy scenario was played out during the height of the travel season, you might have to wait several days to be rescued, since your alternative return would almost surely be on a standby basis.

The possibility of major airline failure isn't a contingency that should deter you from traveling or from electing to use a major U.S. airline. Instead, this discussion is simply a recognition that the major lines have lost some of the lower-risk advantage they once enjoyed, as compared with charters and other alternatives.

## Major Airlines' Other Promotional Fares

APEX and its minor variants aren't the only promotional fares offered by the major airlines. Up to seven other types are available. Specific options vary with individual routes, as described in chapter 11.

## Standby

When you travel on Standby, you go to the airport the day you want to leave, get on a priority list, and wait until flight time. If any Economy-Class seats are available after all the passengers with confirmed reservations have boarded, you get to go. If passengers with confirmed reservations fill the plane and no extra seats are available, you can try another flight, another airline, or another day.

Over the years, Standby has been used mainly for flights to London, with almost no use to any other European capitals. The reason is simply that Sir Freddie Laker's original Skytrain was a standby concept, and the major lines decided to oppose Laker with a similar type of service.

While some Standby fares to London were offered late in January 1986, no major transatlantic airline was offering a Standby fare at the end of last year. But don't be surprised if one of the majors reintroduces it to London this summer, and, of course, if one line offers Standby, the others will all jump on board.

When Standby is available, it's often one of the most attractive alternatives. Fares are generally less than Super APEX, in the 80 to 90 percent range. Of course, there are no advance-purchase restrictions, and since it's a one-way fare, there is no minimum-stay requirement. In fact, Standby is often the only way you can fly one way on a major airline without paying the full Economy fares.

Standby offers excellent value. You fly on a major airline, with major-line flight quality. Most direct U.S.-to-London routes offer at least daily service, and in the peak season there may be several alternatives every day. In most respects, it's a far superior alternative to a charter or to a multi-stop on a low-fare airline.

The obvious drawback is the uncertainty involved—you are not assured of a seat. However, dedicated Standby travelers from prior years report that Standby seats were a real problem only during a few of the very busiest weekends—eastbound mid-June through mid-July, westbound mid-August through mid-September, and around the Easter and year-end holiday seasons. Many business travelers regularly used Standby during its heyday—perhaps one of the reasons that the major lines aren't enthusiastic about reviving it.

No decision on the fate of Standby had been made as of this writing. If it becomes available, however, it surely will be a primary candidate for low-cost travel to and from London this summer.

**Youth Fares**

Last summer, TWA introduced a comprehensive package of youth fares, which was immediately matched by the major competitors. Fares range from slightly lower to much lower than APEX; they're the same all year. As of late 1986, typical year-round, one-way youth fares from Boston, Philadelphia, New York, and Washington to Amsterdam and Brussels were $169; fares to Barcelona, Frankfurt, Geneva, Lisbon, Madrid, and Zurich were $218; fares to Copenhagen, Milan, and Rome were $248; and fares to Cairo and Tel Aviv were $298; fares from the West Coast were $100 higher, in all cases, and there are comparable add-ons from other U.S. cities. Youth-fare tickets are available to travelers aged twelve through twenty-four. On most routes, youth-fare tickets can be bought as one ways, round-trips, or open jaws; a few countries permit only round-trips or open jaws. You can buy tickets at any time, but you can make reservations only within seventy-two hours of departure.

As of late 1986, the British, French, and Greek governments were not allowing youth fares. The British, however, were reported to be "reconsidering" their refusal, and there were indications that the French would approve youth fares for the summer season. It's unlikely that travelers who qualify for youth fares will find any better alternative. If a youth fare isn't available where you want to go this summer, check out the options to adjacent countries—for example, Belgium or Switzerland if you want to visit Britain or France.

**Senior Fares**

So far, only a few airlines have offered fares to the senior market that are any better than regular APEX fares. American offers a 10 percent discount on any transatlantic fare to members of its seniors club, and holders of TWA's systemwide unlimited-travel senior passes can buy an add-on good for one transatlantic round trip for $499 (covering cities as far east as

Zurich) or $599 (covering TWA cities in the Eastern Mediterranean and the Middle East). Most major U.S. airlines have special senior programs covering domestic travel. Don't be surprised to see some additional transatlantic options added by this summer.

**Group and Tour Status Fares**

Several types of group and tour fares are offered on various transatlantic routes. In most cases, the actual fare levels are pegged at essentially the same levels as the least expensive APEX or Super APEX. However, restrictions and conditions of purchase can be quite different.

- **ITX** (inclusive-tour) and **GIT** (group-inclusive-tour) fares are designed as the air-fare component of a complete tour package that also includes a mandatory minimum "land package" of hotel accommodations, sightseeing, and the like.
- **Incentive fares** cover group travel organized by corporations, associations, etc., for travel to special events and/or for travel awarded for some sort of performance or achievement.
- **Weekend round-trip excursion fares** are offered from a few cities during fall, winter, and spring—allowing a maximum stay of only three or four days.

Some of these options weren't offered at all, as of late 1986. Most routes have at least one of the three group, tour, or incentive options, but you can't buy them apart from a complete tour package.

Round the World

Most transatlantic airlines are involved in special round-the-world ticket partnerships. For a set ticket price, travelers can (on most programs) make as many stops as they wish, provided they keep going in the same direction—no backtracking—and stop only once at each stopover city. Of course, you can stop only at those cities served by the two or three airlines involved in the partnerships.

At present, twenty-eight different partnerships of a U.S. airline with one or two foreign lines have special round-the-world fares. All offer Economy-Class tickets, about half offer Business Class, and most offer First-Class options. Price levels depend mainly on the routing used to cross the Pacific. For travel via the North Pacific (including Honolulu), round-the-world costs $1,990–$2,599 in Economy Class, $2,899 in Business Class (where available), and $3,799–$4,399 in First Class. For travel via the South Pacific (including Australia, Fiji, New Zealand, and Tahiti), round-the-world costs $2,099–$2,799 in Economy Class, $3,699–$4,150 in Business Class, and $4,399–$5,399 in First Class. Additional round-the-world services are offered by Canadian airlines in combination with others.

In general, the first leg of the trip is treated as an APEX ticket—you have to reserve and buy tickets no less than twenty-one days in advance. All the remaining legs can be left open if desired, usually for up to six months.

Round-the-world is obviously a good buy for people who want to go around the world. What may be a surprise is that it's sometimes the least expensive way to get to Europe, especially from the West Coast to the Eastern Mediterranean. The reason is the availability of all those stopovers at no extra cost. Most of the least-expensive promotional fares permit no stopovers or—to the Eastern Mediterranean—one or two, at best. So if you want to visit several different points in Europe and the United States as part of your trip, your standard alternative might be a very expensive full-fare Economy-Class ticket, or—even worse—a combination of individual-flight Economy tickets.

The best way to look at round-the-world is as an absolute ceiling on what you should pay for an itinerary that involves multiple stops in internal U.S. and/or European cities. If you need a multistop trip, and if the regular Economy-Class fare for that trip exceeds $2,099, round-the-world can often serve as a lower-cost alternative.

## Specials

Several European governments—notably Belgium, Britain, Germany, the Netherlands, and Switzerland—have adopted fairly liberal airline-regulation policies. Individual airlines are more free than ever to introduce pricing innovations. Although nothing specific is on the horizon as of late 1986, don't be surprised to see some short-term low-fare promotions across the Atlantic that are similar to some of the more dramatic low-fare promotions offered by domestic U.S. airlines last winter.

Full-Fare Economy

Full-fare Economy Class is the world's worst air-travel buy. You receive the same quality of service that you get on APEX at a much higher price. The only difference is the absence of restrictions—with full-fare Economy, you don't have to reserve or buy in advance, and you can buy one-way tickets.

But no sensible traveler should have to pay for full-fare Economy Class and still suffer Economy-Class tight seating and service—not even business travelers who theoretically can't live with APEX restrictions. If you're paying as much as full-fare Economy, you're probably better off paying a little more and moving up to the sharply improved quality of Business Class. Or use one of the low-fare airlines that normally don't apply any restrictions. Or buy a Business- or First-Class frequent traveler coupon from a broker (see chapter 9).

Buying Your Major-Airline Ticket

Obviously, these are the easiest of all tickets to buy. Schedules, fares, and reservations are immediately available through the computers that are now installed in almost all retail travel agencies. You can use major credit cards to buy the tickets. It's as hassle-free as any big-dollar transaction can be.

# 3

# Low-Fare Airlines

*An Idea Whose Time
Has Come . . . and Gone?*

Low-fare airlines are a group of scheduled airlines established specifically to provide low-cost, low-fare, no-frills service. As of this writing, it appears that at least three low-fare airlines will operate scheduled services between the United States and Europe this summer: Icelandair, Tower, and Virgin Atlantic. Continental took over People Express early this year; at this writing, it is not clear how Continental will approach the transatlantic market. A few other lines—in both Europe and the United States—have announced plans to operate this summer, but, in this market, announcement of intent has frequently failed to materialize in actual service.

## A Great Idea

In the major airlines' heyday after World War II, a cozy airline/government establishment made it almost impossible for anybody to operate a low-fare airline on transatlantic routes. International air fares were set by the airlines through the IATA cartel and ratified by the governments involved. Only Icelandair was able to remain outside of IATA and offer competitive low-fare travel.

As in most cartels, prices (fares) were set high enough to protect the weakest, least efficient competitors. Costs inflated by sweetheart labor contracts and home-office bureaucracies were simply passed along to consumers. And the main low-cost alternative—charter travel—was hobbled by all sorts of artificial restrictions and barriers.

But the market changed drastically in the mid-1970s, mainly due to the proconsumer efforts of the U.S. government. First came liberalization of the restrictions on charters. Next came Sir Freddie Laker, with Skytrain, in 1977. Finally, airline deregulation in the United States and much more liberal aviation treaties with European countries opened the transatlantic market to meaningful competition.

### But Great Ideas Don't Always Work

The classic logic of low-fare airline operation is straightforward: operate at low costs; offer low fares. Keep costs low by loading as many people as possible onto each plane and keeping frills to a minimum.

The classic logic of low-fare airline market competition is also straightforward: low-cost, no-frills operators offer low fares; high-cost operators offer extra service at higher fares. The spectrum of market price and quality of service is extended; consumers have increased choices.

But airline-market dynamics aren't dictated by logic; they're dictated by market share. The majors have been willing to allow lower-cost, lower-quality, lower-fare services into the market—but only up to a point. Any time that the low-fare specialists start gaining a substantial share of the total market, the majors react by cutting their fares to match the low-fare line—but keeping their normal, higher-quality service levels.

Icelandair, with its two or three daily narrow-body flights and out-of-the-way European terminal, was tolerated for decades, especially since its fares never got too far below the majors' fares. But Laker, with six flights a day in brand-new DC-10s, couldn't be allowed to keep a significant price advantage. The majors had to match Laker's fares or suffer unacceptable losses in traffic—and they met him head-on. This same scenario has been played out with several subsequent low-fare airline efforts. At various times over the last few years, Air Florida, Capitol, Jet 24, Transamerica, and World have operated scheduled low-fare transatlantic service. These services have lasted from several years (World) to several days (Jet 24). The major obstacle to success has been that competitive major airlines—or the governments that regulate and protect them—have generally not allowed the low-fare airlines to maintain a sufficient price advantage to offset the differences between no-frills flying and the majors' higher-quality services.

So it has come to pass that the simple low-fare airline logic isn't working out the way many airline innovators had hoped. They can still provide low-cost, no-frills service, all right, but without appreciably lower prices to go along with the lower-quality service, they have a tough sell.

The 1987 Outlook

Over the last several years, the major airlines appear to be willing to tolerate slightly lower year-round fares on Icelandair and Virgin Atlantic—and to tolerate substantially lower fares for short periods of time. You can look for more of the same this summer: slightly lower standard fares plus, possibly, some short-term promotions at substantially below major lines' levels. In addition, the low-fare lines generally offer unrestricted fares at levels well below full-fare Economy on major lines. So if you decide to leave for Europe less than twenty-one days in advance, you should surely take a look at one of the low-fare options before you pay the huge premium for a last-minute ticket on a major line.

Specific low-fare levels and restrictions expected in 1987 are discussed for each country in chapter 11. But for the competitive reasons cited this particular aspect of the total picture is among the most uncertain. When it comes to the low-fare lines, the crystal ball gets very cloudy.

Convenience

Low-fare airlines have no inherent convenience differences from the major carriers. Travelers from the West Coast who use Virgin Atlantic or Tower have to stop and/or change planes in New York or Newark, but that's simply because none of them carries enough traffic to justify nonstop service from the West Coast to Europe. There is nothing to prevent low-fare lines from applying for such service when the traffic warrants it.

While it has no U.S. feed, Icelandair has organized special through-fare arrangements with several domestic airlines to feed its international flights from New York, Chicago, Detroit, and Orlando. Icelandair's European terminal in Luxembourg could be considered an inconvenient gateway. Certainly, it's not one of Europe's major destinations. It does, however, provide easy access to some of the more popular destination cities, and the airline has developed some connecting services to facilitate through travel. For example, Icelandair operates free bus connections from Luxembourg to six cities in Germany; it subsidizes a train connection on Swiss Federal Rail to any city in Switzerland or to Paris for just $15 each way, and it also arranges for special connecting air fares to five other nearby European gateway cities. Most Icelandair flights stop in Reykjavik both ways, adding an extra two or three hours to the total trip from the United States to continental Europe, compared with competitors' nonstops to adjacent gateways. Icelandair has the authority to fly nonstop between the United States and Luxembourg, but finds most of its passengers prefer the Reykjavik stop, even if they don't stay over to tour Iceland.

Comfort

Comfort standards on low-fare airlines vary from being comparable to the majors to substantially worse:

- Tower's 747s, with a *CRTL* Comfort Index of 85, are similar to those operated by the major airlines.
- Planes flown by Icelandair and Virgin Atlantic have lower comfort indices than those of most major airlines—you'll definitely notice more crowding on these lines.

Contingencies

Disruption of your travel plans is probably slightly more likely with a low-fare airline than with a major. Whenever any airline has to cancel a flight, its first-choice solution to the problem is to put you on another of its own flights. Obviously, it doesn't want to have to buy a planeload of seats from a competitor if it doesn't have to. Major lines can usually find enough seats on their own flights to cope with most cancellations; if not, the majors routinely accept each others' tickets and passengers, subject to applicable restrictions and space availability.

However, when a low-fare line has to cancel a flight, it may not be as likely to get you a seat on another line. Instead, it can ask you to wait, either for a replacement airplane to show up or for available seats on one of its subsequent flights. If you're traveling with a line that has only a few flights a week—and if bookings are heavy—you might have to wait a long time for another seat on that line.

All in all, the low-fare airlines should make you feel about as confident as if you were on a major line. With the smaller lines, you have to accept some additional uncertainty.

## Buying Your Tickets

Some schedules and fares for the low-fare transatlantic airlines are shown in travel agents' computers, but details seem to be lacking for several. In practice, most agents call these airlines directly for current information.

# 4

# Charters

*Still a Good Bet
if You Buy Wisely*

Charters have traditionally offered the lowest air fares across the Atlantic. Their quality of service record is commensurately low. Almost all of the horror stories you've heard about strandings or delays of several days originate with charter flights. Convenience and comfort factors can be so poor that many first-time charter travelers say "never again."

But tens of thousands of travelers use charters across the Atlantic every year, and probably most of them are repeat customers. They're satisfied with the product and more than satisfied with the price.

An extensive mythology has grown up about charters, much of it based on what used to be true but is no longer. True, you used to have to belong to a club to be eligible for a charter, but that requirement was ended years ago. True, you used to have to go over and back with the same group, but not any longer. True, you used to have no return-schedule flexibility, but you do now. True, charters used to be about the only way to beat high air-fare costs, but that's certainly no longer the case.

But aspects of the mythology remain. Despite some of the problems, charters are still one of the least expensive ways to get to Europe. And despite much consumer-protection regulation, charters are still riskier than scheduled flights on either major or low-fare airlines. And finally, charter flight quality is still apt to be lower than other options.

It's hard to generalize about charters. What counts is the individual charter you select.

## Tour Operators

The main difference between a charter flight and an ordinary scheduled airline flight is that on a charter you buy your transportation from a wholesale tour operator rather than directly from an airline. The tour operator, in turn, contracts with an airline to fly you to Europe and back.

The critical distinction here is that your deal is with the operator, not the airline. The operator is not an agent for the airline, as in the case of a retail travel agent. Instead, operators actually buy seats or flights for their own account—they "own" them and sell them for the best prices they can get.

It's somewhat like buying a suit of clothes or a dress from a department store. Even though the suit or dress carries a manufacturer's label, your transaction is with the store. If you have a complaint, you argue with the store, not the manufacturer.

This analogy isn't exact. Many manufacturers of consumer merchandise provide some sort of guarantee or warranty to backstop the retailer—if the retailer doesn't solve your problem, or goes broke, the manufacturer usually stands behind the product.

Not so with charter flights. Tour operators often charter planes from the world's biggest and best airlines—Pan American, United, Swissair, and the like. But these airlines normally don't offer the equivalent of a manufacturer's warranty. If you have trouble with the operator, you have to settle it with the operator. The airline is just a "hired hand," not a principal.

---

The terminology of charter travel is sometimes confusing. Organizations that operate charter flight programs are called "wholesale tour operators," whether or not the flights include complete tour packages. In fact, most of the operators that run charter programs also offer optional complete tour packages, as well. But even if they run only the charter air trips, they're still called wholesale tour operators.

This difference is critical to the existence of charters. It's the reason they can be cheaper than other kinds of flight—and it's also the root of almost all of the often-serious problems that arise with charters.

## 1987 Charter Fare Outlook

Charter fares are normally tied to scheduled airline fares—by the marketplace, not government regulation. Peak-season charter fares are generally $50 to $100 less than major-airline APEX or Super APEX round-trip to Europe from the East Coast, and $100 to $200 below APEX or Super APEX from the West Coast. You can expect this same sort of differential this summer.

Historically, this price differential has worked well enough as an offset to the convenience and comfort disadvantages of most charters to keep them in business. Lower differentials have caused too much business to shift to the scheduled airlines; higher differentials attract too much business from the scheduled lines, and they retaliate by cutting their fares.

Charter fares, low-fare airline fares, and bulk fares (see chapter 5) between the United States and Europe tend to be quite close. Although substantial differences can exist on some routes, at some times, these three different approaches to below-APEX scheduled-airline fares are generally quite competitive.

Charter pricing is sometimes more finely tuned to the market than scheduled-airline pricing. Rather than having only two or three seasons, many tour operators offer a slightly different price on each flight. This way, the "normal" differential can narrow in periods of the very highest demand and widen somewhat during slower periods. With fares varying every week, your round-trip price is the sum of one-half of the round-trip fares in effect for both legs of the trip. In fact, most charter programs now list fares in "half round-trip" terms.

Over the last few years most charter programs have offered one-way transportation as well as the more traditional round-trip transportation. One-way charter fares are typically $50 to $100 more than one-half of the round-trip fare. Tour operators with charters on more than one route usually allow open-jaw charters with each leg priced on a "half round-trip" basis.

Look for these traditional patterns to continue through the next year. No real innovations in charter fare offers are expected.

Convenience Factors

Charters don't have to be any less convenient than scheduled flights—but they often are. Basically, most charter programs are organized into weekly schedule patterns. Only a few of the most popular programs operate two or three times a week. This is not to say that charter flights to a particular European city don't operate more often—only that the flights of each wholesale tour operator seldom do.

Once-a-week operation can be a drawback to travelers with fixed vacation periods. If your vacation has to start on a Friday evening, and you have to be back at work on a Monday morning, using a weekly charter program with flights during the middle of the week could cost you a lot of the time potentially available for your stay in Europe. Thus, for example, if you had to wait from Friday until Tuesday to leave, and had to come back on a Wednesday, three weeks off work would permit just two full weeks in Europe.

Incidentally, weekly charter-flight patterns also give a minor edge to U.S. charter airlines over European lines. Typically, a U.S. line starts its weekly round-trip with an overnight eastbound departure to Europe, returning westbound the following day. By contrast, a European line starts its round-trip with a daytime westbound flight to the United States, returning eastbound with an overnight flight the same evening. This pattern effectively provides an extra day in Europe on a U.S. carrier.

To see how this works, consider a one-week round-trip charter departing from the United States for Europe on a Saturday night and arriving Sunday morning. With a U.S. carrier, the return flight would leave Europe the following Sunday, allowing seven full days in Europe; with a European carrier, the return flight would leave the following Saturday, allowing just six full days in Europe.

Charter schedules can actually be more convenient than scheduled-airline trips on a few routes. During the peak season, charters will operate nonstop from some U.S. cities

(Cleveland and Buffalo, for example) that do not have any nonstop scheduled-airline service. On the other hand, most charter schedules are no more convenient than those of scheduled flights, and many are less convenient. Scheduled flights from the East Coast normally operate nonstop to their European destinations. Some charters, however, stop to board passengers from more than one East Coast gateway, or drop people off at two or three European cities.

Quite a few of the charters from the West Coast involve stops or connections. Charter flights normally carry more passengers than flights of scheduled airlines, so some are simply too heavy to operate nonstop from California to Europe and have to stop to refuel in the eastern United States or Canada. Other programs feed charter flights departing from New York with passengers originating at many other U.S. cities, through connecting flights on domestic airlines, at special connecting fares. While this kind of program brings charter service to many communities that could not support direct charter flights, the connecting times required in New York are often as long as four to six hours. Travelers on these programs are not allowed to switch to more attractive schedules for these domestic connecting flights.

Charter brochures often fail to mention extra stops or long layovers at connecting points. Travelers interested in finding nonstop or minimum-time flights should specifically check on stops or connections in comparing various charter alternatives.

One additional minor annoyance is that charter operators typically ask passengers to be at the airport for check-in three to four hours before departure, in contrast with the one hour that is advised by scheduled lines. And it's usually for "hurry up and wait" processing; there is often only one check-in position for three hundred or so passengers.

Comfort Factors

The most comfortable charters are generally the ones that use major-airline planes normally assigned to scheduled service. Seating on these is obviously the same as on scheduled service; on most, you can even enjoy the added comfort of Business-Class or First-Class seating at nominal extra cost (see chapter 8).

But most charters use airplanes specifically outfitted for charter service, with all-Economy seating. The best of these are usually 747s, with the standard ten-across seating and pitch equal to or slightly below that of scheduled major airlines. Also reasonably comfortable are those DC-10s and L-1011s that provide either standard 34-inch pitch or nine-across seating, such as found on Balair, Total Air, and in the front and rear cabins (but not the center cabin) on LTU.

The new, tightened federal noise rules have drastically reduced the use of old narrow-body DC-8s and 707s. Enough airlines have put new low-noise engines on their DC-8s—or "hush kits" on the old engines—to operate some charters to Europe this summer. In general, it doesn't pay to put new engines or hush kits on the smaller 707s, but you may see a few 707 charters this summer, as well. With Comfort Indices in the 65–75 range, these are among the least comfortable airplanes you'll find and should be avoided if at all possible.

Finally, several big charter programs that would otherwise be among the best use the least comfortable airplanes. Charter-style DC-10s and L-1011s typically combine ten-across D-class seats (the narrowest on any large jet) with 31- and 32-inch pitch. Any time you find charters with 370 to 380 seats on DC-10s and L-1011s, you know the seating is ultratight. With *CRTL* Comfort Indices as low as 65, sardine-can crowding detracts from the otherwise excellent services found on British Airtours (L-1011), Condor (DC-10), Martinair (DC-10), and Spantax (DC-10).

Contingencies

Charter programs involve two contingencies not associated with flights on major airlines: program cancellation and operator failure. Program cancellation is the less troublesome of the two. In recent years, charter markets have been sufficiently "iffy" that several widely advertised programs have been canceled entirely or severely curtailed. As long as the operator remains solvent, however, this situation doesn't necessarily mean big trouble for travelers.

> Charter flying has been a big business in Europe for years, and the main European-based transatlantic charter airlines are large and stable. Many are divisions or affiliates of the major national airlines. By contrast, U.S. charter airlines have tended to be small and—with a few exceptions—distressingly short-lived. At this time, no U.S. charter line is both big and long-standing. Most are either small (under five wide-body airplanes) or new (less than five years old). Over the last few years, a number were born, grew to substantial size, and faded away over a span of only two or three years. With a large inventory of used airplanes sitting around idle, just about anybody can organize a charter airline, and it sometimes seems that just about everybody has tried. As a result, it's almost impossible to name what might be the main U.S. charter airlines for this summer.

In many instances, an operator who doesn't sell enough seats on a charter program to make it pay simply cancels the charter and cuts a deal with a major airline to accept the few travelers who did buy charter tickets. Travelers in this situation often enjoy a better flight than they expected—a major airline at the charter price. In fact, some large charter operators regularly use this technique to extend their season. Knowing that early and late bookings won't be enough to fill a DC-10, for example, Condor may buy space on Lufthansa for these dates rather than operate their own plane half empty.

Even if the operator doesn't arrange an alternative, as long as the company stays in business, you'll get a refund. Your main worry may be finding replacement space after a late charter program cancellation.

Operator or airline failure, on the other hand, can be a disaster. The specter of tour-operator and airline failure has haunted the U.S. charter industry since its inception. Fear of being stranded has made charter travel an unacceptable alternative for many cautious travelers. Fortunately, there were no major tour-operator failures last year to strand charter passengers in Europe, but a major Caribbean operator folded. One year without a significant failure in Europe doesn't eliminate the risk for 1987.

As mentioned, a successful charter purchase requires performance on the part of two separate suppliers—the wholesale tour operator from which you buy your seats, and the airline that actually provides your travel services. If either supplier drops the ball, you're in trouble. Depending on circumstances, either an operator failure or an airline failure can strand you, delay you, or cause you to lose the money you paid for a charter flight.

Airline failure is usually a less severe problem than operator failure. If an airline fails, the operator normally still has your transportation money and can make deals with other airlines to operate your trip. What happens to you, the traveler, depends on the stage of your trip.

The worst case is when you're already at your destination and about to come home. You'll probably have to wait there while the wholesale tour operator scrounges up a plane from another charter airline or some extra seats on a scheduled airline. During peak travel seasons, this process may take up to a week or so. You normally aren't out any air-fare money, but you may have some extra destination expenses while you're waiting for your alternative flight, and the delay may entail costs of missed work time. If you can't live with the tour operator's "rescue" schedule—which you may not even know about for several days—you may have to pay your own way back.

If an airline fails just before the trip is scheduled to begin, you face a similar sort of problem: a possible delay of days or weeks while the operator arranges alternative airline space. If you can't live with the new schedule, federal regulations require that you get your money back in full—but, of course, you miss the trip. On the other hand, if the failure occurs several weeks or months before your trip is due to start, you might not even notice its effects. The wholesale tour operators can usually find a replacement charter airline within that time.

Operator failure is usually much harder on the travelers involved. Operator failure often means that some or all of the money earmarked for airline payment is gone—the operator has somehow obtained access to it and diverted it to other uses. Without any source of payment, airlines are not obliged to take you anywhere—or bring you back from where they already took you.

Charter passengers theoretically have two government-required "safety nets" to prevent monetary loss: tour operators must post a performance bond, and passengers' charter-flight prepayments are supposed to be placed in trust or escrow accounts to be used only for air-travel payment. Certainly, these protections have decreased consumer problems with operator failure. But the safety net clearly has some gaping holes in it—airlines and operators still fail, and travelers are still stranded. Many travelers find that extra-cost "trip-interruption insurance" is the best protection against potential problems. You can buy it through your travel agent at the same time you book your charter.

Buying Charter Tickets

Charter-flight tickets are sold only through retail travel agents—you cannot buy them directly from a charter airline. Most wholesale tour operators have subsidiary retail outlets, and they often encourage travelers to buy through these in-house subsidiaries. However, any travel agent can obtain charter tickets for you, at standard prices, and earn standard commissions in the process.

---

The 1984 collapse of Jet Exchange, a large West Coast wholesale tour operator, illustrates the range of operator-failure consequences, and ways for travelers to avoid or minimize the risks of failure. At the time it closed, Jet Exchange was involved with two main programs—flights to Germany with the German charter line LTU and flights to France with the French charter airline Minerve.

Immediately after Jet Exchange closed, LTU announced that it would honor all documented reservations for return travel and would even honor reservations for round trips originating within ten days of the failure—despite the fact that management knew it would not be paid. Nobody was stranded, and people leaving within ten days traveled as if nothing had gone wrong.

Minerve, on the other hand, did not honor return reservations or future outbound reservations. Several hundred Minerve travelers were stranded in Europe, and hundreds more suddenly found that the future trips for which they had paid would no longer be provided either by Jet Exchange or by the charter airline.

LTU management deserves full praise for timely, effective, and generous action on behalf of Jet Exchange travelers. In an industry often known for poor standards of business ethics, it's a pleasure to report on a company that went well beyond its legal requirements in order to help travelers who would otherwise have lost hundreds of dollars.

It is also significant that the Jet Exchange program represented only a small portion of the total LTU capacity. The flights had to be flown to fulfill the contract with other operators, in any case. Minerve, on the other hand, took a narrow view of its responsibilities and simply canceled.

Travelers who had prepaid trips on either airline departing later than ten days after the failure wound up with neither their trips nor their money back. Their immediate choices were either to buy alternative tickets from another supplier or forget about their trips.

Neither component of the charter-flight consumer protection system really worked. At an average ticket price of around $500, the required total bond value of $200,000 covered only about four hundred travelers—far fewer than had booked and prepaid through Jet Exchange. In addition, many of the travelers' or travel agents' checks that should have been made out to the trust or escrow accounts were probably made out to Jet Exchange and thus excluded from the protection program.

Of course, the most obvious way to avoid charter-operator or charter-airline failures is to avoid charters altogether. And that's not simply flippant advice, either, since several noncharter alternatives offer fares comparable to charter fares. Best bets include low-fare scheduled airlines and bulk-fare deals (see chapters 3 and 5 for details).

But charters really are the best deals on many routes, and travelers do not have to take unacceptable risks to enjoy their benefits. Here are some of the ways you can avoid—or at least minimize—the chances of being stranded or losing your prepayment:

- Look for programs that use charter airlines with demonstrated records for reliability. Many "name-brand" U.S. and foreign scheduled airlines provide charter service, as well. The biggest foreign-flag charter carriers—Air Charter (France), British Airtours, Balair (Switzerland), Condor (Germany), LTU (Germany), Martinair (Netherlands), and Spantax (Spain)—either are affiliated with major scheduled carriers or, at a minimum, are large independent corporations with extensive intra-European schedules as well as transatlantic services. Your travel agent should be able to advise you about the airlines used in any charter program.
- Look for tour operators with a demonstrated track record for reliability. Probably the safest bets are those wholesale tour operators that are affiliates of top European charter airlines: DER Tours (Condor) and German Charters (LTU) come to mind as among the most stable. But quite a few independents have also developed good reputations: Council (formerly C.I.E.E.), GWV Travel, Wainwrights, Travac, and Unitravel are among the larger tour operators based in the United States with charter programs from major cities all around the country, and many more operate regionally or from single U.S. cities. Unfortunately, however, even a good fifteen-year track record doesn't assure future performance. Until recently, Carefree David, Value Vacations, and Jet Exchange would probably have been on most travel agents' lists of "reliable" operators. Your travel agent should make special inquiries in the trade about how any operator that he or she may have used satisfactorily in the past is doing at the time you're booking your charter.
- Where you have a choice, buy a charter on a program that shares a large airplane with several different wholesale tour operators' programs. That way the fail-

ure of a single operator won't require the entire flight schedule to be canceled.
- Make sure that your check (if you buy direct) or your agent's check is made out to the escrow or trust account established for each charter program. This protection is required by the U.S. government of all charters, yet operators report that over half of the checks they receive are made out to them, rather than to those special accounts. Any charter traveler who makes a check out to a tour operator rather than an escrow or trust account is voluntarily giving up the security available for his investment. Never add unnecessary risk to your travel situation by being uninformed.
- Explore the optional trip interruption insurance programs that are available to protect you against operator or airline failure. The extra cost of such insurance—up to 5 percent of the amount of your fare—should be added to the cost of the charter ticket in your comparisons with alternative transportation options. Also, by the time you read this book, some travel-agent consortiums and cooperative groups may be offering operator- or airline-failure insurance coverage as a "free" benefit to their customers.
- Buy through an accredited travel agency. In bail-out situations, the industry has tended to provide more help to travelers who bought their tickets through agencies than to those who bought directly from a defunct airline or tour operator.

Despite all your best pretrip efforts, you can still get stranded. Probably at least one charter program will strand its passengers next year. If it happens to you, you could be lucky—like the Jet Exchange travelers on LTU—and be able to return with no serious additional expense or schedule delays.

It's more likely, however, that you'll have problems. If you're at the airport, ready to come home, and your promised airplane doesn't show up, keep calm and get all the information available about what is happening.

Unless you are assured of a quick fix, you should immediately face your most important question: how long can you wait for a solution to be found that doesn't require you to pay anything extra? Recognize that it could easily take up to forty-eight hours before you have the full story, and that you might have to wait for as much as a week before your charter airline or tour operator can implement a no-cost-to-you rescue operation.

If you can't accept a delay of one to three days, you might as well resign yourself to extra cost, and immediately start shopping for the "least worst" new ticket home: one way on a low-fare airline, or standby (if available), or a seat on some other charter. But if you take this sort of initiative to get back the quickest way, you'll have to pay separately, with little chance of refund.

If you decide you can wait a day or two, you can expect some sort of bail-out to be organized. If you're lucky, either the tour operator or the airline (whichever did not fold) will have a representative at the airport to keep you informed and to help with whatever arrangements are offered—alternative flights, interim accommodations, meals, and the like.

The worst-case failure scenario is when you really can't find anybody at the airport who knows anything about what has happened. This situation arises at airports where your charter airline doesn't have its own personnel—where the airport itself or some other airline normally handles the check-in and boarding. If that is the case, and unless you're really out of funds, it's probably a good idea to check into an airport-area hotel, if for no other reason than to have a place where people can contact you. Even if you don't get reimbursed, or even if you don't stay all night, it's good insurance. Have at least one person in your party hang around the airport for late developments, and at least one accessible to a telephone in the hotel room or somewhere else a telephone is available.

Then, telephone some friend or relative at home who can contact the wholesale tour operator's home office in the United States (in case of an airline failure) or your retail travel agent (in case of a tour operator failure) to find out what's going on and what you should do. Someone at home can be far more effective than you can be from Europe.

Almost all of the U.S. charter airlines and tour opera-

> tors will likely provide reliable service this year. But the unfortunate fact is that many of them are undercapitalized and potentially vulnerable to failure if something should go wrong, either internally or in the marketplace. Unless you are really confident of the principals, include the cost of trip-interruption insurance coverage when you compare the prices of transatlantic air-fare alternatives.

Charter-flight schedules and fares are not contained in agents' computerized reservations systems. To get the necessary details, agents have to rely on brochures and telephone calls to charter operators.

For that reason, some of the less enterprising travel agents tend to ignore charters—often to bad-mouth them. It's much easier for them to sell you a major-line APEX or a low-fare airline ticket. Any travel agent has the capability to sell you a charter—but finding an agent who will take the time to get details for you is a matter that you will have to investigate for yourself.

# 5

# Bulk Fares

*A New Wrinkle
That Can Save You Big Dollars*

Bulk fares are a recent development, and a very promising one for budget-minded travelers. They can undercut round-trip APEX transatlantic major-airline fares by as much as $200, without entailing any sacrifice in service quality.

Here's how the idea works. One airline might find that its bookings are slow for a particular period. Another wants to start a new European route from a U.S. city that hasn't had nonstop service before and it isn't sure it can sell enough tickets to fill the planes. A third foresees substantial excess capacity on some routes. A fourth is hard up for cash and needs assured revenues. For these—and other reasons—airlines may decide to sell large numbers of seats in bulk to tour operators who will, in turn, market them to the public. The tour operators, often the same ones who run charter programs, commit for the space, and perhaps even pay in advance. It's then the tour operators' job to sell those seats—and they do it by cutting the prices.

The airlines don't like to sell too many of these bulk seats. The "bulk" price they get is far below even the cheapest APEX fare. But by selling in bulk, an airline can guarantee that it will have that income—no matter what happens to traffic. So most bulk-fare programs involve something like twenty-five to one hundred seats per 747 or DC-10 flight, enough to provide a good revenue base, but not so much that planes are filled with low-revenue passengers.

Bulk-fare deals can be made either on major or low-fare airlines. In 1986, bulk-fare deals were made on both types. In fact, some big wholesale tour operators that once ran large charter programs have switched almost exclusively to bulk-fare programs instead. In fact, from the promotions, it's sometimes hard to tell the difference between charter and bulk-fare programs.

## The 1987 Fare Outlook

Bulk fares look like one of the best opportunities for you to cut your transportation bill in 1987. These special fares should be available on several key transatlantic routes. Look for prices that are about $50 to $100 below APEX from the East Coast and $100 to $200 below APEX from the West Coast for comparable periods.

London and Frankfurt will probably be the main European gateways with bulk-fare deals from a dozen or more major U.S. cities. But you should also look for bulk fares to other capital cities such as Amsterdam and Brussels, and perhaps even to some of the usual high-fare bastions in Scandinavia and France, or to some of the more out-of-the way gateways.

Bulk fares will theoretically be available all year. But your best deals will obviously be in the low and shoulder seasons, when many airlines will be very eager to add to their otherwise low revenue base.

## Convenience

There are no inherent convenience differences between bulk-fare travel and regular-ticket travel on the same airline. However, the way airlines offer bulk fares may introduce some convenience differences to be aware of in relation to other options.

Bulk fares are used, for example, to beef up traffic on schedules that aren't competitive. While people willing to pay full APEX fares could go nonstop on some airlines, the lower bulk price compensates for the convenience disadvantage of stops and plane changes for many bargain hunters. Bulk fares are also used to attract travelers through some of the less-used gateways in the United States.

Certainly, not all bulk fares entail less-than-nonstop convenience. Several of the biggest major carriers have already negotiated 1987 peak-season bulk-fare deals on nonstop flights from many different U.S. cities to Europe.

There aren't any standard restrictions on bulk fares. Specific ticket conditions depend on the deals struck between individual airlines and consolidators. Bulk-fare tickets normally have fewer restrictions than APEX; many don't have any. If there are restrictions, the most likely is a minimum stay. Since tour operators want as much time as possible to sell, advance purchase requirements are uncommon with bulk-fare tickets.

Some bulk-fare tickets are limited by season or by day of the week or are sold only for specific flights and dates; others are good for any available flight. Many airlines complained that their 1985 and 1986 peak-season flights were being filled up with too many low-revenue bulk-fare travelers. So for 1987, you can expect some additional seasonal limitations. And there probably won't be a wide selection of bulk-fare seats during the very peak of the season.

Finally, the bulk-fare market is more fluid than the normal APEX market. Some bulk-fare deals are established months in advance for an entire season. But others come up suddenly—if a certain airline runs into a slow period or competition pushes too much capacity on an individual route. So you won't know exactly what is available for any given period until closer to the dates you may want to travel than you will with APEX. For that reason, reliance on bulk fares might be a little more of a gamble in terms of the scheduling of your trip for maximum economy.

Comfort

Nothing in bulk-fare travel is inherently more or less comfortable than travel with any other form of ticket. Since bulk-fare deals are available on scheduled major airlines and low-fare airlines, comfort and service quality standards are apt to be as good or better, on the average, than charter standards.

But comfort depends on the airline, and some scheduled major and low-fare airlines' service-quality levels are actually below those of a few of the better charter lines. If you're considering the bulk-fare option, your first consideration is the airline you'd be taking. Check the data on comfort and service quality for that line in chapters 2, 3, and 4.

> In chapter 4, an analogy was drawn to the purchase of a manufactured article—your deal is with the retailer, not the manufacturer, and if something goes wrong, your only recourse is to the retailer.
>
> With bulk fare, the proper analogy is with buying an insurance policy from a local independent agent. Once you have bought your policy, the insurance company stands behind it, no matter what might happen to the agent.

Contingencies

One of the best advantages to the bulk-fare alternative is that it provides better protection against operator failure than a charter. With bulk fare, your transportation contract is with the airline, not—as in the case of a charter—with a wholesale tour operator. The airline is responsible for getting you home.

The main risk element in bulk fares is that you're totally tied to the airline and operators involved in issuing the tickets. Typically, your bulk-fare ticket will have an endorsement indicating that it is valid only on the issuing airline and cannot be transferred to another.

Accordingly, if your flight is canceled or delayed, you can't take your ticket and expect to get on some other line's next flight. But a bulk-fare ticket is probably no riskier than an APEX ticket. In either case, the airline will obviously put you on its next available flight. And when the issuing line is clearly at fault—for a missed connection, as an example—it may well endorse your ticket over to another line anyhow (if the other line has space available), even though it loses the revenue from your trip.

Buying Bulk-Fare Tickets

Bulk fares are not as widely available as regular APEX or low-fare airline tickets. They are not in the airline-reservations computers most travel agents use. They are not available directly from an airline through the ticket offices, and you can't buy them at the airport.

Instead, bulk-fare deals are normally handled by the same people who organize charters (see chapter 4). These people are already set up to distribute low-priced airline tickets; they make the basic agreements with airlines and sell some seats through their own retail subsidiaries and the rest through other retail travel agents.

To travelers, the distinction between bulk fare and charter may appear to be more of an obscure legal nicety than a significant factor. In fact, the distinction is important when something goes wrong; you're normally better off with a bulk-fare deal than a charter.

Wholesale tour operators in the United States still tend to be small. Many are active in only one major U.S. metropolitan-area market, and a few of the larger ones may operate regionally. They generally advertise in local newspapers that serve their market areas. Accordingly, your best bet to find out about which wholesalers are offering bulk deals—and which agents are handling them—is to read the weekly travel sections of your metropolitan newspapers, usually appearing in the Sunday edition.

In their promotional materials, wholesale tour operators often don't make a clear distinction between their charter and their bulk-fare deals, and prices are often comparable. So if you're looking at options, you have to ask specifically which of the low-fare specials are charters and which are bulk fares. You also have to ask specifically about schedules (check especially on the possibilities of extra stops or changes of plane). And you have to ask about the specific airline—so you can evaluate the comfort and quality standards.

In a few programs, the operators may not know, early in the season, whether any given flight and date will be operated with a charter or a bulk-fare deal. Even when they accept your reservation, they may retain the option of arbitrarily assigning you to either a charter or a bulk-fare deal, depending on how many tickets they sell and the deals they subsequently make with airlines. The normal contracts allow operators this flexibility. So if you want to guarantee a preferred option, you should insist on supplementary written assurance that your trip will be as initially specified. If the operator won't give such assurance, find another operator—or be prepared to accept a lower-quality option than you originally expected.

Despite somewhat greater uncertainties than on APEX tickets, bulk-fare tickets represent a tremendous opportunity to cut your transatlantic transportation bills. Many will find the minor drawbacks more than offset by prices that are as much as $200 below the usual options. On the average, bulk-fare deals probably represent a product slightly superior to charter flights, at about the same prices. You can look for a very big year for bulk fares.

# 6

# Flexible-Schedule Travel

*A Little Flexibility
Pays Big Dividends*

If you can afford to be even slightly flexible in your travel plans—in terms of dates of your trips, the city from which you originate or your destination gateway city—you can often fly to Europe at a substantially lower cost than on any firm-schedule option. Being "flexible" doesn't mean keeping your suitcase by your bedside at all times awaiting a call that sends you racing to the airport. Instead, it means some combination of willingness and ability to:

- delay making your final arrangements until a few weeks before you leave
- remain uncertain about your exact flight date and schedule until a week before you depart
- accept a flight to some European city other than your preferred destination
- conform exactly with someone else's travel plans

Quite a few different kinds of travel marketing organizations have sprung up in recent years to sell various types of flexible-schedule travel, or you can sometimes make deals directly with individuals.

Basically, all the different organizations that sell flexible-schedule travel provide outlets for airline seats (as well as cruise cabins, tours, and hotel rooms) that would almost certainly remain unsold through normal retail travel-agent channels.

These organizations market this excess capacity much the way tickets to Broadway shows that remain unsold by the day of performance are marketed at dramatically reduced prices by a special agency in Times Square.

The suppliers—airlines and tour operators—prefer to use relatively anonymous marketing organizations to sell off their excess capacity. That way they can keep trying to sell at full price through their retail travel-agent channels.

## "Generic" Air Travel

A few travel-marketing organizations specialize in what can be described as "generic air travel." In a parallel with generic medicines and grocery products, this air travel is on fully government-certificated and approved airlines, but with no prior "brand" identification. You never know which airline you'll be flying until you see the plane at the airport. And, like generic drugs and groceries, generic air travel can be a lot less expensive than the identical product sold under its normal "major-brand" label.

The system is based on the premise that there are four important variables in a flight: the originating city, the destination city, the date of travel, and the price. Major-brand airlines allow you to fix origin, destination, and date—for a relatively high price.

Generic air travel provides reduced prices for travelers who can compromise on one or more of the other variables. The generic-travel pioneer Airhitch fixes the price and treats exact date and destination as variables. In 1987 fares will be the same as in 1986: $160 each way from major northeastern airports (Boston, New York, and Washington); $229 each way from the Midwest, Texas, and Denver; and $269 each way from the West Coast. Fares may be even lower on some New York–London and New York–Paris flights this summer.

Travelers register with the generic travel organization, with a fee (approximately $25) that is applied toward the ticket cost; you indicate a departure-date range and a preferred destination gateway city in Europe. Then, about five days before the beginning of the indicated date range, you call a toll-free number to find out what flights will probably be available. You are notified of one or more flights—with dates and departure times—for which you should stand by. At that time, you send in the remainder of the cost and receive a voucher for the flight in the mail. Then, on the designated date, you go to the airport and check in as an Airhitch standby. If seats aren't available, you stand by for the next flight—possibly the same day, more likely the next. If no seats are available during the entire departure-date range, you get a refund. However, Airhitch reports that at no time last year did a week pass without enough seats to Europe to satisfy the demand. Return flights, at the same cost and on the same basis, are arranged with affiliated offices in Europe.

According to the generic-travel organizations, about 90 percent of these flights to "Europe" actually arrive at airports within a 300-mile radius of Brussels. The main gateway airports are London, Amsterdam, Brussels, Frankfurt, Geneva, Madrid, Milan, Munich, Paris, Rome, and Zurich.

Flights can be on "major brand" airlines, low-fare airlines, or charters. Last year, the mix was about half scheduled airlines and half charters. Of course, you don't get your choice: either you take what is offered or lose your fee and your place in line.

The generic-travel organizations' fares stay the same all season. Accordingly, savings are less dramatic for early- and late-season flights, when charter fares are much lower.

Of course, this approach has some risks. It's basically a form of Standby but operated by an outside organization rather than individual airlines. As such, it does not guarantee a seat. And even if you get a seat, a trip to London isn't always an acceptable alternative if you really want to go to Paris, Zurich, or Rome. Getting from where you arrive to where you really want to go could more than eat up the possible fare savings—and add as much as two extra days of arduous land travel. Other costs not to be overlooked may be travel expenses—whether bus or train fares or parking for a car—for potentially more than one trip to the airport if you don't make a flight on your first day. Or even more considerable may be the expense of an overnight stay in your departure city if you live elsewhere and can't return home if your Standby carries over to a second day.

But the Standby system seems to work pretty well. Generic-travel organizations claim that over 99 percent of the travelers get a seat on their first attempt, and 60 percent get their first-choice destination.

The other main drawback is that you may well wind up on one of the very lowest-quality services—a three-stop, twenty-hour endurance test on flights from the West Coast, or a dense-packed seating configuration that might prove excruciating. Operators concede this risk: the system is intended for travelers who care much more about price than quality.

On balance, it would appear that this type of travel is best suited to the youth/student market. Other travelers with a youthful outlook—and more time than money—will also find it attractive.

### Late-Booking Charters

A somewhat more prosaic approach to last-minute travel is the growing practice by wholesale tour operators of selling unsold charter seats at reduced prices. Some large operators even establish a formal late-booking price schedule at the beginning of the season, along with the regular price schedule. Prices from the East Coast (where most of these late-booking flights depart) are generally $100 below the regular prices.

Of course, the fact that last-minute seat prices are established for the entire season does not mean that seats will be available on every flight during the season—or even on any peak-period flight. But enough seats should be available for at least most of the summer to make this a viable option for people who do not require absolute certainty in their travel dates. These last-minute charter seats are available through the same travel agents that handle regular charters.

### Last-Minute Travel Clubs

"Last-minute" travel clubs have recently received extensive publicity. While most of the "product" available on a last-minute basis consists of complete tour packages and cruises, some air-only trips are offered. And the complete tour packages are often really good deals at the reduced prices—even if they aren't especially good deals at their regular prices.

The mix of tours offered through last-minute travel clubs mirrors the main focus of the regular tour market. Most of the action to Europe is during the summer, although some popular destinations are offered year-round.

Last-minute prices represent cuts of 20 to 50 percent off "list" prices on most tours and flights. As might be expected, the price cut tends to be inversely related to the number of selling days left before departure. Typical summer 1986 offerings included the following:

- London package from New York, $444, seven days including airfare and hotel, list price $609
- London/Paris tour from New York, $655, fourteen days including airfare and hotels, list price $879
- Rhine River cruise from New York, $1099, five days including meals and some sightseeing, list price $1500

In an industry rife with "low balling" and promotion of "discounts" that really aren't discounts, last-minute pricing seems to be refreshingly honest and accurate. Most of the last-minute operators routinely cite "regular" prices as well as their selling prices, and a spot check indicated that the regular prices were honestly quoted. Also, quoted last-minute prices are accurate and complete, except occasionally for departure taxes. There are no hidden extras.

Typical lead times for last-minute tours and flights range from a few days to a few weeks. A sampling of offerings last summer indicated that most of the tours sold at any one time were for departures within one to four weeks of the times they were announced. In a very few cases, departures were offered on an "all-year" or "all-summer" basis.

A few organizations indicated that special prices were also available on other travel services, such as rental cars and hotel rooms. These, however, were not listed in any of the bulletins or the hot-line messages; you have to make a special request.

Most last-minute travel-marketing organizations operate as clubs. Travelers have to join officially and pay dues before they are eligible to purchase the travel services. There are no inherent reasons why a club structure is beneficial to purchasers, but the club approach certainly makes life easier for the sellers:

- "Dues" are a significant source of income—a way of generating revenue even from people who may not travel.
- The membership requirement limits access to the toll-free national "hot lines" maintained by several—without such

limitation, telephone costs incurred to deal with curious nontravelers would be excessive.

Club membership is not required by any government or industry regulation, as was the late and unlamented six-month organization-membership requirement for charter-flight eligibility. These clubs will enroll you and sell you tickets at the same time.

Clubs handle communications with their members in two ways. Some use recorded toll-free hot-line telephone messages. Others prefer to use printed listings in the form of bulletins. Both media have advantages and disadvantages.

For one, telephone hot lines can be updated daily. The problem with hot lines is that each user has to listen to the entire rundown, regardless of his or her specific interest. With a large inventory of tours, the recorded message can run five to ten minutes, and listening to a rundown of European air-tour dates and prices, for example, can become extremely tiresome to someone who really wants three days in Las Vegas. And the tours are sometimes rattled off so quickly that you may have to listen through the complete tape twice to make sure you have all the data. Finally, a heavy load of long calls leads to frequent busy signals.

Printed bulletins—mailed or sent by "electronic-mail" service—make it easy for travelers to isolate their special interests and ignore the rest of the inventory. Also, club members who receive bulletins don't have to scribble hasty notes during a recitation of dozens of tour options. On the other hand, printed bulletins can't keep pace with truly last-minute offerings. One operator of a "hot-line" club reported that he often gets his first availability on a tour only a week or two before its departure—which means that there is no way for that particular tour to be offered through a biweekly printed bulletin.

Most last-minute travel clubs are located in the eastern United States and the Midwest. Most of the flight and package tours to Europe they offer originate in the East or Midwest, as well. And, of course, a disproportionate number of tours and flights sold in all markets depart from New York—reflecting the travel industry's traditional overuse of this gateway.

The West is a difficult area for last-minute tours. Most marketers indicated that West Coast airlines and tour operators don't have enough excess capacity to provide a viable market.

There are, however, ways around this problem. For example, clubs can arrange for California passengers to use a low-fare airline to connect with last-minute tours and flights departing from Chicago, Miami, and New York.

Indeed, the main caveat in last-minute travel purchase is the limitation in departure-city options. You might find a spectacularly good deal on a tour departing from New York that exactly suits your needs. But the costs of buying separately ticketed transportation from your home city to New York and back could easily wipe out your saving, compared with a list-price tour or a flight that departs directly from your home city or one that permits a low-cost add-on fare to New York.

Companion Tickets

All of the major domestic airlines in the United States operate some sort of "frequent-traveler" program. These programs offer a mix of "awards" to enrolled members, based on accumulated mileage logged on the sponsoring (or affiliated) airlines. Awards can range from a free upgrade from Coach to First Class to unlimited free system-wide travel for a month. Some of these programs specifically offer awards that include travel benefits for the members' "companions" as well as for the members themselves. Enterprising frequent travelers can opt for these companion awards, and then sell the companion ticket to anyone willing to pay their asking prices.

This practice is perfectly within the airlines' frequent-traveler program rules. Your main limitation as a buyer is that you have to conform your trip to the schedule of the person from whom you buy the companion ticket. Most programs require that companions use the same flights, at least for the "going" portion of a round trip. With some programs, you also have to make your deal far enough in advance to have the companion ticket issued by the airline in your name.

Price levels depend strictly on what the seller thinks he or she can get, and what the buyer is willing to pay. In other words, they're subject to individual negotiation. One ad, for example, offered a First-Class round-trip companion ticket from San Francisco to Germany for $600, surely one of the best travel deals of all time.

Companion travel is especially attractive for single travelers.

Acquiring a companion ticket from a frequent-traveler participant potentially offers a great saving, at least in terms of last year's typical asking prices. The main problem is quite simply that the total number of these opportunities during the course of the year is probably measured in the hundreds, compared with millions of people who want to travel. Still, there's no harm in keeping your eyes on the classified travel ads.

Buying Flexible-Schedule Travel

You can't buy any of these flexible-schedule options from your travel agent. They're not in any of the computer systems, and most are sold direct. The prices allow no room for any travel-agent commissions.

"Generic" flights are available only from the small number of organizations that handle this type of travel:

Airhitch/Worldwide Destinations Unlimited
   (Cooperative for International and Intercultural Exchange)
   2901 Broadway, Suite 100
   New York, NY 10025
   212-864-2000
   Deposit: $25
Access
   250 West Fifty-seventh Street, Room 511
   New York, NY 10019
   212-333-7280
   Membership fee: $45

Several organizations offer last-minute flights and tours:

Discount Travel International
   7563 Haverford Avenue
   Philadelphia, PA 19151
   215-668-2182
   Membership fee: $45 per family
Encore Short Notice
   4501 Forbes Boulevard
   Lanham, MD 20706
   301-459-8082 (800-638-8976 for information)
   Membership fee: $36 per family

Last Minute Travel Club
  6A Glenville Avenue
  Allston, MA 02134
  617-267-9800
  Membership fee: $30 individual; $35 family
Moments Notice
  40 East Forty-ninth Street
  New York, NY 10017
  212-486-0503
  Membership fee: $45
On Call to Travel
  11739 SW Beaverton Highway, Suite 120
  Beaverton, OR 97005
  503-643-7212
  Membership fee: $45 per household
Stand Buys Limited
  311 West Superior Street
  Chicago, IL 60610
  312-943-5737
  Membership fee: $45
Vacations to Go
  5901/D Westheimer
  Houston, TX 77057
  713-974-2121
  Membership fee: $29.95 per family
Worldwide Discount Travel Club
  1674 Meridian Avenue
  Miami Beach, FL 33139
  305-534-2082
  Membership fee: $45

Companion-travel tickets are normally obtained directly from the individuals who "earn" these awards. Individuals with companion tickets to sell generally advertise in the classified sections of major newspapers, under "travel," "tours," "transportation," or "tickets" headings.

# 7

# Discount Tickets

*Caution—You're Bending
the System*

Real discount air tickets were defined in chapter 2 as tickets sold for less than the airlines say those particular tickets should cost. Ticket discounting is wide open for flights across the North Pacific—just about everybody seems to be able to arrange for discount prices that are 20 to 30 percent below the airlines' lowest promotional fares. What started out in the ethnic Oriental communities has definitely moved into the mainstream.

Ticket discounting is considerably less active for travel to Europe than for Asia. Still, more and more discount tickets are coming into the marketplace. It's important for travelers to know about them—what they are, how they work, and who sells them—whether or not they decide to buy.

Discounting—How it Works

True discount (below list price) airline tickets reach the marketplace in three main forms:

**Straight Discount**

The biggest travel discounts originate with the airlines themselves: they often have unused capacity, and they fill those unsold seats by cutting prices. They sell these seats to consolidators, who buy, or commit themselves to buy, a specified portion of an airline's or hotel's yearly or seasonal capacity. By guaranteeing that volume, the consolidators obtain substantial price concessions. They then wholesale their discount-priced air tickets to discount agencies, which sell them to the public below list price. These consolidators are the main source for discount tickets.

This no-pretense discounting is illegal in some countries, and contrary to airline industry rules everywhere, but it takes place anyhow. Every so often the various national regulatory agencies and the international and national airline industry associations clamp down briefly, but economic forces always bring discounting right back.

**Direct Rebate**

Although air fares are still regulated in many markets, travel-agent commissions typically are not. So airlines can effectively circumvent price regulation simply by increasing the amount of "commission" they pay to travel agents. Thus, for example, instead of the usual 8 to 10 percent, an airline can offer "override" commissions of as much as 50 percent. These overrides are supposed to be granted solely as sales incentives for travel agents; the official rules prohibit agents from passing any of this increased commission along to travelers. As a practical matter, however, discount outlets normally rebate all but 10 to 20 percent of these huge margins.

In fact, the line between rebating and straight discounting is often very hard to distinguish. When rebate-ticket dealers talk with their airline suppliers, the usual question is a simple, straightforward, "What is my net price?"

**Indirect Rebate**

Rather than offer a direct (cash-discount) rebate, airlines will often provide indirect rebates. An indirect rebate generally takes the form of some optional add-on travel service that is offered at a below-normal price when purchased in conjunction with an air ticket bought at list price. The add-on travel services usually consist of hotel accommodations or rental cars. Indirect rebates—or, if you prefer, airfare subsidies—avoid some of the stigma attached by the industry and government regulators to price-cutting, but the net effect is the same, if travelers can use the extra services provided at cut-rate prices. Indirect rebates are offered for the same reasons as direct rebates.

Quite often some air fares—even the lowest APEX and Super APEX fares—will turn out to be too high, in light of market conditions, to attract enough business. The most straightforward remedy is to reduce the fares to levels that will attract a satisfactory amount of business.

But straightforward remedies don't always appeal to the airlines or the governments that regulate them. It might be that the United States and the European government involved can't agree on what a new fare level should be, or perhaps they're disagreeing about something entirely different, with air fares serving as a surrogate battleground. Or perhaps a foreign government wants to protect its major airline against competition from a low-fare airline and won't allow the low-fare airline to cut prices. For whatever combinations of reasons, you frequently find situations where airlines prefer to (or have to) subsidize relatively high fares rather than cut them.

As an example, in the winter of 1984–1985, the British government refused to allow British Airways, British Caledonian, Pan American, and TWA to introduce some very low APEX fares to London. The stated reason was that allowing British Airways to cut fares would render it vulnerable to antitrust suits in U.S. courts for predatory competition against Virgin Atlantic. As a result, the comparatively high shoulder-season fares were still in effect during the slow periods of November and early December, as well as (briefly) in January after the holidays. To compensate for these artificially high fares, the airlines flying to London introduced special deals that included "free" hotels, "free" rental cars, or even both. When the British government finally allowed the new fares to go into effect in January, the airlines offered the alternative of the new, low fares without any extras, or the older, higher fares with the freebies.

You may find comparable deals in spring, summer, and fall of 1987. The typical subsidy arrangement does not tie you down any more than the associated airfare. For example, if you find a free hotel or car rental for a week, that doesn't mean that you can only stay in Europe one week on that program. You're free to travel independently as far and as long as you wish, within the return limits of the basic ticket. If you want to keep the car or stay longer at the hotel, you pay for the extra time at regular rates. The land package is simply a way to add value to compensate for the high "list price" of the flight.

These subsidized air-fare deals can be purchased directly from the airlines or through your travel agent. They're usually heavily and conspicuously promoted.

Normally, any subsidy introduced by one major line is quickly copied by its competitors. You very seldom see any one line with an obvious competitive edge. Low-fare airlines' subsidy programs, however, are sometimes ignored by the major lines, especially if the subsidy is obviously designed to compensate for the line's inability to offer as low a fare as it might wish. In any event, however, it might pay to shop around—sometimes one line will have a temporarily superior subsidy package during the specific time you want to travel.

**Throwaway Packages**

The lowest available air fare in many travel markets is a "tour basing" or "group" fare (ITX or GIT) that is officially available only when sold as part of an inclusive tour package, in combination with "land" arrangements—hotel accommodations, rental cars, and the like. In some cases, regulations set by the governments of destination countries specify a minimum qualifying land package (such as, for example, $20 per person per day).

Inclusive tour packages, combining air transportation and hotel accommodations, can sometimes be used to provide inexpensive air fares. When no minimum land package is required, tour operators can sell tour packages that include hotel accommodations that travelers are advised not to use because they are unacceptable or nonexistent. When minimum land costs are required, tour operators can sometimes arrange for a cash refund of the accommodations cost when the travelers arrive at their destinations. The system can even be used for one-way travel, with a land package consisting of a chit for a worthless return trip.

This procedure is obviously within the letter of the applicable laws, even if not within the spirit. Individual airlines may not like this sort of market, but many of the biggest names participate, and use of this type of service entails no risks for consumers beyond the ordinary risks of charter or bulk-fare travel.

The throwaway package system works only when tour-basing airfares are available at levels substantially lower than any airfares that can be purchased without any tour arrangements. At this writing—and for the last several years—there have been no transatlantic tour-basing fares any lower than the least expensive APEX excursions, and it's unlikely to happen this summer. For that reason, you haven't seen any throwaway packages for transatlantic travel. However, this system is widely used to cut the cost of travel within Europe—see chapter 15.

**Agency Discounts**

Smaller discounts—no more than 10 percent and often 5 percent or less—originate with certain travel agents. Even when airlines and hotels don't offer large overrides or net wholesale prices, some agencies give their customers a discount by splitting the regular commission with them. This discount is usually offered in the form of a refund check, given to the customer at the time the ticket is purchased; in a few cases, the discount is in the form of credit for future travel purchases. These agencies often restrict their services to ticketing—their customers have to do their own research and make their own reservations. Alternatively, a small but growing number of agencies charge a fixed fee rather than a percentage for their reservations and ticket-issuing services. Reservations and ticketing services are priced separately. Either way, you can expect to save no more than 10 percent dealing with one of these agencies. While such a saving is better than none, you can usually get a better deal somewhere else.

Travel-Club Discounts

Travel clubs offer modest discounts on transatlantic air tickets. These clubs normally obtain discounts through a captive, in-house travel agency. Because they generate a substantial volume, they are generally eligible for "overrides" from suppliers that increase normal commissions from the 8 to 10 percent base into the region of 12 to 14 percent. But because they typically operate at low costs, they can rebate more than half of the total commission to members in the form of reduced prices.

Before deregulation and the earlier easing of charter rules, travelers had to be bona-fide members of clubs or other established organizations in order to be eligible for charter travel.

During the 1960s and 1970s, several clubs grew to over 100,000 members primarily as the way to become eligible for charter flights. The relaxation of restrictions put most of them out of business, but the largest, United European American Club, managed to hang on as a travel club. Although membership is way down from a peak of over 200,000 families, this club still provides modest discounts on charter flights and bulk-fare deals to its members. Membership fees are currently $15 per year per family, and most members will easily save this amount on a single booking. If interested, contact UEAC at 23929 Valencia Boulevard, Valencia, CA 91355; 805-257-0997.

Discount-Ticket Outlook for 1987

You can expect no shortage of discounts across the Atlantic this year, in view of the uncertainties about the European travel market. Although no specific summer prices were available at the time of this writing, last summer's prices are a good guide for what to expect:

- The lowest prices were on a number of the bigger charter programs. Whenever a charter program doesn't sell out well in advance, discount agencies typically sell seats at prices $50 to $100 below the advertised charter prices, which, in turn, are substantially below the lowest advertised promotional fares on the scheduled airlines.
- Last summer, the lowest transatlantic scheduled-airline prices from New York were on Third-World carriers such as Kuwait Airlines and Pakistan International. Several Eastern European airlines (including JAT) offered low prices to Eastern Europe, the eastern end of Western Europe, and the Eastern Mediterranean. In most cases, the best buys were to cities other than the lines' home-base cities, reached by connecting flights. The reason was that while many foreign airlines offer discounts, they try to protect their home markets.
- Discount tickets on Canadian airlines were available from several major U.S. cities to Europe on connecting flights through Canadian gateway cities. These flights were several hours longer than nonstops from the main U.S. gateways; however, some required extensive layovers at a Canadian

gateway, and you had to backtrack if you left from the East Coast.
- Some excellent discount fares to Europe were available on major U.S. and European airlines, including British Caledonian, Pan American, and TWA. To get the lowest rates, however, you often had to be flexible about schedules. On some lines you specified the dates you wanted to leave and return, but the airline chose the specific dates and flights and confirmed your final schedule a few days before departure.

Convenience

Discount and rebate travel can often be more convenient than costlier APEX excursion travel on the same or comparable airlines. Because of the type of distribution involved, these tickets tend to have less onerous advance-purchase and minimum-stay restrictions than the lowest "list-price" fares. On the other hand, the supplies can be limited, and the best deals sell out quickly.

Discount and rebate travel is usually more convenient than charter travel, too. Service is on scheduled airlines, which means daily or more frequent flights on most routes, compared with the weekly pattern more common for charters. Service quality can often be superior—many of the world's most highly esteemed airlines engage in these deals—although some of the airlines that push discount deals are at the low end of the quality spectrum.

Probably the biggest problem with discount transatlantic deals is that West Coast flights are often on airlines that offer only one- or two-stop rather than nonstop service. Thus, your "price" to save $50 to $150 (coupled with other below-APEX alternatives) may be as much as six hours extra travel time—a price that many travelers aren't willing to pay. And, as is usually the case with any special deals, discount tickets are often unavailable or very scarce during peak periods.

Risks and Uncertainties

These various discount-ticket products entail comparatively few inconveniences and risks. The major limitation is that they are

> Some European governments periodically attempt to "clean up" the airline market place by clamping down on airlines that issue discount tickets. For example, in 1985, the West Germans actually fielded some "tariff police" at their main airports to try to cut down on use of discounted tickets, especially for passengers traveling within Europe and from Europe to Asia. Boarding passengers were randomly selected in check-in lines, and their tickets were examined to detect possible discount sales. When the police observed discrepancies, they asked the travelers for full particulars about how, when, and from whom the tickets were purchased. The travelers themselves weren't hassled, but discounting travel agents, wholesalers, and airlines were.

almost always confined to the single airline that issued them. Itineraries that involve connecting flights require that all flights be on the same airline, or at least on two airlines with established special interline fares. Travelers can't change airlines to enjoy better schedules or to change itineraries. Similarly, refunds for unused tickets are, at best, available only through the issuing agents; in some cases, refunds can be difficult and time-consuming to obtain.

But discount tickets have some advantages, too. Unlike some charter programs, discount-ticket travelers know the identity of the airline they'll be flying before they buy. Also, these tickets avoid the problem of charter tour-operator failure. Passengers' contracts are with the airlines, and the airlines are responsible for fulfillment no matter what might happen to the retail or wholesale agent involved.

Buying Discount Tickets

Discounted tickets obviously are not in the standard airline computer-reservation systems that travel agents use. You can get them only from agencies that operate specifically in this marketplace.

"Bucket shop"—a term appropriated from the securities industry—is the inelegant name given to a travel agency that sells airline tickets at true discount prices. Bucket shops used to be primarily a European and Asian phenomenon, and most European and Asian bucket shops had disreputable overtones.

Over the last three years, however, bucket shops have gained a foothold in U.S. travel markets. And bucket shops in both Europe and the United States have gained a new measure of respectability. While still not on a par with the typical full-service retail travel agencies, bucket shops have moved at least halfway "uptown."

Moreover, more and more full-service agencies are starting to handle discount airline tickets that used to be entirely the province of bucket shops. So if you have a regular travel agent, your first step should be to ask that agent if—and by how much—he or she can beat list-price fares.

If you don't have a regular agent, or if your regular agent can't beat the official prices, you have to find a genuine bucket shop. While no bucket-shop agencies are "household names," they do exist in most major cities. In the United States, the best way to locate them is to check major metropolitan newspapers. Bucket shops advertise themselves as "low-fare" specialists in small space ads in weekend travel sections, and, in some cities, in classified "travel" or "transportation" sections.

Not all travel agents who advertise this way are bucket shops. Some agencies try to promote a low-fare image when, in fact, all they can really claim is expertise in finding the best deal among the many scheduled-airline list-price options. To save yourself time and money, you should first telephone agents that you think may be candidates and ask very specifically if they can beat the list-price options you've found—if they deal in discount, rebate, bulk fare, and throwaway land-package tickets. While some may tell you they "can't discuss prices over the telephone," you should make it clear that you'd be wasting their time as well as yours if they can't beat the standard fares by a substantial margin.

Wherever located, most bucket shops operate on a strictly cash basis—no credit cards, no personal checks. Tickets usually have to be prepaid. In this kind of business, you should protect yourself against possible shady operations. Avoid a final cash payment until the agent is ready to hand you your complete ticket.

Virtually all U.S. bucket shops concentrate on tickets for travel by Coach/Economy Class, low-fare airlines, and charters. There is essentially no U.S. market in discounted tickets for high-quality service—Business Class and First Class—though quite a few European bucket shops advertise themselves as specialists in discount Business- and First-Class tickets. In fact, they're aiming at the many travelers who want something better than the high-density seating and minimal service of Coach/Economy, but still want to save money.

Legal Questions

Discounting individual international airline tickets is currently illegal in the United States. Specifically, it is illegal for airlines and travel agents to rebate any part of the commission to a client, either directly or indirectly. The legal distinction between individual airline-ticket discounting and tour-basing or bulk fares is that the latter are official airline tariffs, while individually discounted tickets, by definition, are not. Incidentally, these same types of discounting and rebating are perfectly legal for domestic travel.

The regulation applies just to airlines and agents. Travelers who buy discounted tickets are not in violation of this regulation.

In practice, the distinction between legal and illegal discounts is almost invisible. Most discount and rebate deals can be structured as bulk-fare deals—or at least made to look enough like bulk-fare deals that virtually nobody could tell the difference.

The U.S. government's enforcement policy on ticket discounting is ambiguous. On one hand, the Department of Transportation insists that discounting should remain illegal, while on the other hand, it admits that it has neither the resources nor the inclination to vigorously enforce the regulation. Enforcement actions are taken only—and only occasionally—when somebody complains loudly enough to attract the department's ear. While the few enforcement actions taken over the last few years have not had a significant impact on the total discount market, the effect of enforcement has unfortunately been to confine ticket discounting to some of the smaller bucket shops and ethnic agencies—and probably to slow its growth.

Of course, many kinds of discounting break self-imposed airline-industry rules and regulations—which shouldn't worry travelers even the least bit. The International Air Transport Association (IATA) keeps preaching to its members about the evils of discounting; the members keep agreeing with IATA—while, at the same time, many keep on discounting.

Discounting may pose something of an ethical dilemma for some travelers. Even though you, as a traveler, are not breaking the law, you may be reluctant to buy the product of an illegal transaction between your suppliers. Clearly, many, if not most, below-list-price air-fare deals are legal. But on some, you might be dealing with an agent or wholesaler who is breaking the law—and it is almost impossible for you to ascertain whether any given deal is in full compliance with the law. If this concerns you, the best way to avoid a potential involvement in an illegal deal is to ask the ticket supplier for some sort of formal, written statement that the ticket is legally obtained. If the supplier is unable or unwilling to make such representation, and you consider it important, shop around for an alternative source.

There's another kind of legal problem, however, that can be a serious concern to travelers. A small number of discount airline tickets result from a complicated scheme in which residents of some Third World countries evade currency-conversion restrictions. A Nigerian, to use a frequent example, can pay a local travel agent in Nigerian currency (which can't be legally converted or taken out of the country). The agent then issues a Miscellaneous Charge Order (MCO) denominated in hard currency at the official exchange rate. The MCO is mailed to a cooperating agency in a hard-currency country, where it can be exchanged at face value for an airline ticket. Of course, the MCO is heavily discounted in all these transactions, so the final selling agent sells the ticket to a traveler at a discount price. The Nigerian receives some hard currency from the agent—much less than the value of the local currency at the official exchange rate, but bankable in Switzerland and beyond the reach of Nigerian officialdom. The ultimate loser in this scheme is the airline, which winds up owning blocked Nigerian currency.

The airlines are trying to stop currency-conversion discounting. Last year, for example, both Pan Am and TWA undertook major efforts to trace the agencies involved in the scheme and invalidate the tickets they issued. Unfortunately, it's sometimes hard to identify such tickets. To protect yourself, avoid any ticket with "MCO" in the "issued in exchange for" box on the face of the ticket. And, to prepare a possible legal recourse, ask the discounter for a written statement that the ticket was not obtained through a currency-conversion scam.

# 8

# Quality Air Travel

*Relief from Rear-Cabin Fever*

Economy Class on major and low-fare airlines, charter flights, and bulk-fare deals is the most popular way to get to Europe, and the least expensive. But what you get is bottom-of-the-line quality. With small (but important) differences, comfort and service range from just above to well below reasonable minimum levels.

Genuine quality air services are available. Unfortunately, most of them are much more expensive—in some cases, ridiculously so. But some quality services are within the reach of even economy-minded travelers, if you know where to find them.

## Business Class

Business Class is the minimum level of transatlantic airline service that can genuinely be described as "comfortable." Seating in 747s is no more crowded than eight seats across in a 2-2-2-2 pattern, and a few lines have only six seats across in a 2-2-2 arrangement. Some lines also have Business Class in the upper deck, at four seats across. In none will you find those detested middle seats. Pitch is at least 36 inches, more generous on some lines. You don't have to worry about comfort even if you're getting the last available seat.

Cabin services are also at a higher level. Drinks and movies are free on all transatlantic airlines. Meal service is usually noticeably better, often with courses served separately on china rather than as a complete meal on a plastic tray—characteristic of Economy-Class meals.

The down side is, of course, that Business-Class fares on most routes are more than double APEX or charter fares. In view of this tremendous price difference, Business Class really isn't a viable alternative for most vacationers, who could otherwise use one of the least costly options. It's a much better buy for those travelers who would otherwise have to pay full-fare Economy because they can't meet the restrictions on APEX and other cheaper services.

The only bargain in Business Class is on El Al flights to Israel. You can upgrade to Business Class from any kind of Economy ticket—even APEX—for $97 each way, from New York, or $207 each way, from Los Angeles. These inexpensive upgrades are available only on through flights; they are not available if you stop over in Western Europe. No other airline offers these upgrades.

First Class

These days, First-Class service across the Atlantic is truly opulent. All the lines that still offer a First-Class service use sleeprette seats with folding leg rests (except for Alia's L-1011s). Seat rows are almost five feet apart. It's the only transatlantic service on which you can actually stretch out. Meal and drink services match the seating opulence.

Of course, the prices are truly opulent, as well—three to six times the cost of APEX or a charter. Clearly, First Class caters to people who can spend a lot of money for top-quality travel.

However, if you want to enjoy the best the airlines have to offer, there are ways to enjoy First-Class service without paying the full tab. As noted in chapter 6, you can sometimes buy a "companion" First-Class trip for about the same cost as an APEX or charter ticket. Also, as described in Chapter 9, you can save up to 70 percent by buying frequent-traveler coupons for First-Class travel from other individuals or from a coupon broker.

First-Class Charter

When a charter program uses airplanes normally used for scheduled service, chances are there will be First-Class and/or

Business-Class sections on that airplane. When this is the case, most charter operators offer the high-quality seating as a premium-price option. In 1986, First-Class charter costs were usually $100 to $300 higher than the regular charter price, but there's no standard range among charter offerings. The premium is set at whatever level the operator thinks will maximize revenues.

In a few cases, the operator features full First-Class service in addition to the seating: unlimited free drinks and the airline's normal First-Class meal service. In most cases, however, only the seating is different—everybody gets the same bar service and meals. Again, it's strictly up to the operator.

The First-Class charter is almost always by far the least expensive way to enjoy a really high-quality trip. Although the premium charged represents a substantial percentage increase over the usual charter price, it's still much less than regular First-Class service on a scheduled airline.

For example, one program last summer employed Swissair DC-10s for nonstop charters from San Francisco and Miami to Zurich. Travelers who rode in the Business-Class seats paid a premium of about $100, round trip (it varied slightly by departure), while travelers who wanted the full sleeperette First-Class seats paid about $300 more. This is less than one-quarter of the normal First-Class fare. On this program, only the seating was different—all passengers received the same cabin service.

Of course, compared with ordinary charters, only the cost and comfort (and possibly the cabin service) are different on First- and Business-Class charters. The convenience and contingency factors are the same.

Premium Service on Low-Fare Airlines

Both Tower and Virgin Atlantic offer a premium service:

- Tower has a few non-sleeperette First-Class seats, which are priced at only $99, each way, over New York–Tel Aviv Economy fares and represent an exceptional value for this long and tedious trip. The one-way fare is $590, and the round-trip fare is $959.
- Virgin Atlantic offers an "Upper Class" option with sleeper-

ette seats, comparable to major airlines' First Class, priced at $1,059 each way. Upper-Class service also includes complimentary helicopter or limo service in both New York and London.

Although these fares are high in relation to the Economy-Class fares on these low-fare airlines, they are far below either First- or even Business-Class fares on the major lines. Accordingly, they represent a good value for travelers who want high-quality service. As in the case of high-quality charter services, however, only the quality is different—convenience and contingency factors are independent of in-flight comfort or class of service.

# 9

# Other Possibilities

*There's Always
Another Approach*

Just in case promotional fares, low-fare airlines, charters, bulk fares, last-minute deals, and discount tickets don't give you enough options, there are still a few other ways you can keep your transatlantic air-travel costs down.

Frequent-Traveler Coupons

Frequent-traveler awards were first mentioned in chapter 6, in connection with "companion" tickets. Most of the awards in these programs, however, consist of upgrades (from Economy to Business or First Class) and "free" trips within various regions. Many provide for trips from the United States to Europe.

These programs are all quite similar. Individuals enroll with any airlines they are apt to use—some programs require a modest entry fee, others do not. Then, the travelers' mileages for each flight taken are logged by the airline and accumulated. On some lines, awards can be earned with as little as 5,000 accumulated miles, while, on others, the minimum awards require as much as 20,000 miles. Obviously, the higher the mileage, the greater the value of the award.

Again, the terminology is a little troublesome. These mileage-based frequent-traveler benefits are properly termed "awards." But since the earliest free-trip awards offered in airline promotional programs were issued in the form of coupons, the term "coupon" has become the unofficial generic expression for any sort of free-travel benefit that can be bought and sold after it has been issued.

Although most members of frequent flier programs use their mileage credits themselves for free travel or upgrades, some prefer to convert their benefits into cash. These frequent fliers—the sellers—supply the inventory for the coupon marketplace. The coupons, however, are not so easily sold—or bought. All airlines require that each coupon for a frequent flier benefit be issued in the name of the traveler who will use it. Once issued, the coupon is not transferable. A seller cannot ask an airline to issue a coupon until he or she can specify the name of the traveler who will use it. Accordingly, the coupon market involves three steps:

1. A frequent flier with accumulated mileage credit (the seller) offers mileage accruals to a coupon broker. The broker pays the seller for the mileage and adds the benefit to the inventory the broker has for sale.
2. When a buyer agrees to purchase a coupon from the broker, the broker provides the buyer's name to the seller of the frequent flier benefit. The seller then asks the airline to issue the specified benefit in that buyer's name. When the seller receives the coupon, he or she forwards it to the broker who, in turn, sends it to the buyer.
3. Using the coupon, the buyer makes reservations and has a ticket issued, either directly by the airline or through a travel agent. The buyer travels under his or her own name.

Since this entire process often takes up to a month, you have to arrange for your coupon well in advance (brokers can arrange express issuance and delivery from some airlines, at your expense). But once you have your coupon, your plans can be flexible. After issue, a coupon giving you a wide range of destinations is usually good for a full year and the ticket you buy with it is also good for a year. Coupon-based tickets typically do not require an advance purchase period, and reservations can be shifted right up to the last minute. Regular coupon users often keep one on hand, ready for use at any time.

Although almost all U.S. airlines have some sort of frequent flier program, coupon brokers concentrate on programs offered by just seven of the larger airlines: American, Continental, Delta, Eastern, Northwest, TWA, and United. Several brokers also sell coupons for travel on foreign airlines, including British Airways, Japan Air Lines, KLM, and Qantas, but these coupons originate with the U.S. airlines that offer flight benefits on the foreign lines. Pan Am's transfer rules are so restrictive that brokers can't effectively buy and sell the benefits.

The main drawback to these coupons—for economy-minded travelers—is that the best deals are for First-Class and Business-Class travel, not Economy Class. To see why, take TWA's award scale as an example. One of the 60,000-mile awards is two free round-trip Economy-Class tickets from anywhere TWA flies in the United States to Europe. As a substitute for APEX tickets this award would be worth $1,200 to $2,400, depending on the origin and destination cities. But for 90,000 miles, the comparable award is two First-Class tickets, valid for travel that would otherwise cost between $7,500 and $11,000. At the average value of the ticket benefits, the Economy-Class award amounts to 3¢ per mile in terms of APEX, while the First-Class award amounts to 10¢ per mile. Other airlines' plans similarly favor First- and Business-Class awards.

Thus in a buy-and-sell market, the per-mile value of First-Class awards is worth two to three times the value of the Economy-Class awards. Coupon dealers obviously ask people who are planning to sell their mileage benefits rather than use them themselves to go for the First-Class awards, and they tend to concentrate on business at the higher end of the market.

It's hard to find any coupon deals through brokers that are less expensive than APEX or Super APEX to Europe. By contrast, First-Class round-trip ticket coupons on major airlines from any domestic U.S. point to any on-line point in Europe or the Middle East were available for about $1,500 to $2,000 in late 1986. These coupons provide for travel that would cost up to $6,000 at regular fares—for round-trip travel from the West Coast to Eastern Mediterranean cities. Business-Class coupons on another major carrier from any domestic point to London or Frankfurt were going for $1,400—including First-Class accommodations on connecting domestic flights. Coupons are clearly an extremely good way to save money if you demand the best quality that air travel has to offer.

Because coupons typically apply to travel from any U.S. point on an issuing airline's system to various points in Europe, savings are obviously greatest for relatively long trips—especially from the West Coast. Also, coupons must save money for travelers who can't abide by APEX advance-purchase and minimum/maximum stay restrictions—but, here, the utility may be limited by the time required to obtain the necessary coupons. The best use of coupons is for high-quality travel at relatively low cost. Savings can easily amount to thousands of dollars per trip.

Buying and selling coupons is not illegal. But the major lines state that transfer by sale or barter—directly or through brokers—is against their rules. Some limit transfers to relatives of program members, but these lines define family broadly (grandparents, cousins, and in-laws), which permits transfers to travelers with different surnames and gives brokers the leeway they need to circumvent the rules. As might be expected, the airlines and brokers take very different positions:

- The airlines state that it is against their rules for frequent flier members to sell benefits or for other travelers to buy them, that these rules are "vigorously" enforced, and that travelers who are detected trying to use tickets obtained with purchase coupons are denied boarding and their tickets are confiscated. The lines warn potential users that they risk having to pay full fare Coach or Economy Class for alternative transportation if they are caught trying to use a ticket obtained through a purchased coupon.
- The brokers respond that, of the thousands of travelers to whom they have sold coupons, only about a dozen or so have been denied boarding by an airline. And most brokers claim that, in such cases, they either issue another coupon on a different airline or cover the cost of alternate transportaiton so that the traveler does not incur out-of-pocket expenses. They also say that several of the travelers who had been denied boarding had openly boasted of their coupon purchase within hearing of airline boarding agents, in effect inviting airline action.

Late last year, two big lines decided to tighten their rules. TWA limited transfer of its popular 90,000-mile award (two free international First Class tickets) to the traveler who won earned the mileage, plus one companion; United added this same restriction to several of its major awards. Presumably, the purpose of these actions was to put a damper on the coupon market. The United and TWA moves may well slow the coupon market. It's too early to tell how coupon brokers will respond to these moves.

Of course, you don't have to deal with a broker. If you know a frequent flier with excess mileage benefits, you can make an arrangement directly—and probably save quite a bit. But these private transactions are also subject to the same limitations as transactions through brokers.

How can you locate a coupon deal? Individual coupon sellers normally advertise in the classified sections of major metropolitan daily newspapers—in the same headings as listed for discount-ticket sources. They also advertise in the classified section of the *Wall Street Journal*, under "Miscellaneous."

But most coupon travelers will probably wind up buying from one of the coupon "brokers" that have come into being in response to the burgeoning frequent-traveler programs. While the coupon market can be quite dynamic, it appears that at any given time prices tend to be uniform—presumably, the various brokers keep themselves aware of other dealers' buy-and-sell prices and make sure that they remain competitive.

Brokers, like individual sellers, advertise in classifieds and travel sections. Recent editions of the *Wall Street Journal* and *The New York Times* carried several ads of coupon brokers interested in buying and selling. A few coupon brokers also have small display ads in business-travel magazines and the travel industry weekly, *Travel Weekly*. The following seem to be among the more aggressive advertisers (there will almost certainly be others this summer): The Coupon Bank, 212-517-8975, 617-227-4676; The Coupon Brokers, 800-247-2891, 303-757-8144; The American Coupon Exchange, 714-644-4112; Travel Deluxe International, 212-826-7025; The Airline Coupon Company, 619-451-2979; International Air Coupon Exchange, 713-661-5234; AGCO, 301-681-8200, 213-459-0404; The Flyer's Edge Agency, 212-466-9300; Travel Enterprises, Inc., 212-533-4440; Price Busters, 619-275-6310; Travel Discounts International, 212-826-8975, 312-922-3831; and Net Fare Corp., 212-645-1080. Others often list their services without names in the classifieds.

Other Coupons

Transatlantic airlines get involved in other coupon promotions from time to time. Late last year, TWA started selling upgrade-discount tickets through catalogs of mail-order companies. Priced at $25 per person, these coupons can be used for either of two purposes:

1. a discount of 25 percent on any type of TWA ticket, from APEX to First Class
2. an upgrade from any type of Economy-Class ticket (including APEX to Europe) to Business Class (Ambassador) on any wide-body flight, or to First Class on a narrow-body flight

The discount offer incorporates quite a few restrictions and blackout dates, but it can still save some transatlantic travelers hundreds of dollars. The upgrade is available on any flight but for international travel is limited to flights costing $800 or more round trip. That peculiar minimum threshhold means that West Coast travelers to Europe can use the coupon to upgrade the cheapest APEX to most if not all European destinations, while travelers from the Midwest and East will have to buy something more expensive than APEX to enjoy the upgrade. Some mail-order houses were still selling these coupons in early 1987. And even if you can't buy them from a catalog, you may find these coupons being offered for sale in the want ads. If so, they're a great way to cut the cost of high-quality travel.

Over the last few years, TWA has been involved in more coupon promotions than any other major line. But you never know which one will try something else. Regardless of the line, however, remember some typical limitations that may not be prominently mentioned in the promotional materials:

- Most ticket discounts are "blacked out" during the most popular travel seasons. In the past, blackout periods typically have included the peak summer season, the Christmas/New Year period, Easter/spring-vacation periods, and even the major four-day weekends.
- Many apply only to Economy-Class service, not Business or First Class.
- Some may provide discounts only on Full-Fare Economy tickets, not such less-expensive promotional fares as APEX. For most travelers, such promotions are a sham—in past promotions of this type, the discounted fares have often been higher than undiscounted APEX fares.

## Foreign-Currency Purchase

International air fares are adjusted only infrequently to compensate for shifts in exchange rates among various major currencies. Also, some fares are established in both Europe and the United States with reference to market "price points," rather than exchange rate parity—at specific prices levels (such as $299.50 for a TV set) that marketers deem especially attractive for a big-ticket purchase. The net result of these factors was that, throughout 1986, airline tickets purchased in European currency were often less expensive than tickets for comparable trips purchased with U.S. dollars.

Foreign-currency purchase represented a fantastic value in late 1984 and early 1985, when the dollar was at all-time high values compared with most European currencies. At that time, some tickets bought in European currencies cost about half of what comparable tickets cost in U.S. dollars.

By 1987, the dollar had dropped some 30 percent against most European currencies, and the values weren't so dramatic. But foreign-currency purchase can still represent good value. With the pound at $1.50, for example, Economy-Class airfares from London to the United States, purchased in pounds, are about 22 percent less than fares from the United States to London, purchased in dollars. Similar disparities exist for fares denominated in most other European currencies.

But exchange-rate disparities don't provide a universal method for cutting air travel costs. The basic problem is that tickets have to be priced in the currency of the country in which the trip originates. Thus, you cannot buy a pound-priced New York–London–New York ticket in New York—and you can't even have a friend buy one for you in London and send it to you. You cannot buy a round-the-world ticket in pounds and start your trip in the United States. If the trip starts in the United States, the ticket has to be sold at the dollar price.

Most of the best major-airline promotional fares—APEX, Super APEX, and similar types—are based on round-trip ticket purchase. Prices are usually much lower than two of the cheapest one-way fares—so much so that you're better off with a dollar-priced promotional fare, even though you may have to pay more for it than a European resident who buys the same kind of ticket to visit the United States.

But you can use the exchange rates to save substantially on

any one-way fares or round-trip fares that are not much less than two one-way fares. So you can buy a one-way dollar-priced ticket from the United States to London and buy a separate one-way pound-priced return ticket after you get to London. Because there aren't any round-trip reductions for Business- or First-Class tickets, cost-conscious business travelers have been buying one-way tickets in dollars for their outbound trips and one-way tickets in pounds for their returns ever since the pound started falling.

Buying a return ticket from Europe in local currency can be advantageous for Standby tickets on major airlines (which are available on a one-way basis) and unrestricted tickets on the several low-fare airlines that have no special round-trip reductions. But low-fare airlines' rates are generally adjusted more frequently, so the advantage may not be as great as with the Business- or First-Class fares on major airlines.

If you fly the Atlantic frequently, you can, of course, enjoy exchange-rates savings on low-cost promotional-fare travel—after your first one-way eastbound trip. You can then buy a series of APEX or Super APEX tickets priced in European currencies for round trips originating in Europe. At the end of the cycle, you buy another one-way trip back. Of course, to make this pay, you have to travel enough to stay within the maximum-stay limits.

Incidentally, you can also buy a cheap one-way ticket to London, then in London a pound-priced round-the-world trip eastward—which will leave you back in the United States with an "open" ticket to London at the end good for six months or a year, depending on the airline, in case you want to start a second trip. Even if you never use that final "open" London return, you would pay less (at current rates) for a round-the-world trip that way than by buying it at the U.S. dollar price.

You do not have to buy these foreign-currency tickets in Europe. As long as you're buying tickets for a trip that originates in Europe (as far as that ticket is concerned), you can buy it here in the United States. Your price is simply the quoted foreign-currency price converted to dollars on the day you buy. Any airline office or travel agent can handle the deal. Note that there is nothing against the law about this kind of foreign currency purchase, nor is it against airline rules. As long as the currency in which you buy is convertible, there's no problem. This kind of purchase is completely different from buying tickets issued against *blocked* currency (see page 89).

Of course, the attractiveness of purchasing tickets in European currencies depends on the exchange rates at the time you're buying. It's clear, however, that any time you're using an option for which a round trip costs the same as two one-way tickets—Standby, low-fare airline, full-fare Economy, Business, or First Class—you should definitely find out what the return trip would cost in European currency as well as in dollars. The airlines will tell you the European fares. Then, get the current exchange rates and calculate the dollar cost of your return ticket in Europe. If it's below the official dollar price, buy your return at foreign-currency prices!

# 10

# Stopovers and Connections

*Coping with Some
Minor Problems*

Travelers to Europe who live in big East Coast cities don't have to worry as much about en route stopovers and connection headaches as people who live in the interior United States or on the West Coast. But for those travelers who do not live in the Northeast, stopovers and connections can be important considerations.

## The Stopover Headache

Many of the most troublesome kinds of traveler questions involve stopovers. Lots of travelers bound for Europe from interior or western U.S. cities apparently would like to stop over in New York, Boston, Washington, Chicago, or Miami on their way—going or coming back—for business or personal reasons.

But the best major-airline promotional fares on most routes, as well as charter and bulk fares, generally do not allow any en route stopovers. The cheapest through fares that officially permit stopovers are full-fare Economy—generally much more expensive than the low-cost alternatives.

A few transatlantic routes do allow East Coast gateway stopovers with APEX or Super APEX fares; see details in chapter 11. Unfortunately, the routes on which stopovers are permitted are generally those to the less popular European gateways. The stopover privileges are, in effect, bonuses designed to make the gateways more competitive. Also, some travelers would like stopovers in the most western European cities on their way to or from some internal point—say, for example, a London or Madrid stopover on a trip to Zurich or Rome. You could buy a promotional-fare ticket to the western gateway and an internal European flight to get to and from the internal point. The catch to this approach is the high internal European air fares. The cheapest internal European round-trip flight of this kind is likely to cost more than your round trip across the Atlantic. A few years ago, a British travel publication (*Business Traveller*) carried a story showing that the cheapest way to travel by air between a certain northern European city and a city in the south of Europe was to go by way of New York!

What can you do? There are four alternatives:

1. If you're visiting the Eastern Mediterranean—Athens, Belgrade, Cairo, Tel Aviv—the APEX fares do allow limited European stopovers, either free or at nominal extra cost.
2. Early in 1986, TWA and Aer Lingus teamed up to offer a special London-Ireland triangular route with a single APEX fare, which allowed you to visit both London and Dublin or Shannon from any American gateway out of which either airline operates. Typical round-trip fares for this route were $639 from New York, $749 from Chicago, and $789 from Texas or $849 from the West Coast. A similar program is expected for 1987 matched by other airlines.
3. If one of the cities you want to visit happens to have a good market in discount tickets (London and Amsterdam have been the best in previous years), you can base your trip on a cheaply priced round-trip ticket to one of these cities, then go to a bucket shop and purchase a separate round-trip ticket to your final destination city. This can be risky and cumbersome, however, since it will take some time for you to find and deal with a bucket shop in Europe, a good bucket-shop flight might not be available when you want to travel, and changes in local markets might dry up the supply of cheap flights when you're looking for one. This should be a "last resort" approach for most Americans.
4. You can sometimes buy two separate promotional fare

tickets—one from your originating city to an East Coast gateway, the other from the East Coast gateway to Europe. Schedule flights to allow you the desired stop over.

Aside from these limited opportunities most travelers resist the generally high costs of internal European flying and arrange stopovers in Europe by car or train or explore using an "open-jaw" APEX fare and take a train between the two cities.

Schedules and Connections

Enough large European cities will have nonstop or direct flights to satisfy many U.S. travelers who live in the largest U.S. cities. But many people who live outside of the top few U.S. metro areas will undoubtedly have to make at least one connection. If so, you'll lower the irritation level substantially if you can avoid connections through Kennedy (New York). Newark, Boston, Washington, Atlanta, Miami, and even O'Hare (Chicago) are usually better alternatives. However, to many European cities, Kennedy is your only choice.

Kennedy does, however, provide one unique schedule advantage: British Airways and Pan American offer daytime nonstops to London. Some of you will welcome them as an alternative to an overnight flight that is the only option for all other eastbound transatlantic flights. If you hate overnight flying, this option is attractive.

In general, the departure and arrival times on flights between the United States and Europe are constrained to a very small "window" by the combination of the elapsed flight times and the differences in European and U.S. time zones. The only time you have any real schedule options is when you start from the West Coast. On routes without nonstop service, you can either (1) fly nonstop to a major European gateway, then take a connecting European flight, or (2) fly to New York or Chicago and connect with a nonstop to your destination. The fares are usually the same; base your choice on convenience.

Many travelers may prefer the first option, especially if the local European connection is relatively short because:

- Total flight times can be several hours less—because the nonstop "polar route" West Coast–to–Europe flights are

> Kennedy, of course, has a tremendous volume of international traffic—and almost all of it arrives and departs at the same times. The resulting congestion causes what seems like endless delay: You taxi around, apparently at random, then wait at the end of the runway for takeoff clearance. Getting airborne can easily consume at least an hour on good days, and more time when the weather's bad or during peak summer travel. Be especially wary of Kennedy connections involving different airlines—the internal circulation roads frequently bog down in gridlock on heavy travel days.

hundreds of miles shorter than connecting routes through New York or Chicago.
- By splitting your eastbound flight into one long segment (nine to twelve hours, West Coast to Europe) and a short add-on, you allow more time to relax (maybe even to sleep) on the overnight segment. The alternative New York connection involves shorter overnight transatlantic flights; when you figure the time required for takeoff and climb, drink and dinner service, and (possibly) a movie, you have almost no time left to get any rest. Westbound, this factor isn't as important.
- With this option, you'll probably leave in the afternoon and arrive at your final destination the next evening—perhaps later than you'd like.

But the other option has some advantages, too. If your connection in Europe would require a long European flight (for example, London to Athens), you might well be better off connecting through New York. The Economy-Class service-quality standards on most intra-European flights are poor. With this option, you typically leave the West Coast early in the morning and arrive at your final destination the next morning or early afternoon.

# 11

# Projected 1987 Transatlantic Air Fares

*How It Looks for the Summer*

The following listing presents a summary of peak-season 1987 transatlantic air fares to twenty-five major gateways in Europe and the Eastern Mediterranean as they were being quoted in late 1986. Fare increases are anticipated for late spring by all the major carriers. However, if you are ticketed for a lower fare prior to its being increased, the airline will honor the previously ticketed fare. Our greatest emphasis is on the least expensive type of major airline fare available in each market. Other major airline fare levels are also listed, along with some comments and predictions about low-fare airline, charter, and bulk-fare opportunities.

Fares are quoted for four U.S. origin areas. Chicago and New York are obvious departure points. Texas refers to either Dallas or Houston, depending on which city has the most direct service on each route, and West Coast refers to either Los Angeles or San Francisco, on the same basis.

To facilitate comparison, all fares are shown as round trips—even fares that are also available one way. One-way fares for Full-fare Economy, Business, and First Class are usually half of the round-trip figures shown.

Fares quoted apply to the most direct (preferably nonstop) services available. Occasionally (especially on Business and First Class), some airlines offer lower fares on flights that require connections; these fares are not listed, but you should ask your travel agent about them if you don't mind an extra stop or connection. However, you aren't apt to find any such reductions on the lowest APEX fares.

The intent of this comparison is to illustrate the substantial differences between the various classes of fares and the different patterns that prevail to different destinations. This book should *not* be your definitive reference for complete or up-to-date fares on any one route. As an indication of the complexity in air fares, consider that the computer printouts used to construct this simplified list often show 30 to 40 different fares for each route. Make sure that your travel agent, the airline ticket office, or anyone else making your reservations double-checks to ensure that you are receiving the lowest possible fare within your requirements.

In general, the season in which your trip originates determines the seasonal fare to be paid. However, if your itinerary includes, say, a weekend flight going over but a midweek flight coming back, your fare will usually be one-half of the sum of the two different round-trip fares. Open-jaw trips (see page 13) are figured the same way: the fare is half of the round trip to (or from) each of the two points.

### Alternative Gateways

Your itinerary will normally establish the gateway city, or cities, in Europe to and from which you'll fly. Your attention should therefore be directed to finding the best alternative for those specific destinations.

Look at it this way. You'll probably pay something between $500 and $1,000 for your air travel—minimum—plus something like $400 for local travel within Europe. Depending on your standards, your daily hotel and meal costs will be anywhere from $30 to $100, per person. So on a three-week trip your average per-person out-of-pocket cost for just being in Europe—the overhead cost—will be between $75 and $170 a day. Clearly, then, you would have to save at least double that amount per ticket before you could justify flying to an alternative gateway that required an extra day of ground travel to get to or from the places you really wanted to visit.

In rare cases, however, it will be to your advantage to use a different gateway city, in a different country, just to save on air travel—prevailing high fares to one city may make a flight to a less expensive gateway an attractive option. You should give careful consideration to this approach in cases where you're looking for fares substantially less than major airline APEX fares, but you can't find any low-fare airline service, charters, bulk-fare deals, or discounts to your preferred destination.

If, however, you are planning a "grand tour" of several countries, you might be relatively indifferent about which gateways to use. Your range of options, then, will be broadened: you can let relative air-fare levels (as well as car rental levels, if you're driving) help determine the route you take. In this connection, note in chapter 14 that Belgium, Germany, Luxembourg, and the Netherlands offer attractive combinations of low air-fare options and low rental car costs, compared with adjacent countries. If you're visiting these countries anyhow, they look like especially attractive gateways this year.

In any case, the only way to get a handle on what you can expect to spend is to tabulate your options on a country-by-country basis.

For 1987, all APEX fares carry a $75 cancellation fee or 10 percent of the fare, whichever is greater. There is now a $5 per ticket customs fee that will be added to the cost of the ticket at the time of purchase.

**Amsterdam**

*Major Airlines*

| | Round-trip fares to Amsterdam from | | | |
|---|---|---|---|---|
| Fare basis | New York | Chicago | Texas | West Coast |
| *Excursions* | | | | |
| Lowest available round-trip | $ 738 | $ 828 | $ 918 | $ 968 |
| Lowest available one-way | — | — | — | — |
| *Full fare* | | | | |
| Economy | 1,442 | 1,668 | 1,930 | 2,102 |
| Business Class | 1,676 | 1,874 | 2,184 | 2,328 |
| First Class | 3,212 | 3,606 | 3,636 | 4,162 |

**Restrictions on lowest available fare**
Peak season: June 1–September 14
Advance purchase: twenty-one days
Minimum stay: one day

Weekend supplement: $50 each way
Stopovers: none
Children's fare: 67 percent
Cancellation penalty: $75

*Low-Fare Airlines*
While there is no direct low-fare airline service currently available to Amsterdam, a traveler may take Virgin Atlantic to London and use their $25 add-on fare to Maastricht, Holland (about one hour's driving time from Amsterdam).

*Charter and Bulk Fare*
Amsterdam has always been a major charter destination, so look for some large programs this summer. Dutch charter specialist Martinair operated nonstop or direct charters from many U.S. charter cities in 1986 and will probably repeat this year. Peak summer fares should be about $400–$450 from New York, around $500–$550 from Chicago, and around $625–$700 from the West Coast.

## Athens

*Major Airlines*

|  | Round-trip fares to Athens from |  |  |  |
|---|---|---|---|---|
| Fare basis | New York | Chicago | Texas | West Coast |
| *Excursions* | | | | |
| Lowest available round-trip | $ 997 | $1,497 | $1,226 | $1,696 |
| Lowest available one-way | — | — | — | — |
| *Full fare* | | | | |
| Economy | 1,818 | 2,100 | 2,136 | 2,396 |
| Business Class | 2,500 | 2,806 | 2,900 | 3,250 |
| First Class | 4,400 | 4,600 | 4,800 | 5,204 |

**Restrictions on lowest available fare**
Peak season: June 1–August 31
Advance purchase: fourteen days
Minimum stay: seven days
Weekend supplement: none
Stopovers: none
Children's fare: 67 percent
Cancellation penalty: $50

*Low-Fare Airlines*
There has been no low-fare airline service direct to Athens in the past, and none is likely for 1987.

*Charter and Bulk Fare*
Charter volume has been heavy in recent years. You can expect the same for 1987. Summer fares from New York should range from $550–$650 with one-ways available around $350–$400. Most of the action is from New York; don't expect much from the interior cities or the West Coast. There may be some bulk-fare service at about the same prices as charters.

## Belgrade

*Major Airlines*

|  | Round-trip fares to Belgrade from | | | |
|---|---|---|---|---|
| Fare basis | New York | Chicago | Texas | West Coast |
| *Excursions* | | | | |
| Lowest available round-trip | $ 849 | $ 949 | $1,517 | $1,757 |
| Lowest available one-way | — | — | — | — |
| *Full fare* | | | | |
| Economy | 1,646 | 1,812 | 2,314 | 2,554 |
| Business Class | 1,844 | 2,010 | 2,732 | 2,890 |
| First Class | 3,386 | 3,590 | — | — |

**Restrictions on lowest available fare**
Peak season: June 1–August 14
Advance purchase: twenty-one days
Minimum stay: fourteen days
Weekend supplement: $50 each way
Stopovers: none
Children's fare: 67 percent
Cancellation penalty: $75

*Low-Fare Airlines*
No low-fare airlines serve Yugoslavia, and nothing is likely to change that in 1987.

*Charter and Bulk Fare*
Nothing dramatic is expected. Yugoslavia is a fairly minor destination for Americans and is generally isolated from some of the more competitive market forces.

## Brussels

*Major Airlines*

|  | Round-trip fares to Brussels from |  |  |  |
|---|---|---|---|---|
| Fare basis | New York | Chicago | Texas | West Coast |
| *Excursions* | | | | |
| Lowest available round-trip | $ 738 | $ 858 | $ 918 | $ 968 |
| Lowest available one-way | — | — | — | — |
| *Full fare* | | | | |
| Economy | 1,442 | 1,668 | 1,936 | 2,102 |
| Business Class | 1,676 | 1,874 | 2,184 | 2,328 |
| First Class | 3,212 | 3,606 | 3,606 | 4,162 |

**Restrictions on lowest available fare**
Peak season: June 1–September 14
Advance purchase: seven days
Minimum stay: seven days
Weekend supplement: none
Stopovers: one at each U.S. gateway; extra cost: none
Children's fare: 67 percent
Cancellation penalty: $75
Other special conditions: $75 for one change

*Low-Fare Airlines*
There is no low-fare airline serving Brussels from the United States.

*Charter and Bulk Fare*
Most of the low-fare service to Brussels seems to be through bulk-fare deals, rather than charters. Bulk-fare deals were offered in 1986 at around $500 from New York and $700 from the West Coast. A few charter programs will also be offered in 1987.

## Cairo

*Major Airlines*

| Fare basis | Round-trip fares to Cairo from |||| 
|---|---|---|---|---|
| | New York | Chicago | Texas | West Coast |
| *Excursions* | | | | |
| Lowest available round-trip | $ 999 | $1,117 | $1,162 | $1,182 |
| Lowest available one-way | — | — | — | — |
| *Full fare* | | | | |
| Economy | 2,076 | 1,986 | 1,997 | 2,128 |
| Business Class | 2,284 | 2,536 | 2,744 | 3,194 |
| First Class | 3,832 | 4,526 | 4,684 | 5,194 |

**Restrictions on lowest available fare**
Peak season: May 15–September 14
Advance purchase: twenty-one days
Minimum stay: six days
Weekend supplement: none
Stopovers: one in either Rome or Athens. Others: $75 each
Children's fare: 67 percent
Cancellation penalty: $75

*Low-Fare Airlines*
There is no low-fare airline serving Cairo from the United States.

*Charter and Bulk Fare*
Don't expect any charters to Cairo this summer, though you may see some bulk-fare tickets in the range of $650–$700 from New York.

## Copenhagen

*Major Airlines*

| Fare basis | Round-trip fares to Copenhagen from ||||
|---|---|---|---|---|
| | New York | Chicago | Texas | West Coast |
| *Excursions* | | | | |
| Lowest available round-trip | $ 825 | $ 974 | $1,971 | $1,108 |
| Lowest available one-way | — | — | — | — |
| *Full fare* | | | | |
| Economy | 1,464 | 1,700 | 1,812 | 2,216 |
| Business Class | 1,464 | 1,700 | 1,812 | 2,216 |
| First Class | 2,582 | 3,628 | 4,410 | 4,166 |

**Restrictions on lowest available fare**
Peak season: June 1–August 14
Advance purchase: twenty-one days
Minimum stay: ten days
Weekend supplement: $50 each way
Stopovers: none
Children's fare: 67 percent
Cancellation penalty: $75
Other special conditions: ticketing required at the time of reservation

*Comment:* Look for fares to Scandinavia to remain slightly to moderately higher than fares to other European cities for comparable distances. All passengers who pay full-fare Economy are entitled to Business Class.

*Low-Fare Airlines*
Early this year, Tower received permission to fly from the United States to Copenhagen. At this writing, Tower's fares have not been established.

*Charter and Bulk Fare*
Scandinavia has permitted only a trickle of charter service from the United States in the past. You probably won't see much this year either.

**Dublin**

*Major Airlines*

| Fare basis | Round-trip fares to Dublin from |||| 
|---|---|---|---|---|
| | New York | Chicago | Texas | West Coast |
| *Excursions* | | | | |
| Lowest available round-trip | $ 629 | $ 712 | $ 698 | $ 812 |
| Lowest available one-way | — | — | — | — |
| *Full fare* | | | | |
| Economy | 1,108 | 1,618 | 1,694 | 1,926 |
| Business Class | 1,400 | 1,660 | 1,694 | 1,926 |
| First Class | 2,840 | 2,868 | 3,160 | 3,250 |

**Restrictions on lowest available fare**
Peak season: June 1–September 14
Advance purchase: twenty-one days
Minimum stay: seven days

Weekend supplement: $25 each way (except New York)
Stopovers: at U.S. gateway
Children's fare: 67 percent
Cancellation penalty: $75
Other special conditions: $100 for one change

*Low-Fare Airlines*
No direct or nonstop low-fare airline service to Ireland is expected. If you want to use a low-fare airline, your best bet is to take Virgin Atlantic to London, and then fly directly, take the train/ferry (BritRail Pass), or take a fly/drive package option.

*Charter and Bulk Fare*
Ireland has enjoyed good charter service over the years, but most flights serve Shannon (see page 129).

**Frankfurt**

*Major Airlines*

| | Round-trip fares to Frankfurt from | | | | |
|---|---|---|---|---|---|
| Fare basis | New York | Chicago | Dallas (Texas) | Houston (Texas) | West Coast |
| *Excursions* | | | | | |
| Lowest available round-trip | $ 756 | $ 847 | $ 896 | $ 896 | $1,024 |
| Lowest available one-way | — | — | — | — | — |
| *Full fare* | | | | | |
| Economy | 1,190 | 1,301 | 1,333 | 1,330 | 1,546 |
| Business Class | 1,824 | 2,184 | 2,200 | 2,200 | 2,270 |
| First Class | 3,212 | 3,606 | 3,680 | 3,685 | 4,120 |

**Restrictions on lowest available fare**
Peak season: June 1–September 14
Advance purchase: twenty-one days
Minimum stay: seven days
Weekend supplement: approximately $50
Stopovers: none
Children's fare: 67 percent
Cancellation penalty: $75

## Low-Fare Airlines
No low-fare airline flies to Germany. Virgin Atlantic offers a $25 add-on fare from London to Maastricht, Holland (about one hour's driving time from Germany).

## Charter and Bulk Fare
Germany is an extremely active charter and bulk-fare destination, with big programs on its two charter airlines—Condor and LTU—as well as on U.S. carriers. Charter programs were run from over a dozen U.S. cities in 1986, and the pattern should continue for 1987. Peak summer round-trip fares should be $475–$550 from New York, $550–$650 from Chicago, $600–$700 from Texas, and $700–$850 from the West Coast.

## Geneva

### Major Airlines

| Fare basis | Round-trip fares to Geneva from |  |  |  |
|---|---|---|---|---|
|  | New York | Chicago | Texas | West Coast |
| *Excursions* |  |  |  |  |
| Lowest available round-trip | $ 948 | $ 847 | $ 996 | $1,052 |
| Lowest available one-way | — | — | — | — |
| *Full fare* |  |  |  |  |
| Economy | 1,506 | 1,694 | 1,698 | 2,414 |
| Business Class | 1,694 | 1,916 | 2,174 | 2,916 |
| First Class | 3,228 | 3,614 | 4,096 | 4,590 |

**Restrictions on lowest available fare**
Peak season: June 1–September 14
Advance purchase: twenty-one days
Minimum stay: seven days
Weekend supplement: $100 round trip ($50 each way)
Stopovers: none
Children's fare: 67 percent
Cancellation penalty: $75

## Low-Fare Airlines
Despite the new country-of origin treaty, no low-fare airline had started flying to Geneva as of late 1986. But you may see some low-fare flights scheduled this summer.

## Charter and Bulk Fare

Several operators plan to offer low-cost charters to Switzerland this summer, serving both Geneva and Zurich. Peak-season round-trip fares should be about $500–$600 from New York, $650 from Chicago and Texas, and $800–$900 from the West Coast.

## Helsinki

### Major Airlines

| Fare basis | Round-trip fares to Helsinki from ||||
|---|---|---|---|---|
| | New York | Chicago | Texas | West Coast |
| *Excursions* | | | | |
| Lowest available round-trip | $ 985 | $1,131 | $1,205 | $1,238 |
| Lowest available one-way | — | — | — | — |
| *Full fare* | | | | |
| Economy | 1,548 | — | 1,706 | 2,120 |
| Business Class | 1,862 | — | 2,500 | 2,520 |
| First Class | 3,038 | — | 3,866 | 3,916 |

**Restrictions on lowest available fare**
Peak season: June 1–August 14
Advance purchase: twenty-one days
Minimum stay: seven days
Weekend supplement: yes
Stopovers: none
Children's fare: 67 percent
Cancellation penalty: $75

### Low-Fare Airlines

There was no activity in 1986, and none is expected in 1987.

### Charter and Bulk Fare

Scandinavia has permitted only a trickle of charter service from the United States in the past. You probably won't see much this year either.

## Lisbon

*Major Airlines*

| Fare basis | Round-trip fares to Lisbon from |  |  |  |
|---|---|---|---|---|
| | New York | Chicago | Texas | West Coast |
| *Excursions* | | | | |
| Lowest available round-trip | $ 664 | $1,142 | $1,234 | $1,324 |
| Lowest available one-way | — | — | — | — |
| *Full fare* | | | | |
| Economy | 1,268 | 1,794 | 1,801 | 1,825 |
| Business Class | 1,922 | 2,676 | 2,882 | 3,222 |
| First Class | 3,535 | 4,288 | 4,406 | 4,900 |

**Restrictions on lowest available fare**
Peak season: June 15–August 14
Advance purchase: fourteen days (mid-week); twenty-one days (weekend)
Minimum stay: seven days
Weekend supplement: $100 round trip
Stopovers: none
Children's fare: 67 percent
Cancellation penalty: $75

*Low-Fare Airlines*
There was no activity in 1986, and none is expected in 1987.

*Charter and Bulk Fare*
Several charter programs operate to Portugal each year, especially from U.S. cities with strong ethnic ties—Boston, New York, and San Jose, California. Look for round-trip fares at about the same level as last year—around $500–$600 from the East Coast. As of press time charters from San Jose have not yet been announced. But check for them later in the season if the Bay Area is a convenient departure gateway for you.

## London

*Major Airlines*

| Fare basis | Round-trip fares to London from |||||
|---|---|---|---|---|---|
| | New York | Chicago | Texas* Dallas | Texas* Houston | West Coast |
| *Excursions* | | | | | |
| Lowest available round-trip | $ 688 | $ 758 | $ 698 | $ 649 | $ 888 |
| Lowest available one-way | — | — | — | — | — |
| *Full fare* | | | | | |
| Economy | 938 | 1,096 | 1,090 | 950 | 1,326 |
| Business Class | 2,478 | 2,328 | 2,310 | — | 3,064 |
| First Class | 4,174 | 4,918 | 3,570 | — | 4,926 |
| Concorde | 5,358 | — | — | — | — |

*Fares from Texas quoted from British Caledonian Airways (BCAL).

**Restrictions on lowest available fare**
Peak season: June 1–September 30
Advance purchase: twenty-one days
Minimum stay: seven days
Weekend supplement: $50–$70 each way (no supplement on BCAL)
Stopovers: none
Children's fare: 67 percent
Cancellation penalty: $50
Other special conditions: $50 for one change.

*Low-Fare Airlines*
London has been an active low-fare airline market, but with the demise of People Express, the outlook for this summer is unclear. Virgin Atlantic, however, may keep things very competitive.

*Charter and Bulk Fare*
London has been an active charter market for some years, with service from about a dozen U.S. cities on a regular basis. Bulk-fare seats were widely offered in 1985–1986. What happens this summer may well depend on how much authority the low-fare airlines get to increase their schedules. Look for charters at peak-season round-trip fares around $400–$500 from New York, $550–$650 from Chicago, and $600–$750 from the West Coast.

## Luxembourg

*Major Airlines*

| Fare basis | Round-trip fares to Luxembourg from ||||
|---|---|---|---|---|
| | New York | Chicago | Texas | West Coast |
| *Excursions* | | | | |
| Lowest available round-trip | $ 738 | $ 689 | $ 989 | — |
| Lowest available one-way | 239 | 299 | — | — |
| *Full fare* | | | | |
| Economy | 801 | — | — | — |
| Business Class | 838 | 888 | — | — |
| First Class | — | — | — | — |

**Restrictions on lowest available fare**
Peak season: June 15–September 14
Advance purchase: twenty-one days
Minimum stay: seven days
Weekend supplement: $25 each way
Stopovers: free in Iceland
Children's fare: 67 percent

*Comments:* Icelandair will likely retain its special place in the scheme of transatlantic travel with its competitive fares to well-located Luxembourg. The airline recently added additional U.S. gateways—Baltimore, Detroit, and Orlando—offering passengers the option of not having to connect through New York. Icelandair's new Saga (business) class provides extra leg room but retains very tight, 3-3 across seating.

Icelandair may be particularly attractive to travelers who can't conform with the usual advance-purchase requirements or minimum/maximum stay requirements of APEX fares. As well, the airline offers easy connections to numerous destinations within Europe. Icelandair provides free bus service from Luxembourg to eight cities in Germany, three cities in Belgium, and three cities in Holland. In addition, the airline offers passengers a special $15 rail fare to Paris or any city in Switzerland on Swiss Federal Railways. For passengers destined for Stockholm, Bergen, Oslo, and Copenhagen, there is a free twenty-four-hour stopover for one-way flights and a forty-eight-hour stopover for round-trips in the unique city of Reykjavik, Iceland.

*Low-Fare Airlines*
Icelandair is the continent's only low-fare airline.

*Charter and Bulk Fare*
Icelandair preempts all the action here.

**Madrid**

*Major Airlines*

| Fare basis | Round-trip fares to Madrid from |||| 
|---|---|---|---|---|
| | New York | Chicago | Texas | West Coast |
| *Excursions* | | | | |
| Lowest available round-trip | $ 672 | $ 733 | $ 770 | $ 825 |
| Lowest available one-way | — | — | — | — |
| *Full fare* | | | | |
| Economy | 1,298 | 1,798 | 1,966 | 2,206 |
| Business Class | 2,150 | 2,650 | 2,856 | 3,196 |
| First Class | 3,540 | 4,290 | 4,408 | 4,902 |

**Restrictions on lowest available fare**
Peak season: June 15–August 14
Advance purchase: fourteen days (mid-week); twenty-one days (weekends)
Minimum stay: seven days
Weekend supplement: $100 round trip
Stopovers: none
Children's fare: 67 percent
Cancellation penalty: $75

*Low-Fare Airlines*
There was no activity in 1986, and none is expected for 1987.

*Charter and Bulk Fare*
Several charter programs operate to Spain each year with service from the East, Midwest, and West Coast. Fares will probably range from $450–$550 from the East Coast and $650–$750 from the West Coast.

## Milan

*Major Airlines*

|  | Round-trip fares to Milan from |  |  |  |
|---|---|---|---|---|
| Fare basis | New York | Chicago | Texas | West Coast |
| *Excursions* | | | | |
| Lowest available round-trip | $ 809 | $ 879 | $ 938 | $1,008 |
| Lowest available one-way | — | — | — | — |
| *Full fare* | | | | |
| Economy | 1,468 | 1,668 | 2,137 | 1,966 |
| Business Class: | 2,108 | 2,408 | 2,422 | 2,892 |
| First Class | 3,906 | 4,536 | 4,408 | 5,082 |

**Restrictions on lowest available fare**
Peak season: June 1–September 14
Advance purchase: twenty-one days
Minimum stay: seven days
Weekend supplement: yes
Stopovers: none; open-jaw permitted
Children's fare: 67 percent
Cancellation penalty: $75

*Low-Fare Airlines*
There has been no low-fare airline service from the United States to Italy, and nothing new is likely this summer.

*Charter and Bulk Fare*
Italy is a major charter destination, especially from the East Coast. Last summer, a number of programs operated from Boston, New York, and Philadelphia. Charters to Milan this year will probably be about $550–$650 from the East Coast, $700–$800 from Chicago and Texas, and $800–$900 from the West Coast.

## Munich

*Major Airlines*

| Fare basis | Round-trip fares to Munich from ||||| 
| --- | --- | --- | --- | --- | --- |
| | New York | Chicago | Texas Dallas | Texas Houston | West Coast |
| *Excursions* | | | | | |
| Lowest available round-trip | $ 811 | $ 876 | $ 968 | $ 988 | $1,989 |
| Lowest available one-way | — | — | — | — | — |
| *Full fare* | | | | | |
| Economy | 1,652 | 1,990 | 1,050 | 2,050 | 2,222 |
| Business Class | 1,870 | 2,240 | 2,304 | 2,310 | 2,490 |
| First Class | 3,250 | 3,642 | 3,642 | 3,701 | 4,200 |

**Restrictions on lowest available fare**
Peak season: June 1–September 14
Advance purchase: twenty-one days
Minimum stay: seven days
Weekend supplement: approximately $50
Stopovers: none
Children's fare: 67 percent
Cancellation penalty: $75

*Low-Fare Airlines*
There was no activity in 1986, and none is expected for 1987.

*Charter and Bulk Fare*
Germany is an extremely active charter and bulk-fare destination, with big programs on its two charter airlines—Condor and LTU—as well as on U.S. carriers. Fares this summer will probably be about $50 more than charter fares to Frankfurt from the U.S. gateways cited above.

## Nice

*Major Airlines*

|  | \multicolumn{4}{c}{Round-trip fares to Nice from} |
| --- | --- | --- | --- | --- |
| Fare basis | New York | Chicago | Texas | West Coast |
| *Excursions* | | | | |
| Lowest available round-trip | $ 862 | $1,010 | $1,008 | $1,043 |
| Lowest available one-way | — | — | — | — |
| *Full fare* | | | | |
| Economy | 1,838 | 2,164 | 2,344 | 2,580 |
| Business Class | 2,128 | 2,430 | 2,744 | 2,962 |
| First Class | 3,748 | 4,152 | 3,992 | 4,770 |

**Restrictions on lowest available fare**
Peak season: May 15–September 30
Advance purchase: twenty-one days
Minimum stay: seven days
Weekend supplement: $100 round trip ($50 each way)
Stopovers: none
Children's fare: 67 percent
Cancellation penalty: $75

*Comments:* Lowest available fares to France from U.S. cities other than New York have generally been about $100 more than fares to other European cities of comparable distances, while New York fares have been more competitive. This pattern is expected to continue this summer.

*Low-Fare Airlines*
There are no low-fare airlines presently serving Nice, and none is expected to do so in the near future. The only low-fare alternative would be a charter.

*Charter and Bulk Fare*
Air Charter, a subsidiary of Air France, will offer charter service from New York this summer in the $500–$600 range.

## Oslo

*Major Airlines*

|  | Round-trip fares to Oslo from | | | |
|---|---|---|---|---|
| Fare basis | New York | Chicago | Texas | West Coast |
| *Excursions* | | | | |
| Lowest available round-trip | $ 865 | $ 974 | $1,966 | $1,085 |
| Lowest available one-way | — | — | — | — |
| *Full fare* | | | | |
| Economy | 1,464 | 1,700 | 1,798 | 2,216 |
| Business Class | 1,464 | 1,700 | 1,798 | 2,216 |
| First Class | 3,583 | 3,628 | 4,017 | 4,166 |

**Restrictions on lowest available fare**
Peak season: June 1–August 14
Advance purchase: twenty-one days
Minimum stay: ten days
Weekend supplement: $50 each way
Stopovers: none
Children's fare: 67 percent
Cancellation penalty: $75
Other special conditions: ticketing required at time of reservation

*Comments:* Look for fares to Scandinavia to remain slightly to moderately higher than airfares to other European cities of comparable distances.

*Low-Fare Airlines*
Any low-fare airline service to Oslo this year is extremely unlikely.

*Charter and Bulk Fare*
Scandinavia has permitted only a trickle of charter service from the United States. You probably won't see much in 1987. Dedicated low-fare travelers will have to try nearby gateways—especially Frankfurt and Hamburg.

## Paris

*Major Airlines*

|  | Round-trip fares to Paris from | | | |
|---|---|---|---|---|
| Fare basis | New York | Chicago | Texas | West Coast |
| *Excursions* | | | | |
| Lowest available round-trip | $ 739 | $ 894 | $ 908 | $1,015 |
| Lowest available one-way | — | — | — | — |
| *Full fare* | | | | |
| Economy | 1,654 | 1,980 | 2,210 | 2,396 |
| Business Class | 1,994 | 2,246 | 2,888 | 2,778 |
| First Class | 3,562 | 3,970 | 3,808 | 4,586 |
| Concorde | 4,296 | — | — | — |

**Restrictions on lowest available fare**
Peak season: May 15–September 30
Advance purchase: twenty-one days
Minimum stay: seven days
Weekend supplement: $100 round-trip ($50 each way)
Stopovers: none
Children's fare: 67 percent
Cancellation penalty: $75
Other special conditions: Indicated lowest fares require ticketing at the time reservations are made. Where this is impractical, ordinary APEX is available at $30 to $50 higher, depending on departure city.

*Comments:* Lowest available fares to France from U.S. cities other than New York have generally been about $100 more than fares to other European cities of comparable distances, while New York fares have been more competitive. This pattern is expected to continue this summer.

*Low-Fare Airlines*
At present, no low-fare airlines operate from the United States to France. While some carriers are interested, the French government has taken a dim view of any fares that undercut Air France.

*Charter and Bulk Fare*
Charters and bulk-fare seats to France should have a big year again in 1987. Air France has moved into the transatlantic

charter market, which adds considerable impetus. Look for direct charters from several U.S. cities this summer, although some of the biggest programs will involve a domestic connection to a charter originating in New York. Typical peak-season fares will be $500–$600 from New York and $700–$800 from the West Coast.

## Rome

*Major Airlines*

|  | Round-trip fares to Rome from | | | |
|---|---|---|---|---|
| Fare basis | New York | Chicago | Texas | West Coast |
| *Excursions* | | | | |
| Lowest available round-trip | $ 840 | $ 910 | $ 978 | $1,049 |
| Lowest available one-way | — | — | — | — |
| *Full fare* | | | | |
| Economy | 1,210 | 1,710 | 2,177 | 2,008 |
| Business Class | 2,260 | 2,560 | 2,966 | 3,044 |
| First Class | 4,082 | 4,712 | 4,950 | 5,248 |

**Restrictions on lowest available fare**
Peak season: June 1–September 14
Advance purchase: twenty-one days
Minimum stay: seven days
Weekend supplement: $35 each way
Stopovers: none; open-jaw permitted
Children's fare: 67 percent
Cancellation penalty: $75

*Low-Fare Airlines*
There has been no low-fare airline service from the United States to Italy, and nothing new is likely this summer.

*Charter and Bulk Fare*
Italy is a major charter destination, especially from the East Coast. Last summer, a number of programs operated from Boston, New York, and Philadelphia. Charters to Rome this year will probably be about $550–$650 from the East Coast, $700–$800 from Chicago and Texas, and $800–$900 from the West Coast.

## Shannon

*Major Airlines*

|  | Round-trip fares to Shannon from | | | |
| --- | --- | --- | --- | --- |
| Fare basis | New York | Chicago | Texas | West Coast |
| *Excursions* | | | | |
| Lowest available round-trip | $ 599 | $ 699 | $ 668 | $ 782 |
| Lowest available one-way | — | — | — | — |
| *Full fare* | | | | |
| Economy | 1,128 | 1,246 | 1,280 | 1,426 |
| Business Class | 1,470 | 1,620 | 1,654 | 1,886 |
| First Class | 2,800 | 2,828 | 3,120 | 3,210 |

*Special promotional fare

**Restrictions on lowest available fare**
Peak season: June 1–September 14
Advance purchase: twenty-one days
Minimum stay: seven days
Weekend supplement: $25 each way (except New York)
Stopovers: one at a U.S. gateway
Children's fare: 67 percent
Cancellation penalty: $50
Other special conditions: $100 for one change

*Low-Fare Airlines*
No direct or nonstop low-fare airline service to Ireland is expected to operate this year.

*Charter and Bulk Fare*
Ireland has enjoyed good charter service over the years, and 1986 should see a repeat. Look for peak-season round-trip fares at around $425–$500 from the East Coast.

## Stockholm

*Major Airlines*

| Fare basis | Round-trip fares to Stockholm from ||||
|---|---|---|---|---|
| | New York | Chicago | Texas | West Coast |
| *Excursions* | | | | |
| Lowest available round-trip | $ 929 | $1,040 | $1,075 | $1,149 |
| Lowest available one-way | — | — | — | — |
| *Full fare* | | | | |
| Economy | 1,600 | 1,836 | 2,268 | 2,352 |
| Business Class | 1,600 | 1,836 | 2,268 | 2,352 |
| First Class | 3,796 | 3,840 | 4,662 | 4,378 |

**Restrictions on lowest available fare**
Peak season: June 1–August 14
Advance purchase: twenty-one days
Minimum stay: ten days
Weekend supplement: $50 each way
Stopovers: none
Children's fare: 67 percent
Cancellation penalty: $75

*Comments:* Look for fares to Scandinavia to remain slightly to moderately higher than airfares to other European cities of comparable distances.

*Low-Fare Airlines*
New low-fare airline service to Stockholm is extremely unlikely this year.

*Charter and Bulk Fare*
Scandinavia has permitted only a trickle of charter service from the United States. You probably won't see much activity in 1987. There's no market for low-fare airlines, either. Dedicated low-fare travelers will have to try nearby gateways—especially Frankfurt and Hamburg.

## Tel Aviv

*Major Airlines*

|  | \multicolumn{5}{c}{Round-trip fares to Tel Aviv from} |
|---|---|---|---|---|---|
| Fare basis | New York | Chicago | Texas Dallas | Texas Houston | West Coast |
| *Excursions* | | | | | |
| Lowest available round-trip | $ 949 | $1,449 | $1,617 | $1,666 | $1,857 |
| Lowest available one-way | 769 | 889 | 973 | 985 | 1,091 |
| *Full fare* | | | | | |
| Economy: | 1,498 | 1,624 | 1,648 | 1,666 | 1,863 |
| Business Class | 2,818 | 3,318 | 3,524 | 3,524 | 3,864 |
| First Class | 4,422 | 5,172 | 5,290 | 5,290 | 5,784 |

**Restrictions on lowest available fare**
Peak season: June 14–July 14
Advance purchase: ten days
Minimum stay: six days
Weekend supplement: none
Stopovers: one free in Europe and one free at U.S. gateway
Children's fare: 75 percent
Cancellation penalty: $75

*Low-Fare Airlines*
Tower Air is pushing service to Israel. It is currently quoting an $869 round-trip fare from New York in the peak season and $719–$749 for most of the rest of the year. New York to Tel Aviv has always been a very competitive route, and it should remain so in summer 1987. Tower has discontinued its service from the West Coast.

*Charter and Bulk Fare*
Israel has historically been a reasonably good market, but the low-fare airlines seem to be providing most of the cheaper opportunities on a scheduled (and possibly bulk-fare) basis rather than charter. Still, you can expect some flights, and at the same prices as the low-fare lines.

**Vienna**

*Major Airlines*

|  | Round-trip fares to Vienna from | | | |
|---|---|---|---|---|
| Fare basis | New York | Chicago | Texas | West Coast |
| *Excursions* | | | | |
| Lowest available round-trip | $ 844 | $1,344 | $1,512 | $1,610 |
| Lowest available one-way | — | — | — | — |
| *Full fare* | | | | |
| Economy | 1,458 | 1,958 | 2,126 | 2,366 |
| Business Class | 1,978 | 2,478 | 2,684 | 3,024 |
| First Class | 3,446 | 4,196 | 4,314 | 4,802 |

**Restrictions on lowest available fare**
Peak season: June 1–September 14
Advance purchase: twenty-one days
Minimum stay: seven days
Weekend supplement: $30 (Friday, Saturday, and Sunday)
Stopovers: none
Children's fare: 67 percent
Cancellation penalty: $75
Other special conditions: $100 to change return date

*Comments:* Alia (Jordan) is the only airline with nonstop service from Chicago and New York to Vienna, plus through service from Los Angeles. The airline also offers the lowest fares. Other carriers serve Vienna with connections.

*Low-Fare Airlines*
There has been no low-fare airline to Vienna, and none is likely this year. Alia is probably the best bet.

*Charter and Bulk Fare*
Over the past few years, a few sporadic charter programs have been operated to Vienna. 1986's low-price action was either with bulk fares or with group-tour rates on Tarom, the Romanian airline. You can expect the same this year—few charters, but several comparable low-cost options.

## Zurich

*Major Airlines*

|  | Round-trip fares to Zurich from | | | |
|---|---|---|---|---|
| Fare basis | New York | Chicago | Texas | West Coast |
| *Excursions* | | | | |
| Lowest available round-trip | $ 776 | $ 844 | $ 996 | $1,052 |
| Lowest available one-way | — | — | — | — |
| *Full fare* | | | | |
| Economy | 1,506 | 1,916 | 2,176 | 2,414 |
| Business Class | 1,694 | 2,092 | 2,576 | 2,916 |
| First Class | 3,228 | 3,618 | 4,096 | 4,590 |

**Restrictions on lowest available fare**
Peak season: June 1–September 14
Advance purchase: twenty-one days
Minimum stay: seven days
Weekend supplement: $100 round-trip ($50 each way)
Stopovers: none
Children's fare: 67 percent
Cancellation penalty: $75

*Low-Fare Airlines*
Despite the new country-of-origin treaty, no low-fare airline had started flying to Zurich as of late 1986. But you may see some low-fare flights scheduled this summer.

*Charter and Bulk Fare*
Several operators plan to offer low-cost charters to Switzerland this summer, serving both Geneva and Zurich. Peak-season round-trip fares should be about $500–$600 from New York, $650 from Chicago and Texas, and $800–$900 from the West Coast.

# Part II

# Getting Around Europe

# 12

# Internal European Transportation Options

*Make the Best Choice for Your
Own Individual Trip*

If you're going to spend your entire European vacation exploring a single city, you don't need to worry about travel within Europe. You can skip this and the next three chapters. But a clear majority of travelers visit at least two cities or regions on their trips. Chances are you're interested in knowing about the most efficient and pleasant ways to travel from place to place.

Getting around in Europe normally means some combination of three alternatives: flying, taking trains, or driving in a rented car—the latter two in combination with a few boat or ferry trips to get across some of the channels and seas. Perhaps you'll take a few bus trips, as well, but mainly for short, local excursions. The European countries have emphasized railroads rather than buses as the basic form of public surface travel. As with transatlantic air travel, your choices of internal transportation in Europe will be discussed in terms of cost, convenience, comfort, and contingency factors.

Cost Comparisons

A good way to compare the costs of traveling around Europe by different modes is to compare per-person costs of some "standard" trips that are typical of those that Americans might take:

- A twenty-one-day trip of 1,500 miles, or about 70 miles a day average, typical of a fairly intensive exploration within a single country or smaller multicountry region, for example, Frankfurt-Zurich-Paris-Frankfurt, with a generous allowance for sightseeing side-trip excursions.
- A twenty-one-day trip of 3,000 miles, or about 140 miles a day average, typical of a "see as much as you can" multicountry trip. A trip from Amsterdam to Naples and back, with liberal allowance for sightseeing excursions, would be representative of this "standard."
- A sixty-day trip of 3,000 miles, or about 50 miles a day average, typical of an all summer stay that minimizes long-distance travel.
- A sixty-day trip of 8,000 miles, typical of a multicountry trip that gets you to most of Europe's high spots over the course of a full summer.

Costs for these trips by the three major modes—rental car, rail, and air—are shown in Table 5 (page 147).

**Rental-Car Costs**

Estimates of car-rental costs in the figures are based on the least-expensive car rentals available from one or more of the eleven major European car-rental companies. The figures reflect the summer 1986 rates plus 15 percent inflation anticipated for 1987 in one of the four European countries with the lowest overall car-rental costs. In the case of the two-month trips, automobile costs are based on use of one of the lowest-priced leases. Costs for the "subcompact" car are for a *standard* subcompact, as defined in chapter 14—something like a Ford Fiesta or Renault 5 le Car. Costs for a "compact" car are based on a slightly larger model, such as a Ford Escort or VW Jetta. Finally, costs for the "midsize" car are based on a four-door model of a Ford Sierra, Opel Ascona, or VW Passat. The cost calculations used to derive the figure *include* collision damage waiver expenses—even though it's optional, most Americans driving in Europe buy it.

The costs of operating a car in Europe are higher than at

home, largely because gasoline currently can cost up to $3.00 a gallon in many European countries. European automobiles continue to use leaded high-octane gasoline to power high-compression engines, without clean-air modifications required in the United States, so fuel economy tends to be somewhat better than here. Even so, the net effect is average operating costs of at least 50 percent higher than at home for comparable car models. Data reflected in the figures are based on operating costs of 10¢ a mile for a subcompact, 12¢ a mile for a compact, and 14¢ a mile for a four-passenger car.

There are some additional costs in driving that are not incorporated into the cost-comparison calculations. As at home, parking may be the biggest. Very few downtown European hotels have free parking; many have none at all, and parking your car in a garage can easily add at least $5 to $10 a day to your total transportation costs. You'll have trouble parking free or at nominal cost at the main city-center tourist attractions, as well. And even off-the-beaten-track cities have discovered parking meters.

A second additional cost becomes apparent as soon as you hit the open road. The "motorways" in France, Italy, and Spain are toll roads, and—as on the big turnpikes in our eastern states—those tolls can add up to some hefty totals on long trips. Also, you'll find no shortage of toll bridges and tunnels in many European countries.

## Rail Costs

Rail cost estimates in the figures are shown both for Eurailpass and for individual tickets, estimated at 10¢ a mile in Second Class and 15¢ a mile in First Class. These average costs are typical of the railroad ticket rates in the larger of the main tourist countries: Austria, Denmark, France, Germany, Italy, and the United Kingdom. Costs are substantially lower in several European countries. Also, use of passes limited to single countries sometimes results in still lower trip costs.

Three additional costs of rail travel are not incorporated into these calculations.

First is the fact that rail passes or ordinary tickets do not usually cover local transportation costs once you've arrived in a city. So you must plan on either municipal transit or taxi fares for travel between rail stations and hotels and for local sightseeing trips. These can easily add up to several dollars each day.

Second is that train travelers tend to stay at city-center hotels and eat at downtown restaurants accessible to train stations. Almost universally, city hotel accommodations are substantially more expensive than comparable quality accommodations in the countryside. When you're budgeting, you should generally figure on spending somewhere between $5 and $25 per person per day more—depending on your standards and the area in which you'll be traveling—for accommodations and meals when you travel by train than when you drive a rented car.

Third, you have to pay a fee of at least $1 to reserve a seat on the main express trains. Some of the best trains, e.g., TALGO, T.G.V.s, or *La Nouvelle Première* require a surcharge. You must pay these separately whether you are using individual tickets, Eurailpass, or a national unlimited-mileage pass.

**Air-Travel Costs**

The air-travel cost estimates in the figures are especially "soft." They're based on typical costs of around 30¢ a mile for the short trips and 25¢ a mile for the 3,000- and 8,000-mile trips. But the fares for any individual trip can differ substantially from these averages, depending on specific trip characteristics and which of a bewildering variety of special ticket deals you might find available for each individual itinerary.

The additional costs of air travel, beyond the ticket, are similar to those of rail travel, though potentially larger. Access to and from airports by special bus, train, or taxi can easily add up to $5 to $30 a person every time you move from one city to the next.

Convenience Factors

Some of the most successful U.S. guidebook writers recommend train travel as the most convenient way to see Europe, as well as the most economical. Express trains run on most of the main routes every hour during the day, and many of these trains run through some of Europe's most scenic areas. You can get a close look at the countryside without keeping your eyes on the road, coping with unfamiliar roads and traffic patterns, or worrying about taking a wrong turn. You arrive and depart right in the center of most cities—no fighting city and suburban traffic to get out of town; no hassles about buses to the airport. And rail travel is fast—express trains almost everywhere zip along at 70 to 90 miles an hour, and the new high-tech French T.G.V. *(Train à Grand Vitesse)* and the British H.S.T. (High-Speed Train) cruise at 125 to 160 miles an hour.

Rail travel has some experiential drawbacks, too. You can't have the train stop while you take a few pictures of that spectacular scene you just passed, or have it wait for you to explore an interesting castle or church. You'll miss the joys of the smaller villages and of staying in countryside hotels or resorts that may be well off the beaten track; you won't have the chance to have that delightful meal in an inexpensive countryside inn.

Driving a rented car, for many, is the ideal way to travel through Europe. The advantages of touring by car are not much different in Europe from the way they are at home. You can stop whenever you wish. You can change your plans on impulse to explore intriguing sights that you may encounter. And traveling by car allows you to get off the beaten track—to adventure and explore a region in depth, if you want. Your luggage can remain in the trunk much of the time—you're not obliged to handle all your belongings every time you move to a new city. And you can enjoy dining and staying overnight in countryside inns or picnicking in scenic locales—special experiences that may be money saving too.

Driving really isn't a very good way to travel if you're staying mainly in the bigger cities. The benefits of flexibility generally don't compensate adequately for the hassles of trying to cope with traffic and parking. And even in the countryside, where driving is most advantageous, touring Americans can sometimes run into considerable difficulties if they get lost or need some mechanical assistance in a small community where nobody speaks English.

Speed is the main advantage of flying as a means of getting around Europe. It's probably the only advantage—and, in many cases, not a very important one. When you consider the extra time of getting to and from airports, plus the requirement that you be at the airport at least an hour before flight time for most international services, you find that an express train is competitive with flying for total elapsed time, city-center-to-city-center or door-to-door, for trips of 300 miles or less.

However, if your itinerary calls for visits to a few points that are widely separated, or requires you to get across one or more of the seas, the airplane may be your only practical alternative. For example, if your trip consists of visits to London and Athens, or Copenhagen, Helsinki, and Rome, you almost have to fly. Even the fastest surface travel could eat up two or three days for each leg of your journey.

## Comfort Factors

The comfort implications of driving, pro and con, are essentially the same in Europe as at home—at least in terms of physical comfort. "Mental" comfort may be another question. Some Americans are apprehensive about driving in unfamiliar circumstances, and driving along a narrow country lane used by oxcarts as much as by automobiles can be pretty "unfamiliar" to many. Also, a driver accustomed to the 55 miles per hour speed limit on U.S. interstate highways may be intimidated by a steady stream of big Mercedes sedans cruising along at 90 to 100, flashing their headlights at anyone timid enough to be moving more slowly. But the adjustment is easier than many might think. Traffic signs throughout Europe use the same international pictorial symbols that require absolutely no special language capability, direction signs are at least as good as those at home, European road maps are excellent, and European gas stations and garages are pretty well accustomed to serving American visitors in their rental cars.

European rail travel is generally quite comfortable, especially on the main through-express services. Even Second Class provides wider seats and more leg room than Coach or Economy air service, and First-Class train seats are as roomy and comfortable as those you find on First-Class air services. During peak travel periods, however, Second-Class trains can get very full, to the point that aisles are crammed with standees, and Second-Class comfort standards in Spain, Italy, and Greece leave a lot to be desired at any time.

Intra-European air services tend to be considerably less comfortable than domestic U.S. services. If you think that seats on U.S. airlines are crowded too close together, you have quite a surprise coming when you get on your first intra-European flight.

## Contingencies

There's not much to say about contingencies that you don't already know. Especially in the summer, drivers don't have to worry much about snowbound mountain passes or washed-away bridges. The trains and planes run like clockwork—except when there's a strike. All in all, you can pretty well count on making your targeted itineraries by any of the modes.

Theft of luggage, cameras, and other personal valuables can be a problem in both cars and trains. Luggage and valuables are not necessarily secure in the trunk of your car—rental cars (with their company decals) are too often the targets of thieves who are very skilled at opening car locks. There have also been frequent reports of light-fingered pickpockets plying their trade on European trains: travelers trying to get some sleep on overnight trips are especially vulnerable, as are Americans, who seem to be easy to identify and who are apparently considered especially inviting targets.

## Sample Trips

In addition to the "standard" trips used for the overall comparison of auto, rail, and air travel within Europe, here are two real trips—one long, one short—costed out by different modes of transportation, in per-person terms, for travel during the peak 1986 summer season. Train fares are point-to-point:

**Trip 1: London-Paris-Zurich-Milan-Venice-Athens-London**

    Economy-Class air:   $715 (quoted by a travel agent); $731 (quoted by an airline)
    First-Class rail*:   $546
    Second-Class rail*:   $376

*For travel between Venice and Athens, the fare is calculated for rail through Yugoslavia. For travel between Athens and London, the fare is also calculated as traveling by rail through the Eastern Bloc and picking up the ferry at Ostende, Belgium. This is the lowest-priced route.

Driving, including cost of three-week rental and Channel ferry: $446 (two people in a subcompact); $304 (four people in a midsize car)

**Trip 2: Frankfurt-Munich-Zurich-Paris-Frankfurt**

Economy-Class air:   $460 (quoted by a travel agent); $502 (quoted by an airline)
First-Class rail:   $226
Second-Class rail:   $148
Driving, including the cost of a two-week rental:   $226 (two people in a subcompact); $167 (four people in a midsize car)
Driving, including cost of a one-week rental:   $158 (two people in a subcompact); $108 (four people in a midsize car)

Trip 2 illustrates one other interesting factor about traveling in Europe. Determining the best air fare for a complicated itinerary in Europe is as much black art as science. These fares are not immediately available through the computers (you have to get a quote from the rate desk), and there are different ways to figure them.

## The Channel Crossing

The English Channel crossing has been a barrier to European travelers since Roman times. And even in today's supposedly high-tech age, it still presents a challenge to travelers who want to visit both England and one or more Continental countries during a short trip.

Of course, you can fly from London to Paris, Amsterdam, Brussels, Frankfurt, Zurich, or most other nearby continental points in three to four hours, city-center to city-center. The problem is that most Americans would want to do this trip on a one-way basis, in combination with open-jaw APEX or charter transatlantic flights. And the cheapest one-way flights are expensive, in the range of $80 to $150 from London to some of the nearby big continental gateways.

For the many travelers who will be in the market for a less expensive mode of crossing, the best is the combined rail-Hovercraft or rail-boat service. One-way tickets are about $36 from London to Paris, $28 to Amsterdam, and $31 to Brussels. The drawback to these trips is that they use up the better part of an entire day, with all the various connections and queuing times.

The fastest London-Paris service is the rail–Hovercraft, which takes about five and a half hours; the London-Brussels rail-hydrofoil takes about seven hours (plus a $13 hydrofoil supplement); and the London-Amsterdam rail-ferry service takes about eleven hours. These surface crossings can eat into your touring time, especially if you're spending only a short time in Europe, but they're still the preferable alternative to the higher cost of flying.

Bus-ferry travel provides rock-bottom prices for the Channel crossing. Express bus and connecting ferry services link London with Paris, Brussels, and Amsterdam, at a cost of about $24 one way. But you trade a lot in convenience to save a few dollars; these trips typically require eleven to twelve hours travel time. Most travelers prefer to economize on some other part of their itinerary and take the much faster and more comfortable rail alternatives to cross the Channel.

One other possibility is popular with some American travelers. Overnight ferries operate on some of the longer Channel crossings, from Southhampton or Portsmouth to Le Havre for instance, and you can get a mini-stateroom for about $30 per person, plus the basic fare. Since you'd pay at least that for an overnight stay in many hotels, it's not a bad way to go—at Le Havre, you're less than two hours out of Paris by train. Similar overnight (or longer) services are available connecting England with other French ports plus ports in Holland, Germany, Denmark, and Sweden.

Your Best Deal

The detailed comparisons between car, rail, and air demonstrate some overall points:

- Rail and rental cars are generally competitive in cost for a wide variety of trips. Eurailpass has the edge for the high-mileage trips; four people sharing a car can travel very inexpensively for most trip patterns.

- Individual tickets—rather than Eurailpass—are considerably less expensive for trips with a low average daily mileage, especially if you're willing to travel Second Class.
- Rail is about the only economically practical way for the single traveler to get around in Europe.
- Traveling around in Europe by air is competitive only for those rare cases when you travel for relatively short distances during long periods of stay, or if you're visiting a few widely spaced points. For most other types of trip, flying is substantially more expensive.

For most travelers, the practical choice is between rail and car. Since the costs are generally competitive, the decision therefore hinges on the travel style that suits you best:

- Rent a car if you're interested in seeing a lot of the countryside and enjoy almost total flexibility in where and when you go.
- Use the train if you're concentrating mainly on visits to Europe's bigger cities or if driving in a foreign country makes you apprehensive or if you're traveling by yourself.

### Be Multimodal

If you elect to use Eurailpass or a single-country rail pass or to rent a car, you're pretty much committed to that mode of travel throughout your visit. After all, if you're paying for unlimited mileage, the more you use, the less each mile costs.

But you don't have to settle for just one form of transportation, especially if your trip consists mainly of visits to a few of the bigger cities. After all, you don't need a car *or* a rail pass when you're exploring one of the major cities. Instead, you might consider individually purchased train tickets for your longer hauls; then, for special excursions outside major cities, you can rent cars for the days that you actually need one. Although daily rentals are more expensive per day than weekly rentals, the total cost should be much less if you just rent for a few individual days.

### Table 5 European Transportation Costs (U.S. dollars)

| Means of travel | 21 days 1,500 mi | 21 days 3,000 mi | 60 days 3,000 mi | 60 days 8,000 mi |
|---|---|---|---|---|
| **Subcompact car, two people** | | | | |
| Rental/lease | $500 | $500 | $980 | $980 |
| Operations at 10¢/mile | 150 | 300 | 300 | 800 |
| Trip cost | | | | |
|   Total | 650 | 800 | 1,280 | 1,780 |
|   Per person | 325 | 400 | 640 | 890 |
| Per person per day | 15 | 9 | 11 | 15 |
| **Compact car, two people** | | | | |
| Rental/lease | $570 | $570 | $1,090 | $1,090 |
| Operations at 12¢/mile | 180 | 360 | 360 | 960 |
| Trip cost | | | | |
|   Total | 750 | 930 | 1,450 | 2,050 |
|   Per person | 375 | 465 | 725 | 1,025 |
| Per person per day | 18 | 22 | 12 | 17 |
| **Midsize car, four people** | | | | |
| Rental/lease | $700 | $700 | $1,150 | $1,150 |
| Operations at 14¢/mile | 210 | 420 | 420 | 1,120 |
| Trip cost | | | | |
|   Total | 910 | 1,120 | 1,570 | 2,270 |
|   Per person | 228 | 280 | 393 | 568 |
| Per person per day | 11 | 13 | 7 | 9 |
| **Rail (Eurailpass)** | | | | |
| Trip cost | | | | |
|   Per person | $350 | $350 | $620 | $620 |
| Per person per day | 17 | 17 | 10 | 10 |
| **Rail (Individual ticket)** | | | | |
| Trip cost (Second Class) | | | | |
|   Per person | $150 | $300 | $300 | $800 |
| Per person per day | 7 | 14 | 5 | 13 |
| Trip cost (First Class) | | | | |
|   Per person | $225 | $450 | $450 | $1,120 |
| Per person per day | 11 | 21 | 8 | 20 |
| **Air Travel** | | | | |
| Trip cost (Economy) | | | | |
|   Per person | $450 | $600 | $600 | $1,600 |
| Per person per day | 21 | 29 | 10 | 27 |

## Don't Be Too Frugal

Finally, when it comes to internal transportation in Europe, experienced travelers know that trying to shave every last dollar off the final cost is often false economy. It simply doesn't make sense to try to stuff more than two adults and one medium size or two small children into a typical European subcompact car. For all the time you spend driving, a few extra dollars spent on a slightly larger car will pay handsome dividends in more comfort and less stress for all concerned.

Similarly, traveling through Europe by train is perhaps the one time even dedicated money savers should consider First Class. It's hard to justify a First-Class air-fare premium of, say, $1,000 for an eight-hour trip: $125 an hour is a very stiff price to pay for a more comfortable seat and a few drinks. But on a two-week rail pass (for example, the one in Germany), the difference between First and Second class is $55. You could probably travel at least 1,500 miles with this pass, so, at an average of 50 miles an hour, you'd be riding trains for 30 hours. Thus the premium for First Class amounts to less than $2 an hour—a reasonable price for the genuine roominess and comfort of First-Class travel.

# 13

# Rail Travel

*Enjoy a Superb
Transportation System*

Fewer Americans have been on an intercity train than on a commercial airplane. In fact, most Americans probably have little idea of how efficient and pleasant rail travel can be. If you elect to travel around Europe by train, you'll find that it's a most satisfying way to get where you're going.

About the only rail service in the United States that comes even close to European standards of speed and schedule convenience is in the "Northeast Corridor" between Boston and Washington. In Western Europe, almost all main intercity corridors enjoy rail service that's almost as fast as the Metroliner, operates more frequently, and is better maintained. Many countries have achieved a standard of one fast train per hour on major trunk routes and more frequently scheduled local and branch-line service.

There are three ways you can buy rail transportation within Europe. Eurailpass and the comparable Britrail Pass are best known. These tickets provide unlimited rail travel throughout Europe and throughout Britain, respectively, for a set number of days; the British term "rover" is a particularly suitable generic name for them. But there are quite a few other types of individual country rover tickets as well that may suit you better. And, finally, you can buy individual tickets for your trips as you need them.

## Eurailpass

Eurailpass is probably the best-known European rail ticket. This summer's prices have already been established. The regular Eurailpass is available for First Class only:

|  | *First Class* |
|---|---|
| 15 days | $280 |
| 21 days | $350 |
| 1 month | $440 |
| 2 months | $620 |
| 3 months | $760 |

Children under twelve years of age pay half fare. Children under four years travel free.

In 1985, Eurailpass introduced a new offer it called "Eurail Saverpass" for groups of three or more persons traveling together (two persons in the off season—good October 1 through March 31). It is limited to fifteen days of consecutive First-Class travel at the rate of $210 per person. In addition, a Eurail Youthpass is available to travelers under twenty-six years of age, entitling them to one month of unlimited Second-Class travel for $310, or two months for $400.

These Eurailpass tickets offer unlimited no-extra-cost rail travel on the national railroad systems of sixteen countries: Austria, Belgium, Denmark, Finland, France, West Germany, Greece, Ireland, Italy, Luxembourg, Netherlands, Norway, Portugal, Spain, Sweden, and Switzerland. In addition, they allow free travel on a wide variety of specialized railways, buses, and ferries or steamers—most notably the services from Brindisi (Italy) to Patras (Greece), Cherbourg and Le Havre (France) to Cork and Rosslare (Ireland), Stockholm to Turku and Helsinki (Finland), and the links between Denmark and Sweden. They also qualify the holder to discounts on a number of other travel services.

Reservation fees, meals, refreshments, *La Nouvelle Première* (New First Class) and overnight TALGO supplements (special through-trains that operate between Paris and Madrid and Paris and Barcelona) are not included. The *Nouvelle Première* surcharge costs approximately $6.20, or 15 percent of the price of a First-Class ticket. Currently being run on a trial basis by the S.N.C.F. (French National Railroads), it is a deluxe rail service offered on two trains between Paris and Strasbourg. Also, there is an $8 high-season supplement on steamers between Brindisi and Patras. It is also suggested that reservations be made in advance for all rail journeys as seats can sell out quickly in the summer.

The Eurailpass system has two main gaps. It does not include Great Britain (England, Scotland, and Wales) and Yugoslavia—which means that Greece can only be reached by steamer with Eurailpass.

Eurailpass prices are established in U.S. dollars and are not subject to change due to exchange rate fluctuations. You have to buy your tickets before you reach Europe. The pound-priced versions sold in Great Britain offer no bargains for U.S. travelers.

Eurailpass is easy to buy and easy to use. Any travel agent can get one for you. It is one of the most successful products ever offered to the American travel market—mainly because it represents a solid value that's hard to top.

## Individual Country Rovers

Most European countries have individual rovers valid only within their own systems, and several adjacent countries have regional multicountry rovers. Britrail is the best known because it's usually sold as the complement to Eurailpass for travel in Great Britain.

Individual national rovers are less expensive than Eurailpass for First-Class travel and significantly less expensive for travelers willing to ride Second Class, an option not available to adults on Eurailpass. Most countries also have quite a few other rovers and special tickets, which are detailed in the individual country summaries that follow.

## Individual Tickets

Eurailpass, Britrail Pass, and the other rovers are widely publicized. U.S. travel agents find them easy to sell. But rovers are not always the best way to buy European rail travel.

Your best rail deal depends mainly on the number of miles you'll be traveling. If you're going to travel extensively in more

## The Orient Express

Another way to see many of the same countries is on one of the two renovated Orient Express trains. These trains are really "land cruises" re-creating the glamour, intrigue, and elegance of the 1920s. Both the Venice Simplon Orient Express and Nostalgia-Istanbul Orient Express are variations of the original train that operated between Paris and Istanbul; both are operated under license with the French National Railroads. Each line has completely refurbished its carriages, restoring them to their original opulence. Neither is cheap, but each offers the traveler a unique, one-of-a-kind rail journey that does a fairly convincing job of bringing to life a bygone era.

The 1987 Venice Simplon Orient Express schedule runs between March 25 and November 16, 1987. The northbound routing includes the following cities: Venice, Innsbruck, Zurich, Paris, and London and returns with two round trips a week. These journeys take two days and one night (thirty-two hours approximately). Sample one-way fares are $820 London to Venice, $870 after September 1, 1987, and $620 Paris to Zurich per person, double occupancy, including meals, tax, service charges, and one stopover. Children under twelve pay half fare.

The Nostalgia-Istanbul Orient Express re-creates the original journey to Istanbul from Zurich, taking nine days. The train operates two eastbound (May 20 and Sept. 26, 1987) trips annually on original renovated Wagons-Lits carriages. Each stop includes off-train sightseeing and some additional meals. The cost per person will be about $5,500 and includes all rail transportation, meals, excursions, tips, taxes, escorts, and overnight hotels in Zurich and Istanbul.

than a few different countries, Eurailpass is, in fact, likely to be your best deal, and the individual country rovers are great for extensive exploration of single countries. But when your total trip mileage will be fairly limited, it's often much cheaper simply to buy individual tickets for individual trips. Basically, you have to determine whether Eurailpass is really a good deal on the basis of how much you plan to use it.

Take a three-week trip as an example. Figuring the average cost for First-Class rail travel among the Eurailpass countries at somewhere near 15¢ a mile, you'd have to travel 2,333 miles or more on individual tickets to equal the $350 Eurailpass price. If you're willing to travel Second Class, at an average fare of about 10¢ a mile, your break-even point would be something like 3,500 miles. If your itinerary calls for substantially less travel, you're better off buying individual tickets.

The individual-country rover in Germany isn't much cheaper than Eurailpass for First-Class travel. Its main advantages are the Second-Class option and availability for shorter time periods. But the Italian, Austrian, Benelux, Swiss, and Scandinavian rovers can be considerably less expensive than Eurailpass for both First- and Second-Class travel if you're staying within a single country or region.

Of course, break-even points calculated with average per-mile costs are just for general guidance. For a precise determination, you have to compare costs for your individual trip. It's really quite easy. You can approximate your total mileage from maps. Or if you're really interested in detail, the Thomas Cook *Continental Timetable*, widely available in U.S. travel bookstores, shows exact point-to-point rail distances (in kilometers, which you divide by 1.61 to convert to miles). Then use the average rail costs for the country or countries you plan to tour to estimate the total cost of your trip with individual tickets and compare this total with the cost(s) of one or more rover tickets that would cover your trip. The following railfare listings should give you the information for each country to figure the most economical way to buy your tickets.

Buying Rail Tickets

You have to buy Eurailpass before you arrive in Continental Europe, and you have to buy most other single and multi-country unlimited-mileage rover tickets before you arrive in the country or countries in which you'll use them. You can buy them either through your travel agent or direct from the various national tourist offices or national railroad offices in the United States. In the listings that follow, the prices for rovers available in the United States are given in U.S. dollars. Those rover passes available only in Europe are listed in U.S. dollars for ease of comparison, though they must, in fact, be purchased in local currencies.

Regional rover tickets and a few of the national rovers can usually be bought after you arrive. It's probably better to buy these tickets when you're ready to use them rather than beforehand, so that you can choose the options that best suit your immediate needs. You can generally buy them at major city railroad stations or from local travel agents.

When you buy a ticket for international travel within Europe, you may find that some of the eligibility requirements (especially for children's half-fare tickets) are quite different from those for travel entirely within the country where your trip originates. Make sure to check these specific rules carefully before you buy tickets.

Many of the best rail-ticket programs require some sort of proof of foreign residence, age, or status. Your U.S. passport will serve in most cases. However, students may be required to show additional identification in a few situations. If you're a student, check with your school registration office for some sort of official ID.

Finally, you'll note that most of the special "youth" deals are available only in Second Class. Family groups that include both adults and youths who want to travel together on Eurailpass will therefore have to buy regular adult Eurailpasses for the youths as well as the adults—or else the adults will have to ride in Second Class, even though they've paid for First. This same problem can crop up with some of the individual country passes, too.

European trains sometimes consist of several parts that at some point split and go to several different destinations. However, individual cars are always clearly marked, and the ticket inspectors take care to inform passengers if they are in the wrong car for their desired destination.

In a few instances, 1987 rates were not available at press time. These are noted in the text.

## Austria

*Unlimited Mileage Passes*

| Type of ticket or pass | Valid for | Cost (U.S. dollars) First Class | Second Class |
|---|---|---|---|
| *Bundesnetzkarte* | 9 days | $149 | $ 99 |
|  | 16 days | 203 | 135 |
|  | 30 days | 321 | 214 |
| Austria ticket | 9 days | — | 66 |
| Youth | 16 days | — | 93 |
| Provincial ticket | 9 days | 60 | 40 |
|  | 16 days | 87 | 58 |
|  | 30 days | 134 | 90 |

The *Bundesnetzkarte* can be bought in the United States, Austria, and in some German train stations. The Provincial Tickets, a regional rover pass good for travel in any one of the nine individual provinces, are obtainable only in Austria. The Austria Ticket is valid for travelers under the age of twenty-six and can also be used on government post buses. Both tickets allow discounts of 50 percent on DDSG Steamships (on the Danube, for example) and mountain cog railways.

*Other Special Tickets and Passes*
"Kilometric Tickets" are also available for Second-Class rail travel and may be good buys for families. Basically, you multiply the distance you plan to travel by the number of people in your party and buy the appropriate kilometric ticket. A 2,000-kilometric ticket costs AS 1,700; a 5,000-kilometric ticket, AS 4,100; a 10,000-kilometric ticket, AS 8,000.

Senior citizens (women over sixty, men over sixty-five) can buy a pass good for one calendar year (January through December only) for $11 (AS 155), which gives a 50 percent reduction on any ticket. Passport identification is required.

Children under six years of age travel free; those from six to fifteen years of age travel at half fare.

*Individually Purchased Tickets*
Average or standard cost per mile:
  First Class    14¢
  Second Class   9¢

*Comment:* If you want to travel from one part of Austria to another on a corridor that crosses Italian or German territory, try to travel on a *korridorzuge* (corridor train). These trains cross frontiers without the usual passport formalities because they do not board or discharge passengers outside Austria.

**Belgium**

*Unlimited Mileage Passes*

| Type of ticket or pass | Valid for | Cost (U.S. dollars) First Class | Second Class |
|---|---|---|---|
| Benelux-Tourrail | | | |
| Adult | 5/17 days | $71.60 | $47.80 |
| Youth (12–26) | 5/17 days | 53.60 | 35.80 |
| Child (6–12) | 5/17 days | 35.80 | 23.80 |
| Belgium-Tourrail | | | |
| One price Adult | 16 consecutive days | 87.80 | 58.40 |
|  | 5/16 days | 47.00 | 31.00 |
|  | 8/16 days | 61.60 | 41.00 |
| Youth (12–26) | 5/16 days | 35.20 | 23.40 |
|  | 8/16 days | 46.20 | 31.00 |
| Child (6–12) | 5/16 days | 23.40 | 15.60 |
|  | 8/16 days | 31.00 | 20.60 |
| Half-fare card | 1 month | 14.40 | 9.60 |

The Benelux-Tourrail pass covers travel in all Benelux countries—Belgium, the Netherlands, and Luxembourg. Belgium-Tourrail, as the name suggests, is confined to Belgium.

Both Benelux-Tourrail and Belgium-Tourrail can be used on a specified number of days within a longer total time limitation. In the validity notation used above, the number before the slash (/) indicates the number of days on which the ticket may be used, and the number after the slash indicates the total maximum validity period. Thus, for example, 5/16 indicates that a pass can be used on any five days during a 16-day period.

The Benelux-Tourrail can be bought in Belgium (as well as in The Netherlands and Luxembourg). It is valid only during the major tourist season: between April 1 and October 31. The Belgium-Tourrail can be purchased only in Belgium and is valid between April 1 and September 30. Both require passport or other identification; youth- and child-fare passes require proof of age. The rates noted above are for 1986. However, little change is expected for 1987.

Half-fare cards, available year-round, allow a 50 percent discount on all rail travel within Belgium. The price is the same for all travelers, regardless of age.

*Other Special Tickets and Passes*

Inexpensive weekend-excursion tickets, for example, to the Belgian beaches or to the Ardennes forest, are available for travel from Friday evening to Monday morning. Day-excursion tickets to the same areas are available only during the summer. Benelux Weekend Tickets are special round-trip fares for long weekend trips to the other Benelux countries.

"A Beautiful Day . . ." tickets offer reduced fares for excursions to local points of interest and include admission to museums, boating parks, etc.

Children travel free up to six years of age; between six and twelve years of age children pay half fare.

*Individually Purchased Tickets*

Average or standard cost per mile:

    First Class     13¢
    Second Class   9¢

## Denmark

*Unlimited Mileage Passes*

| Type of ticket or pass | Valid for | Cost (U.S. dollars) First Class | Second Class |
|---|---|---|---|
| Danish Rail Pass | 1 month | $168 | $140 |
| Scandinavian Rail Pass | 21 days | 263 | 176 |

The Danish Rail Pass, available outside Denmark, is good for one month's unlimited travel on Danish State Railways (DSB). Children under twelve are half price.

The Scandinavian Rail Pass is called *Nordturist* ticket and permits unlimited rail travel in Denmark, Finland, Norway, and Sweden. The ticket is also valid on ferries between Helsingor and Helsingborg; on all domestic DSB ferries in Denmark; plus the route that serves Rodby Faerge–Puttgarden, and the route serving Mitte See and Geder–Warnemünde Mitte See; on the boat lines between Stockholm-Turku, Goteborg-Frederikshavn, and Kristiansand-Hirashals; on the DSB bus from Storlien to Trondheim; and on the combined boat and bus route between Halden/Sarpsborg and Stromstad. Cabin rates are additional on boats.

The pass also entitles the user to other discounts:

- 15 to 40 percent off at more than 100 First-Class hotels between June 1 and September 1
- 50 percent discount on boats between Stockholm-Helsinki, Larvik-Frederikshavn, Havnegard (Copenhagen)–Malmö (by hydrofoil), Copenhagen-Oslo, Stavanger-Bergen, Umea-Vaasa, and on the private railway from Hirtals and Hjorring in Denmark
- free admission to the railway museums in the four countries

*Other Special Tickets and Passes*

Senior citizens can travel for half fares during off-peak periods, for round-trip tickets only; an identification card is issued at stations. These tickets cannot be used during the following periods: 2:00 PM–7:00 PM Friday, 8:00 AM–noon Saturday, and 2:00 PM–midnight Sunday.

Groups (minimum two adults and one child) can travel at a 30 percent or more reduction on individual fares. The discounts vary from midweek (more) to weekends (less) and the number of persons traveling together.

Children under four years of age travel free; between four and twelve years of age children pay half fare.

*Individually Purchased Tickets*

Average or standard cost per mile:

    First Class    16¢
    Second Class  12¢

*Comment:* Because Denmark is small and flat as a pancake, most train trips are no more than commuter runs. Rail stations also sell tickets for connecting ferries and buses. Seat reservations are generally required on longer trips. Reservations are essential for all services using the Great Belt Ferry (see chapter 16).

**France**

*Unlimited Mileage Passes*

| Type of ticket or pass | Valid for | Cost (U.S. dollars) First Class | Second Class |
|---|---|---|---|
| France Railpass | 4 days | $ 89 | $ 69 |
|  | 9 days | 190 | 130 |
|  | 16 days | 250 | 170 |
| France Saverpass (for 2 people) | 9 days | $299 | $199 |

The France Railpass consists of coupons for four, nine, or sixteen nonconsecutive days of rail travel to be used within a fifteen-day (for the four-day pass) or one-month period.

*Other Special Tickets and Passes*

The *Carte Jeune* and *Carré Jeune* both offer 50 percent reductions on fares on "blue days" (off-peak periods) to people age twenty-five or younger. Both cost approximately $22 and are valid for Second-Class travel only. The *Carte* permits unlimited travel during the period between June 1 and September 30 and allows one free couchette on any route. The *Carré* allows four single uses at any time throughout the year. The suburban rail network around Paris is excluded from both passes. These can be purchased only in France.

*Sejour* return tickets offer a 25 percent discount off any return journey (to point of origin) totaling over 1,000 kilometers with a five-day minimum stay requirement between outbound and return trips. These tickets must be used only on "blue days."

Children under four years of age travel free (provided they do not require a seat when the train is full); children four to twelve years of age pay half fare.

*Individually Purchased Tickets*
Average cost per mile:

    First Class    15¢
    Second Class  10¢

*Comment:* The French boast the fastest train in the world. The *trains à grande vitesse* (TGVs) regularly reach speeds of 168 miles (270 kilometers) per hour. Traveling time between Lyons and Paris (265 miles) is two hours. There is a compulsory seat reservation fee on the TGV of about $4. TEEs (Trans Europe Expresses) require a surcharge at all times, unless you are traveling on a railpass.

The TGV is very cramped and spartan in Second Class. First Class is recommended for all but the most hardy. Buffet food is limited and expensive; the full meals are a better value but must be ordered at the time of booking. During peak periods, there is a supplemental charge.

Recently, the French National Railroads introduced a new service entitled *La Nouvelle Première*, or New First Class. It is currently being offered on two trains between Paris and Strasbourg. There is a 15 percent surcharge over present First Class, which amounts to about $6.20. The new deluxe service provides for redecorated carriages and three-star dining. All Eurailpass and France. Railpass travelers are required to pay the surcharge for the deluxe service if it is desired on the routes on which it is currently available.

To get English-language train information in Paris, call 43-80-50-50.

## West Germany

*Unlimited Mileage Passes*

| Type of ticket or pass | Valid for | Cost (U.S. dollars) First Class | Second Class |
|---|---|---|---|
| Tourist card | 4 days | $110 | $ 75 |
|  | 9 days | 170 | 115 |
|  | 16 days | 230 | 160 |
| Youth card (junior tourist card) | 9 days | — | 75 |
|  | 16 days | — | 95 |

Both cards can be bought in the United States and in other countries in Europe, but not in the Federal Republic. Purchasers must have a valid passport. Besides offering the user unlimited rail travel throughout the Federal Republic, they also provide:

- free motorcoach and bus transportation on the "Romantic Road" along the Rhine from Munich or Fuessen to Rocthenburg, Wuerzburg, and Wiesbaden from June to September (reservations required)
- free motorcoach transportation on the scenic Rhine/Moselle routes; all routes of the Touring Company are included free of charge
- free KD Rhineline sightseeing steamers traversing the Rhine, Main, and Moselle rivers
- reduced fares on rail travel to Berlin with a free city sightseeing tour and free transit visa to East Berlin (not available with the four-day card).
- free bicycle rentals at three hundred railway stations in West Germany

No supplement is paid on Intercity or fast trains, and holders of First-Class cards can travel on the 125 mile-per-hour TEE Rheingold Express.

The Youth Card or Junior Tourist Card is available to persons under twenty-six years of age and is good for Second-Class travel. A valid passport with proof of age is required.

*Other Special Tickets and Passes*

Senior citizens (women over sixty, men over sixty-five) can buy a discount pass for DM 110 (approximately $55) allowing half-fare purchases throughout the system for one year on trips over 50 kilometers. Proof of age is required. These passes are sold at German railway stations.

"Tramper" tickets allow unlimited Second-Class travel for one month for travelers under the age of twenty-two, or for those under twenty-six who have valid student identification. Travel without supplement on Intercity trains (ICs) is allowed. These tickets cost DM 245 (approximately $122) and are also sold only at German railway stations.

*Tourenkarte* (Regional Rail Rovers) are available to travelers who also hold a rail ticket for a return journey, in which the entire trip totals over 200 kilometers each way. These tickets can be purchased only in Germany and provide for unlimited

Second-Class rail travel, including most buses, for ten days within a period of twenty-one days in a particular region, for example, Bavaria. They cost DM 46 for one person, DM 62 for two persons traveling together, and DM 77 for a family traveling together with any number of children under eighteen years of age.

*Bezirkswochenkarte* (Weekly District Tickets) provide the same type of travel as the *Tourenkarte* but do not require the long-distance rail ticket. The cost is DM 125 First Class, DM 83 Second Class per person. Children ages four to eleven years travel for half fare.

*Vorzugkarten* (Reduced Return Tickets) provide a 20 percent discount on return tickets for a distance totaling more than 201 kilometers round trip. *Vorzugkarten* are purchased in Germany and also require the user to stay over a Saturday night.

A new type of ticket that was offered for 1986 and will be available in 1987 is the "Rail and Fly" for travelers holding a valid return airline ticket. This special ticket gives the user a reduced fare for the journey to and from the airport. The cost in First Class for one person is DM 100 and DM 70 in Second Class. For two people traveling together the cost in first class is DM 160 and DM 110 for Second Class; for each additional person the cost is First Class DM 60 and Second Class DM 40. Children under seventeen can ride on this ticket for DM 10 in both classes.

*Individually Purchased Tickets*
Average or standard cost per mile:
   First Class:    15¢
   Second Class:   10¢

Children under four years of age travel free; from four to eleven years of age children pay half fare.

*Comment:* GermanRail operates many Intercity (IC) trains that serve over fifty cities on five lines within the Federal Republic, Austria, and the Netherlands. Many of these IC trains stop at Frankfurt Airport. We've received reports of last-minute platform changes on main IC routes from those shown on the indicator boards. Double-check that you are on the right platform before boarding.

A supplement on tickets purchased in Germany of DM 5,

including seat reservation, is required on all Intercity trains; a supplement of DM 10 on TEE trains within Germany; a supplement of DM 3 on "D" trains for travel of less than 50 kilometers. If supplements are paid on the train, rather than paid at the ticket window, an additional DM 1 is required. The Rheingold Express carries a supplement of DM 10 over regular First-Class fare, which includes a seat reservation. There is generally a charge for seat reservations.

### Greece

*Unlimited Mileage Passes*

| Type of ticket or pass | Valid for | Cost (U.S. dollars) First Class | Second Class |
|---|---|---|---|
| Touring card | 10 days | — | $26 |
|  | 20 days | — | 42 |
|  | 30 days | — | 57 |

Touring cards can be obtained for unlimited Second-Class travel on the Greek Railway Network (OSE) or the railway's buses, either in the United States or in Greece. Depending on the number of people traveling together, there may be a further discount off the rate quoted for the basic touring card. OSE also offers Season Tickets that allow the user unlimited travel along a specific route for a specified period.

*Other Special Tickets and Passes*
Senior citizen cards are available (sixty years old and older) with valid passport. They cost Drs 3,000 (approximately $22) for "A" class (or First-Class) travel and Drs 2,000 (approximately $14) for "B" class (or Second-Class) travel, allowing five free one-way trips, except on certain dates around Christmas, Easter, and during the summer (July through September). They also provide for a 50 percent reduction on all additional trips on the inland network or on the OSE buses.

Children under four years of age travel free; from four to twelve years of age children pay half fare.

*Individually Purchased Tickets*
Average or standard cost per mile:
  First Class    5¢
  Second Class   3¢

*Comment:* The main rail route into Greece is through Yugoslavia. International express trains enter the country via Belgrade. Because Yugoslavia is not part of the Eurail network, Eurailpass holders must travel via Italy and the ferry at Brindisi to reach Greece. Service from Athens to Salonika and from Athens to Corinth is adequate; poor by comparison to the rest of Europe.

**Ireland**

*Unlimited Mileage Passes*

| Type of ticket or pass | Valid for | Cost (U.S. dollars) Standard Class |
|---|---|---|
| Rambler (rail only) | 8 days | $ 57 |
|  | 15 days | 84 |
| Rambler (rail and bus) | 8 days | 72 |
|  | 15 days | 104 |
| Youth Rambler (rail and bus) | 8 days | 61 |
|  | 15 days | 89 |
| Irish Overlander (Republic of Northern Ireland) | 15 days | 119 |
| (Children 5–16 years of age) |  | 45 |

Ramblers are available in the United States or in Ireland. Youth Ramblers can be purchased in the United States through a single source: C.I.E. Tours International (New York). The bus and rail Rambler is usually a better value for traveling around the country since buses and trains are more complementary than competitive.

The age limit on Youth Ramblers is twenty-five; proof of age is required. Ramblers may be purchased at bus depots and railway stations in Ireland or through C.I.E. Tours in the United States (800-CIE-TOURS; 212-972-5600).

*Other Special Tickets or Passes*
None.
Children under fourteen years travel at half fare.

*Individually Purchased Tickets*
Average or standard cost per mile:

    First Class    23¢
    Second Class  18¢

Standard rail tickets are priced according to the period of time between beginning and end of a trip. Sample fares for 250 kilometers (156 miles) out and 250 kilometers return covering various periods:

| | |
|---|---|
| Single | $23 |
| Monthly return | $30 |
| 8-day return | $25 |
| 4-day return | $25 |
| Weekend return (with stayover Saturday) | $16 |

*Comment:* Rail service in the Republic of Ireland provides limited geographical coverage compared with most other European countries. Although all major cities are connected by rail, service does not extend into many of the most scenic parts of the country.

## Italy

*Unlimited Mileage Passes*

| Type of ticket or pass | Valid for | Cost (U.S. dollars) First Class | Second Class |
|---|---|---|---|
| Italian Unlimited Rail Pass | 8 days | $134 | $ 85 |
| (B.T.L.C. Italian Tourist | 15 days | 164 | 103 |
| Ticket) | 21 days | 190 | 120 |
| | 30 days | 238 | 150 |

The Italian Unlimited Rail Pass also called the B.T.L.C. Italian Tourist Ticket, can be purchased outside of Italy as well as in Rome and in border cities. The ticket allows travel on the *Rapido* without supplement.

*Other Special Tickets and Passes*
The Italian kilometric ticket provides for 3000 kilometers of travel in up to twenty trips, by as many as five people at one time. It is valid for two months. When the ticket is used simultaneously by more than one person, the distance traveled is multiplied by the number of users and the total deducted from the 3000-kilometer limit. Kilometric tickets must be date stamped and may be purchased only in Italy. They cost $165 for First Class and $93 for Second Class.

Tourists are given a 15 percent discount on day-return tickets with a maximum distance traveled of 50 kilometers. A three-day return ticket is available, which grants the same discount on journeys of 250 kilometers traveled.

Family rates are given for members of a household (minimum 3 persons) traveling together. The reduction is about 20 percent for adults and 65 percent for children. Travel-at-Will tickets are available for children under twelve at half of adult fares; children under four years travel free.

*Individually Purchased Tickets*
Average or standard cost per mile:

  First Class 6¢
  Second Class 4¢

Standard fares on Italian State Railways are based on distance traveled. Seat reservations are advisable on intracontinental journeys.

*Comment:* Rail service between the major Italian cities is fast, frequent, and relatively inexpensive. The best *Rapido* services require a supplement over the individual ticket rates quoted that is calculated on distance traveled at approximately 30 percent over the regular fare. Some *Rapidos* offer only First Class.

## Luxembourg
### Unlimited Mileage Passes

| Type of ticket or pass | Valid for | Cost (U.S. dollars) First Class | Second Class |
|---|---|---|---|
| Benelux-Tourrail | | | |
| Adult | 5/17 days | $84.00 | $56.00 |
| Youth (12–26) | 5/17 days | $62.00 | $42.00 |
| Child (4–11) | 5/17 days | $42.00 | $28.00 |
| Network tickets | | | |
| | Weekend/holiday | Half fare on return | |
| | 1 day | — | $ 4.50 |
| | 5 days | — | $13.00 |
| | 1 month | — | $35.00 |

The Benelux-Tourrail pass covers rail travel in all Benelux countries—Luxembourg, the Netherlands, and Belgium. It can be purchased in Luxembourg at any railway station as well as in other Benelux countries. It is valid only between April 1 and October 31 each year. The rates quoted above were in effect for 1986. Little change is expected for 1987. See the rail listing under Belgium for a discussion of valid dates.

Network tickets are valid for unlimited travel on the Luxembourg National Railway and bus system.

### Other Special Tickets and Passes
Senior citizens (over 65 years) pay half fare for First- and Second-Class travel on trains and buses. Children between four and twelve years also pay half fare; children under four years travel free.

### Individually Purchased Tickets
Average or standard cost per mile:

    First Class    9¢
    Second Class  6¢

*Comment:* Luxembourg has an integrated rail and bus network operated by the Luxembourg National Railways.

## Netherlands

*Unlimited Mileage Passes*

| Type of ticket or pass | Valid for | Cost (U.S. dollars) First Class | Second Class |
|---|---|---|---|
| Netherlands Pass | 3 days | $36.25 | $24.00 |
| | 7 days | 48.25 | 33.50 |
| Benelux-Tourrail | | | |
| Adult | 5/17 days | $80.00 | $54.00 |
| Youth (12–26) | 5/17 days | 59.00 | 39.00 |
| Child (4–11) | 5/17 days | 40.00 | 27.00 |

The Netherlands Pass is available in the Netherlands or in the United Kingdom from Dutch Railways or Britrail. A photograph is required for the seven-day pass.

The Benelux–Tourrail pass covers travel in all Benelux countries—the Netherlands, Belgium, and Luxembourg. It can be purchased in the Netherlands at any railway station as well as in the other Benelux countries. It is valid only between March 15 and October 31 each year. The rates quoted above were in effect for 1986. Little change is expected for 1987. See the rail listing under Belgium for a discussion of valid dates.

*Other Special Tickets and Passes*
A Public Transport Link Rover (add-on to the Netherlands Pass), allows unlimited travel on all buses (except KLM Airport Bus), trams, and metros. It is available from Dutch Railways in the Netherlands or the United Kingdom. Priced in Dutch guilders, this pass runs, for one day, Dfl 4.75 (approximately $2.10); three days, Dfl 9.25 (approximately $4); seven days, Dfl 18.50 (approximately $8).

Day Rovers are available for unlimited travel during any single twenty-four-hour period and cost Dfl 78 ($34) First Class and Dfl 52 ($23) Second Class. These are more economical only if you plan to travel more than 210 kilometers.

Teenage Rovers, for youths under nineteen, are available for unlimited Second-Class travel on any four out of ten days duration of the ticket for Dfl 40 ($18). Family Rover tickets are also available for unlimited travel on any four out of ten days—First Class, Dfl 200 ($88); Second Class, Dfl 140 ($61).

Multi-Rover tickets are also available for any group of two to six persons traveling together over long distances giving one day's unlimited travel in Second Class. They can be used Monday through Friday after 9:00 AM and all day on weekends and holidays. They cost for two persons, Dfl 72 ($31.50); for three persons, Dfl 87 ($38); for four persons, Dfl 101 ($44); for five persons, Dfl 115 ($50); and for six persons, Dfl 129 ($57).

Senior citizens can purchase a half-price card good for either three months or one year.

Children under four years of age travel free; from four to ten years of age, they travel at half fare. Those with international tickets pay half fare to age twelve.

*Individually Purchased Tickets*
Average or standard cost per mile:

    First Class    17¢
    Second Class  13¢

*Comment:* The Netherlands has a sliding fare structure based on total distance traveled, and 250 kilometers is about as far as you can go in Holland.

## Norway

*Unlimited Mileage Passes*

| Type of ticket or pass | Valid for | Cost (U.S. dollars) First Class | Second Class |
|---|---|---|---|
| Scandinavian Rail Pass | 21 days | $263 | $176 |

See the entry under Denmark in this chapter for complete information on the Scandinavian Rail Pass.

*Other Special Tickets and Passes*
Mini-groups of two or more persons can obtain reductions of 25 percent off regular rail fare on journeys of 100 kilometers or more.

Senior citizens (over sixty-seven years) pay half fare; younger spouses of a qualifying senior can also use these tickets. Proof of age is required. Identification cards are available at railway stations.

Children under four years travel free; those from four to sixteen years of age pay half fare. Those with international tickets pay half fare to age twelve.

*Individually Purchased Tickets*
Average or standard cost per mile:

   First Class    24¢
   Second Class   15¢

Fares per mile are reduced as distance increases.

*Comment:* Norway's rail network offers some of Europe's most spectacular scenery. Trains often require reservations (obligatory on express). Seat reservations cost NOR 10. It's a good idea to purchase tickets a day in advance for night trains leaving the country.

**Portugal**

*Unlimited Mileage Passes*

| Type of ticket or pass | Valid for | Cost (U.S. dollars) First Class | Second Class |
|---|---|---|---|
| Tourist ticket | 7 days | $ 56.45 | — |
|  | 14 days | 90.00 | — |
|  | 21 days | 128.60 | — |

This pass is available both in Portugal and outside it.

*Other Special Tickets and Passes*
Family tickets are available: the first adult pays full fare, other family members pay half fares except children four through eleven years, who pay one-quarter fare.

Children between four and twelve years pay half fare; children under four travel free.

Senior citizens (sixty-five years and older) pay half fare with proof of age.

*Individually Purchased Tickets*
Average or standard cost per mile:

    First Class
        Express     8¢
        Standard   6¢
    Second Class
        Express     5¢
        Standard   4¢

*Comment:* Supplements are required on services classed as *Rapido*, but there are not many of them. Some stations in the Algarve are quite a distance from the center of the towns that they serve. A few local services still use woodburning trains. Train times should always be checked with the latest wall timetable at the station of departure; the standard international timetable references may not be accurate.

The rates above for all train services may be affected by a 10 percent fare increase expected during 1987.

Train information can be obtained by telephone in Lisbon from: 864181, 866101, or 869760.

**Spain**

*Unlimited Mileage Passes*

| Type of ticket or pass | Valid for | Cost (U.S. dollars) First Class | Second Class |
|---|---|---|---|
| Tarjeta Turista (Tourist Card) | 8 days | $100 | $ 69 |
| | 15 days | 162 | 115 |
| | 22 days | 192 | 146 |

The *Tarjeta Turistica* can only be purchased in Spain at any railroad station or Rente Travel Office. It provides unlimited rail travel on over 12,700 kilometers of track and is valid all year.

*Other Special Tickets and Passes*
*Chequetren* is a special rail pass or voucher that may be purchased only in Spain at any main railway station or local travel

agency. The pass may be used by a maximum of six people traveling together to gain a savings of 15 percent off normal fares. The pass can be purchased for about 21,250 to 29,750 pesetas ($157–$219) in advance for services that value 25,000 and 35,000 pesetas ($184–$258) worth of rides.

Round-trip discounts are effective on so-called "blue days" that the Spanish National Railroad (RENFE) establishes at the beginning of the year. A copy of the calendar can be obtained at the information office of any railway station. This discount is applied to the basic ticket price, but not to supplements for special trains.

There is no longer a senior-citizen discount for tourists. It is now available only to Spanish citizens.

Children under three years of age travel free; between four and twelve years of age children pay half fare. Children with international tickets pay half fare to age twelve.

*Individually Purchased Tickets*
Average or standard cost per mile:

    First Class    6¢
    Second Class  4¢

*Comment:* Service is efficient on the fast trains between major cities, but Second-Class trains, although cheap, can be slow and crowded. Supplements are required on fast trains. The already low fares limit the number of cheap tickets available.

**Sweden**

*Unlimited Mileage Passes*

| Type of ticket or pass | Valid for | Cost (U.S. dollars) First Class | Second Class |
|---|---|---|---|
| Scandinavian Rail Pass | 21 days | $263 | $176 |

See the entry under Denmark in this chapter for complete information on the Scandinavian Rail Pass.

*Other Special Tickets and Passes*
The Eurailpass and Eurail Youthpass are both good on the Swedish Rail system and on some ferries.

Children under six years of age travel free; between six and twelve years of age children pay half fare.

*Individually Purchased Tickets*
Average or standard cost per mile:

    First Class    28¢
    Second Class  12¢

*Comment:* Some trains are designated in schedules with an "R" in a square; reservations are mandatory on these trains over all sectors. Other trains that are marked with a solid black square have compulsory reservations only for passengers' trips beginning at the start of the train's journey (at the first few stations). On trains that are marked with a solid black triangle, reservations are recommended.

## Switzerland

*Unlimited Mileage Passes*

| Type of ticket or pass | Valid for | Cost (U.S. dollars) First Class | Second Class |
|---|---|---|---|
| Swiss Holiday Card | 4 days | $118 | $ 80 |
|  | 8 days | 138 | 94 |
|  | 15 days | 165 | 113 |
|  | 1 month | 231 | 157 |

The Swiss Holiday Card can be bought outside of Switzerland from the agencies of the Swiss National Tourist Office or at major rail stations in Switzerland, also at Zurich and Geneva airports. It is valid for unlimited travel on the Swiss Federal Railway plus all boats and postal buses within the country. Holders may also buy reduced tickets (20–50 percent discounts) for excursions to mountaintops on *telepheriques* (aerial cableways and cablecars). Children between the ages of six and sixteen pay half fare on the Holiday Cards.

Regional Holiday Season Tickets provide reduced-price travel within various regions of Switzerland. These tickets can be purchased at the railway stations within the region of planned travel and are valid for a total of fifteen days. They allow for unlimited travel on five of those fifteen days, and half-fare travel on the other ten days. Unlimited travel is allowed in the Locarno/Ascona and Lugano regions on any of the seven days.

*Other Special Tickets and Passes*
The Half-Fare Travel Card, also called the "Elite Season Ticket," is sold at all Swiss rail stations and allows a 50 percent reduction on all federal trains, post buses, lake steamers, and private trains. It costs SFr. 60 ($28) for fifteen days or SFr 75 ($34) for thirty days. The Junior Half-Fare Card is for youths between the ages of sixteen and twenty-six, and costs $16 for a month. Holders of Half-Fare Travel Cards can buy "day tickets," each good for a free day of unlimited travel while the Half-Fare Card is valid. The "day tickets" can only be purchased in Switzerland and cost SFr 190 ($112) for four days or SFr 370 ($219) for ten days in First Class, and SFr 125 ($92) for four days or SF. 240 ($142) for ten days in Second Class.

Within Switzerland and available to anyone are numerous unlimited travel cards—*Abonnements*—which are slightly more expensive than the Swiss Holiday Card. Family, group, and excursion tickets are available and are valid for two days at a 20 percent reduction off standard fares (including mountain railways and *telepheriques*) or regional travel passes (*Passeport du Promeneur*). In most cases, these are not particularly a good deal unless they fit your travel plans perfectly.

Children under six years of age travel free; children six through sixteen years of age pay half fare.

Senior citizens (women over sixty-two, men over sixty-five) can buy an annual half-fare pass for SFr 125 ($74). A current photo and proof of age are required.

*Individually Purchased Tickets*
Average or standard cost per kilometer:

    First Class    36¢
    Second Class   26¢

Switzerland operates a sliding-fare structure that offers cheaper round-trip than one-way tickets.

*Comment:* Examine your planned itinerary carefully to determine whether the Swiss Holiday Card or the Half-Fare Travel Card is the better buy. If you can't take advantage of a special program, remember that a round-trip ticket is up to 20 percent cheaper than two one-ways.

Seat reservations cannot be made on internal train services except by groups of ten or more people traveling together.

Ordinary and excursion tickets for local areas can now be purchased conveniently at automatic ticket dispensers on station concourses. These take coins and SFr 20 notes, and they give change.

Switzerland has one of the most integrated railway networks in Europe with more than 3,000 miles of electrified lines. Zurich International Airport has its own railway station with 160 direct trains a day to all parts of the country.

**United Kingdom**

*Unlimited Mileage Passes*

| Type of ticket or pass | Valid for | Cost (U.S. dollars) First Class | Economy Class |
|---|---|---|---|
| Britrail Pass | 7 days | $210 | $149 |
| | 15 days | 315 | 225 |
| | 22 days | 400 | 285 |
| | 1 month | 470 | 335 |
| Senior Citizen Britrail | 7 days | 180 | — |
| | 15 days | 270 | — |
| | 22 days | 340 | — |
| | 1 month | 400 | — |
| Youth Britrail | 7 days | — | 130 |
| | 15 days | — | 190 |
| | 22 days | — | 240 |
| | 1 month | — | 285 |
| Child Britrail | 7 days | 105 | 75 |
| | 15 days | 158 | 113 |
| | 22 days | 200 | 143 |
| | 1 month | 235 | 168 |
| Freedom of Scotland Ticket | 7 days | — | 50 |
| | 14 days | — | 73 |

The above rates will be valid from April 1987 through December 31, 1987. These passes can be bought only outside of Britain. Persons sixty and older qualify for the Senior Citizen Britrail Pass. The Youth pass is for those sixteen through twenty-five years of age; the children's pass is for five through fifteen year olds.

The Freedom of Scotland Ticket is good throughout Scotland, the extreme north country of England (Carlisle and Berwick), and the ferries in the Firth of Clyde.

Many other regional passes are available.

*Other Special Tickets and Passes*

"Annual Railcards" are sold only in the United Kingdom for senior citizens, families, and young persons (formerly designated as students), allowing half-fare travel with certain restrictions at peak hours. Senior Citizens must show senior ID and/or passport. The young person railcard applies to any person under the age of twenty-three, or anyone who is a student at a British college.

There are "Saver" and/or "Low Saver" tickets, sold only in the United Kingdom, for metropolitan travel in all big cities. The restrictions, conditions, and amount of discount vary from city to city. There are also "blue days"—low-traffic periods during which discounts are greater. If you opt for discount tickets of this kind, be sure to check out all the stipulations. Railcard holders receive one-third off the price of Savers.

"Day Returns" apply to trips within approximately 50 miles of London and are sold only in the United Kingdom. Fares depend on the region and division. For instance, Day Returns to Brighton and Dover are £6.60 ($9.50) and £9.00 ($13), respectively. A Saver on the same South East Division of the Southern Region to Dover is £12 ($17). Basically, check out the various fares to see which is better for you.

"The London Travel Pak" is another promotional fare, again, sold only in the United Kingdom. This ticket includes round-trip rail from Gatwick Airport to Victoria Station or round-trip transfers from Heathrow Airport to central London by Airbus or Underground, a London Explorer pass good for three consecutive days of travel on the Underground and Red buses, and a four-day Britrail pass for unlimited travel in Britain. Prices in U.S. dollars are noted below. The "Travel Pak" can only be purchased in the United States.

|  | 1986 rates | |
|---|---|---|
| Type | First Class | Economy Class |
| Adult | $155 | $115 |
| Child (5–15 years old) | 80 | 60 |
| Senior Citizen (65 or older) | 135 | — |

*Individually Purchased Tickets*
Average and standard cost per mile:

    First Class     21¢
    Second (Economy) Class   14¢

Previously, the fare structure was based on the duration of your rail trip. Now, it is based on market conditions and extremely complex factors producing many anomalies between city pairs. We suggest that you try to buy one of the tickets discussed in this section to avoid a potentially confusing experience trying to puzzle through the other fares.

*Comment:* There are no supplements on the InterCity 125 trains.

**Yugoslavia**

*Unlimited Mileage Passes*
None.

*Other Special Tickets and Passes*
None.

*Individually Purchased Tickets*
Average or standard cost per mile:

    First Class    1¢
    Second Class   0.6¢

*Comment:* The country has two major northwest and southeast travel corridors linked laterally by three or four smaller routes. The large eastern cities are served by slow but reliable trains. There is no railway service along the coast. Connections from inland cities to Dubrovnik and other major resort centers are slow.

Train service is very inexpensive in Yugoslavia. However, supplements are charged on all internal express (rapid) trains.

To obtain information on the rail services described in this chapter, please contact the railroads and companies noted below.

National Railways

**Belgian National Railroad**
745 Fifth Avenue
New York, NY 10151
212-758-8130

**Britrail**
630 Third Avenue
New York, NY 10017
212-599-5400

333 N. Michigan Avenue
Chicago, IL 60601
312-263-1910

800 Hope Street
Los Angeles, CA 90017
213-624-8787

**Eurailpass**
610 Fifth Avenue
New York, NY 10020
212-586-0091

**French National Railroads (SNCF)**
610 Fifth Avenue
New York, NY 10020
212-582-2816

**German Federal Railroad (Germanrail)**
747 Third Ave., 33rd Floor
New York, NY 10017
212-308-3100

**Italian State Railways**
666 Fifth Ave., 6th Floor
New York, NY 10103
212-397-2667

**Swiss Federal Railways**
608 Fifth Avenue
New York, NY 10020
212-757-5944


Orient Express

**Venice Simplon–Orient Express, Inc.**
One World Trade Center, Suite 1235
New York, NY 10048
212-938-6830
800-524-2420 Nationwide

**Nostalgia-Istanbul Orient Express**
Society Expeditions
723 Broadway East
Seattle, WA 98102
206-285-9400

# 14

# Rental and Lease Cars

*If You Really Want to See
the Countryside, Drive It*

Driving can be both an economical and enjoyable way to get around Europe, as illustrated by the comparisons in chapter 12. While the enjoyment is not dependent on where you rent, costs are. Car rentals are much more expensive in some countries than others. This cost disparity is due both to differences in basic rates and to differences in the Value Added Tax (VAT)—a surcharge tax imposed by national governments (somewhat like our state sales taxes, but at higher rates) that can add up to as much as 25 percent of the price of the rental. Rates among different rental companies can also vary substantially for the same country or region.

Lowest Cost Rentals in Each Country

Table 6 (page 181) shows the lowest weekly rental costs, including taxes, for a standard subcompact car in seventeen European countries (plus Israel) last summer. The lowest cost rental in Finland, at $303, is so high that it would run off the chart. The cost figure used for each country reflects the rates of the rental company that offered the lowest rates in that country. Rates for 1987 were not available in time for publication. If you're interested in driving, contact the rental companies for the most current rates. Meanwhile, adding 10 to 15 percent to 1986 rates will give you a reasonable estimate of what you'll pay this summer.

**Table 6  1986 Weekly Rental Costs for Standard Subcompact Car
(U.S. dollars, taxes included)**

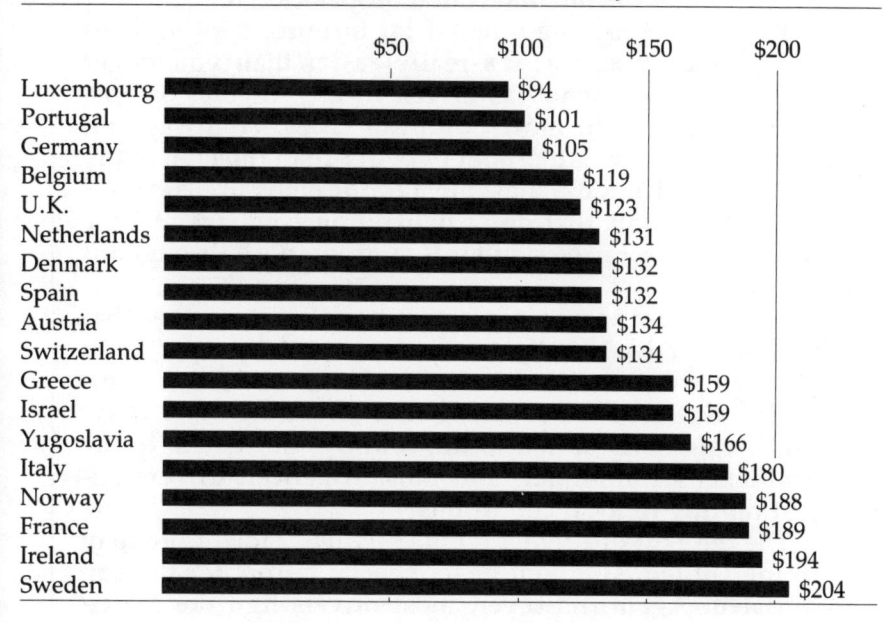

|  |  |
|---|---|
| Luxembourg | $94 |
| Portugal | $101 |
| Germany | $105 |
| Belgium | $119 |
| U.K. | $123 |
| Netherlands | $131 |
| Denmark | $132 |
| Spain | $132 |
| Austria | $134 |
| Switzerland | $134 |
| Greece | $159 |
| Israel | $159 |
| Yugoslavia | $166 |
| Italy | $180 |
| Norway | $188 |
| France | $189 |
| Ireland | $194 |
| Sweden | $204 |

The table highlights the range in cost for what is essentially the same product, depending on the country in which you rent. Although not specifically included in the table, the country-by-country cost pattern for a standard subcompact should also hold for larger car rentals, as well.

The figures used in Table 6, as well as in the subsequent detailed analyses, apply to special rental programs designed for tourists from the United States. In most cases, they are substantially lower than the rates you would pay if you just walked into a local car-rental office in Europe. Also, these cost figures include applicable VAT taxes. They do not include optional collision damage-waiver coverage, which reduces the collision deductible to zero, or any other optional insurance coverage sold by the rental companies.

Up to three unlimited-mileage weekly car-rental rates are

A few words for the first-time European driver.
The idea of driving a rental car in Europe intimidates some Americans, but it's really easier than you might think. Anybody who has driven in Los Angeles or Boston can cope with most European cities. Highway and destination signs are probably better than those in many parts of the United States; most traffic signs use standard graphic symbols that don't depend on language. Traffic rules are also fairly standard—and simple—throughout Europe.

If your main worry is heavy city traffic, remember that a rental car isn't really the best form of transportation for seeing cities. If your trip involves mainly the major capital cities, you're usually better off on the train. Driving is especially suited to the countryside, where traffic problems are minimal, and most American drivers adjust rapidly to local conditions.

The thought of driving on the "wrong" side of the road in the United Kingdom poses special terrors for the uninitiated. Again, however, most drivers find the anticipation worse than the fact. It takes perhaps 10 or 20 minutes and then you begin to feel surprisingly adjusted.

But don't sign up for an expensive long-term rental if you're really hesitant about driving in Europe. Instead we suggest you take a one- or two-day trial rental. If you're comfortable, extend your rental, or plan on extended driving the next time.

When you decide to try a rental car, you'll need your regular state driver's license and a major credit card—it's like renting a car in the United States. Check with your car rental company for full particulars on documentation—especially if any driver in your party is under twenty-one or over seventy years old.

shown for each country in the country and company comparisons at the end of this chapter:

- The weekly cost for an unrestricted rental (no special limitations on length of rental, office location, and the like), for

a standard subcompact car, with unlimited mileage, as summarized by Table 6.
- The weekly cost for the least expensive car rental available in the country. These rentals may be restricted in some way, they may provide for a sub-subcompact car that is smaller, older, or less powerful than a standard subcompact, or they may be both restricted *and* sub-subcompact.
- The weekly cost for a standard midsize car sufficiently large to accommodate four passengers and their luggage. Where lower cost restricted rentals are available, the figures for four-passenger cars apply to restricted rentals.

**Restrictions**

Most unrestricted rental programs offer a high degree of flexibility—about what you'd expect from the major rental companies here at home. In most countries you can return cars to different locations within the same country at no additional charge. There are rental offices in most primary and many secondary cities in each country and at virtually all the international gateway airports. Service is generally available during extended hours, seven days a week, at the bigger city and airport locations. The main limitation is that you have to rent a car for a minimum of one week to qualify for the tourist rates.

A few of the rental companies also offer cheaper restricted deals, and offer them in their busiest locations. These restrictions differ among the various rental companies but involve one or more limiting factors.

- advance purchase, similar to APEX airline tickets
- limited rental-office locations, either at major airports or main city-center offices
- pick up and turn in only during normal weekday office hours
- mandatory return to the location where the car was rented

**Standard Subcompacts**

Almost all European car rental companies offer one or more of six standard subcompacts in most of their locations: Fiat Uno, Ford Fiesta, Opel Corsa, Renault 5 *le Car*, Volkswagen Golf (Rabbit), and Austin Metro. The Ford, Renault, and VW

> Most rental companies use a letter-group system for classifying the cars in their fleets. Although no official industry-wide standards have been adopted, the standard subcompacts are placed in each rental company's Group A more often than in any other. However, in countries where sub-subcompacts are common, the standard subcompacts are often in a more expensive Group B, and the Group A cars are the sub-subcompacts. If the standard subcompacts are in Group A, the cheaper sub-subcompacts (where available) are called Group O or Group X. Similarly, the standard four-passenger models used for this comparison can be found anywhere from group C to group G.
>
> These disparities aren't just the result of different rental car company practices either. A single company often lists identical cars differently in different countries. Thus, for example, Avis lists an Opel Corsa as Group B in Luxembourg and Group A in Germany.
>
> Obviously, to be realistic, company-by-company and country-by-country price comparisons have to be among *comparable car models,* not necessarily among the *same letter groups.* It's all too easy for a rental company to engage in group inflation that would mislead you completely if you based your comparison shopping strictly on letter groups.

are widely sold in the United States and should be familiar to most American motorists; the others are very similar. They're fine city and road cars for two adults and their baggage. They are adequate for two adults plus one child under ten years old or for two adults plus two younger children. Almost all of these models are furnished in two-door or three-door (hatchback) versions. Adults will find it tough getting in and out of the rear seats. Also, neither automatic transmissions nor air conditioning are featured on any of these cars, even as extra-cost options.

Some companies offer even smaller or older model cars at some locations—for example, Citroen CV6, Renault 4, Austin

Mini, VW Beetle, and Fiat Panda. Of the companies that offer these sub-subcompact cars, some do caution that they are suitable for city driving only.

**Insurance**

As with U.S. car rentals, the basic European rates include coverage for "third party," fire, and theft claims. They also include collision coverage, with a substantial deductible ($500 and up) for which the renter is liable. This liability can be reduced to zero by a "collision-damage waiver" (CDW) payment, which typically adds about $5 to $10 a day to the rental contract. Most American drivers' own automobile liability policies cover rental-car collision damage, even in Europe. But many travel experts recommend CDW to avoid what might become serious inconveniences and interruptions of travel plans while the renter may be detained for verification of his U.S. coverage.

CDW is a very poor buy when compared with other insurance. But you shouldn't look at it strictly as insurance against accident liability. Instead, view it as insurance against having your trip spoiled or sidetracked by hassles and delays. What you're really paying for is peace of mind.

The special lease programs typically include full zero-deductible collision insurance.

Trading Up

With three adults—or two adults and two kids about six to ten years old—you'll probably want a car slightly larger than a standard subcompact, such as a Fiat Ritmo, Ford Escort, Opel Kadett, Renault 9, and VW Jetta. Costs for stick-shift models of these cars run anywhere from $20 to $70 higher per week (including taxes) than the standard subcompacts. These cars are usually in Groups B and C, and car-rental companies often describe the cars as "suitable for four adults." But many Americans feel pretty crowded driving substantial distances with four adults in these models, because many rental companies furnish them mainly in their two- or three-door versions.

You probably shouldn't consider anything smaller than a

car in the next larger group for four adults. This group normally includes Fiat Regata, Ford Sierra, Opel Ascona, Renault 18, VW Passat, and the like. Most rental companies categorize them as Group D in most countries, but they can be found from Group C to Group G on occasion. Stick-shift models rent for between $50 and $150 more per week than the standard subcompact Group A models.

Automatic transmissions are about $5 a day extra, but they're not usually offered as options on the standard subcompact models, even at extra cost. You have to go up one size class— to models usually offered as stick-shift options in Group B— to get an automatic. With automatics, these cars are usually priced as Group C. Thus, the least expensive automatic you can get will run at least $50 to $100 a week more than the standard subcompact.

Even in hot countries such as Italy and Spain, air conditioning is an expensive luxury. The cheapest air-conditioned models in Italy, for example, are in the $400 to $450 a week range.

Of course, you can also go the luxury or sporty route in a European car, so long as you're willing to pay. For example, a Mercedes 280SE or Porsche 944 will run in the vicinity of $400 to $500 a week. Large parties can rent a VW microbus for something in the range of $300 to $400 a week.

Finally, parties so inclined can rent recreational vehicles (RVs) for camping through Europe. Vehicles suitable for four to six travelers start at about $400 a week in the high season, with extra charges for mileage in excess of 1,750 kilometers (1,090 miles) a week. Off-season rentals are about 40 percent less. Europe is full of well-located campgrounds, and RV travel style has become quite popular. Of course, as here at home, operating expenses are at least double those of an efficient compact car, and putting lots of miles on a gas-guzzling RV with the price of gasoline at anywhere from $2.50 to $3.00 a gallon can add up to a big expense. For a less expensive camping trip, try tent camping with an efficient compact car instead.

One-Way Rentals

Several of the independent rental companies have "Continental One-Way" programs. Weekly costs are somewhat higher than most single-country rentals. But no drop-off charge is required so long as you rent and return the car in any combination of up to twenty-five cities in fourteen countries. The costs, as illustrated, are the tax-free rates that are valid for this special rental in all countries except Denmark and France. (If you begin this one-way program in either Denmark or France, you'll have to pay 22 or 33 percent taxes in addition to the rates shown.) For rentals longer than one week, the prices drop sharply after the first week.

A few companies offer two one-way deals: one that's available in most major cities, and another lower-priced offer that's limited to just a few of the company's key locations (with limited pickup and drop-off options). Check with rental companies for details.

Avis, Hertz, and National, on the other hand, provide free drop-off between some of the larger European cities as a feature of their regular programs, but add drop-off charges for other locations. These rentals are always based on regular rates in the originating country, which—depending on your starting point—may often be much lower than the special one-way program rates. Check Avis, Hertz, and National brochures for specifics.

### Leases

For several years, a purchase-repurchase lease has been the best deal for travelers needing a car for longer periods—three weeks or more. These leases are available in both Belgium and France. They're actually purchase-repurchase contracts. You buy a factory-new car on a contract that obligates you to sell it back after you have driven it. The rental company takes care of all the paperwork and financing—you're never really aware that you theoretically own the car rather than hold a lease on it. This deal beats ordinary renting because of some complicated combination of circumstances involving "export" sales and special markets for slightly used cars.

The one caution is that you're driving a literally new car. You are required to abide by special break-in procedures, and you may have to cope with minor new-car mechanical adjustments. You can get service, however, at any dealership that handles the brand of car you've leased, and, of course, it's at no additional charge.

The best standard sixty-day lease arrangements for 1986 ran from $900 in Belgium and $850 in France for standard subcompacts, and from $1,250 in Belgium and $1,000 in France for one of the standard four-passenger models. Leases are tax-free, and include full zero-deductible insurance; pick up and return options are limited.

### Airline Deals

Airlines offer rental car tie-ins that are sometimes less costly than any separate arrangements. This summer you can expect a variety of such promotions.

As indicated in chapter 9, the best of these deals actually amount to an air-fare subsidy. The current marketing gimmick seems to be pricing these subsidized rentals at $1 a week or even free. That's only for the first week, of course; extra weeks are usually priced at the cooperating rental company's normal rates. These deals are based on a minimum of two people traveling together, who are usually given a standard subcompact car. Singles can enjoy a subcompact for a modest supplement, and larger parties qualify for larger cars.

Airline tie-ins offering only modest rate reductions are more common, especially during the peak season. But many of these airline tie-in rates require a minimum of two participants. Whenever you're checking on a car-rental promotion, be sure to determine if the price is for the car, regardless of how many use it, or if it is quoted on a per-person basis.

The airline deals called *Fly/Drives* are often very good, provided they can be used with the lowest available air fare. In fact, a good rental car deal may well be the most important factor in airline selection. But watch out for what look like great deals that require you to buy a much more expensive type of air fare than you'd normally use to qualify. One of the heavily publicized deals a few years ago was good only for travelers who used a noncompetitively high weekend fare, rather than the cheaper midweek fare.

### Rental Companies

Six of the eleven organizations specializing in European rentals are multinational car-rental companies with operating di-

> **Note of caution:** If you elect to go with one of the international car-rental chains, and you want to pay by credit card at the time you turn the car in, be sure to pay with a bank card (such as MasterCard or Visa) or a T&E card (such as American Express or Diners Club) rather than a car-rental company credit card. In prior years, some car-rental companies have seriously gouged their customers by using unofficial exchange rates well below the actual bank rates prevailing at the time of the charge. While it's too early to say how the companies will operate this year, you're certainly safe with one of the bank cards. They typically give you the official rate on any converted-currency billings. T&E cards charge a 1 percent exchange fee, but they also give you the official rate.

visions or affiliates in both the United States and Europe. International giants Avis and Hertz are very active in the market, with fully competitive rates in many countries. Second-tier multinational operations American International and Budget are also prominent. National in the United States represents Europcar in Europe, and the U.S. Dollar is affiliated with the international interRent.

The other five U.S. car rental companies that specialize in European auto rentals and leases are wholesale tour operators. Cortel and Kemwel are major full-line European tour operators that include aggressive car-rental programs, along with many other travel services, while Auto Europe, Europe by Car, and Foremost Euro-Car stick with just the automobile field. In any case, these companies do not have rental operations; they merely package and market the rentals. In fact, on-the-spot service on a rental from one of these operators is usually provided by one of the major multinationals.

Finally, some European car dealers in the United States can arrange purchase-repurchase leases for their makes of car. The leases are operated out of Belgium and France, regardless of where the car is manufactured.

The different kinds of companies offer what are generally competitive rates. And to get these rates, you have to reserve in advance. As mentioned, you'll have to pay much more if you just show up at a rental counter. But there are also some important operational differences among the companies, too.

- The multinational car-rental companies typically allow you either to pay in advance or to pay at the end of your rental, by cash or with a major credit card, depending on your preference, while the tour operators require full payment in advance.
- Avis, Budget, and Europcar now require reservations only forty-eight hours in advance; Hertz, interRent, and Ansa require one week; the tour operators have no minimum, but late rentals (within two or three weeks) usually entail extra late charges and special fees for telephone and telex messages.
- Most firms have a minimum one-week rental to qualify for the special tourist rates, but Cortell offers special tourist rates on rentals as short as three days. However, per-day prices for the shorter rentals are quite a bit higher than for weekly rentals.

**Pricing**

Most rental companies' brochures show European rental rates in U.S. dollars. With some, these dollar prices are official—they're what you pay no matter what happens to exchange rates. All Auto Europe and Cortell (and some Europe by Car) rentals are established officially in U.S. dollars. Of course, these rental companies reserve the right to readjust their rates in the event of a substantial shift in currency-exchange levels.

For others, the official rates are established in the local currencies of individual countries (except that rentals in Israel and Yugoslavia are expressed by all rental companies in U.S. dollars, and in a few other countries by some rental companies, as well). U.S. dollar figures cited in brochures are "for guidance only," and what you really pay is the dollar equivalent of the foreign-currency rental rate at exchange rates that prevail when you pay—before or after. When comparing rates from different rental companies you may have to recalculate the dollar cost of any rentals officially priced in local currency to reflect the latest value of that currency.

A second note of caution: Several years ago, some car rental companies either deliberately or inadvertently used very unrealistic exchange rates to calculate those "for guidance only" dollar figures in their rental brochures. Thus, for example, in its first in-depth look at European auto rentals, *Economy Traveler* found companies that used exchange rates overstating the value of the dollar by as much as 10 percent, thereby understating the actual cost of their rentals by 10 percent. Moreover, the newsletter found that the dollar had never been at the inflated value used to calculate the "guidance" rates at any time during the period when prices were established and brochures printed.

Three years ago, the dollar's steady climb against European currency resulted in overstatement in dollar figures of the actual rental costs from those companies that quote their offical prices in local currency. So nobody was hit with an unexpectedly high rental bill because of understated dollar rates. Even though the dollar is weaker this year than in previous years, it will probably remain steady during the summer. You may again see accidentally or deliberately understated dollar costs from some of the companies that price officially in local currency. Your protection? Read the small print and recalculate any dollar equivalents of local currency.

### Adjacent-Country Renting

If you take the lowest cost unrestricted rental for a standard subcompact car as an overall index of the car-rental cost levels in each European country—a pretty good standard of comparison, by the way—you'll see that car-rental costs in Belgium, West Germany, and Luxembourg are substantially lower than in some adjacent countries that are important tourist destinations. With rental costs in Luxembourg set as a standard, for example, costs in Austria and Switzerland are 43 percent higher, costs in Italy 91 percent higher, and costs in France more than double.

This disparity naturally gives rise to the thought that renting a car in one of the low-cost countries, even if you're mainly interested in using it in one of the higher-cost countries, may be the most economical way to go. There's no overall advice to be given here, but two major guidelines can be drawn:

1. If your trip involves driving through both high- and low-cost car-rental countries, it's clearly advantageous to arrange your itinerary to take advantage of the car-rental rates in a low-cost country. Your decision to do this is made even easier by the fact that the countries with low-cost rentals are also generally the countries with the lowest airfares from the United States. Thus, Brussels, Frankfurt/Dusseldorf, and Luxembourg are excellent choices of arrival gateway, even if much of your trip involves driving through Austria, France, Italy, or Switzerland.
2. If you *don't* really want to spend much time in one of the low-cost countries, the choice is harder. Remember (from chapter 11) that your "overhead" cost of just *being* in Europe is $75 to $170 a day. So it doesn't pay to spend an extra day or two driving from a low-cost gateway to a high-cost country to save less than this amount on car rental expenses. On the other hand, if your itinerary calls for travel near one of the low-cost gateways anyhow, you could save a substantial amount on a car rental (and possibly air fare, as well) by using an alternative low-cost gateway. Thus if you're visiting northern France, consider Brussels, Frankfurt, or Luxembourg as gateways; if you plan to drive through southern France, consider Barcelona as a gateway; for trips to Italy, look at Munich and Zurich as alternative gateways.

Country and Company Comparisons

The following listing identifies the rental companies offering the lowest cost weekly rentals in each country in 1986 for unrestricted standard subcompact rentals, minimum cost rentals (subcompact cars, restricted rentals, or, in some cases, restricted subcompact rentals), and four-passenger car rentals (some restricted).

## Austria

Lowest cost and competitive suppliers:

Standard subcompact, standard rental, $134: Budget
Minimum cost rental, $134: Budget
Four-passenger car rental, $196: Budget

*Comments:* Austrian rates are based on a VAT reduced from the usual 31 percent to a special tourist rate of 21.3 percent, available on rentals up to twenty-one days. If you're renting for twenty-two days or more, consider renting in Germany.

## Belgium

Lowest cost and competitive suppliers:

Standard subcompact, standard rental, $117–119: Avis, Budget
Minimum cost rental, $99–104: Auto Europe, Foremost, Kemwel
Four-passenger car rental, $194–208: Avis, Budget, Kemwel

*Comments:* Belgium is one of the best European rental locations; Belgian leases are probably the best available all-around long-term car arrangements. The good auto-rental rates make Brussels a very desirable gateway.

## Denmark

Lowest cost and competitive suppliers:

Standard subcompact, standard rental, $132: Budget
Minimum cost rental, $132–136: Auto Europe, Budget, Europe by Car
Four-passenger car rental, $207–208: Ansa, Avis

## Finland

Lowest cost and competitive suppliers:

Standard subcompact, standard rental, $303–306: Ansa, Budget
Minimum cost rental, $303–306: Ansa, Auto Europe, Budget
Four-passenger car rental, $406: Kemwel

*Comments:* Sky-high rates, but, in this isolated market, lack of competition keeps prices high. Train fares are surely a better value.

### France

Lowest cost and competitive suppliers:

Standard subcompact, standard rental, $189: Budget
Minimum cost rental, $161–169: Auto Europe, Kemwel
Four-passenger car rental, $296: Budget

*Comments:* The French VAT at 33 percent is the highest in Europe. Unless you're willing to submit to this degree of taxation, consider planning your arrival by air to a gateway in nearby Belgium, Germany, Luxembourg, or Spain; renting a car there at a much lower rate, touring France, and then returning the car to your point of origin (or if you have a one-way deal, you may be able to drop the car off in France). Or use one of the tax-free leases, even for trips as short as three weeks.

### Germany

Lowest cost and competitive suppliers:

Standard subcompact, standard rental, $103–105: Europe by Car, Foremost
Minimum cost rental, $94: Europe by Car, Kemwel
Four-passenger car rental, $174: Europe by Car

### Greece

Lowest cost and competitive suppliers:

Standard subcompact, standard rental, $159–167: Budget, Kemwel
Minimum cost rental, $122: Kemwel
Four-passenger car rental, $275–282: Budget, Kemwel

### Ireland

Lowest cost and competitive suppliers:

Standard subcompact, standard rental, $194–202: Auto Europe, Budget, Europe by Car, Foremost

Minimum cost rental, $161–164: Auto Europe, Kemwel
Four-passenger car rental, $275: Budget

**Israel**

Lowest cost and competitive suppliers:

Standard subcompact, standard rental, $159: Kemwel
Minimum cost rental: $159: Kemwel
Four-passenger car rental, $274–275: Budget, Europcar

*Comments:* Costs reflect waiver of taxes for tourists' rentals. Make sure your contract shows no tax charge.

**Italy**

Lowest cost and competitive suppliers:

Standard subcompact, standard rental, $158: Foremost
Minimum cost rental, $136–147: Auto Europe, Europe by Car, Kemwel
Four-passenger car rental, $240–249, Ansa, Budget, Foremost

**Luxembourg**

Lowest cost and competitive suppliers:

Standard subcompact, standard rental, $94–106: Auto Europe, Budget, Europe by Car, Foremost
Minimum cost rental, $66: Kemwel
Four-passenger car rental, $155: Budget

*Comments:* Luxembourg can boast Europe's lowest car-rental rates. Cheap rentals here are a good complement to low-cost airline Icelandair, for which Luxembourg is the continental gateway.

**Netherlands**

Lowest cost and competitive suppliers:

Standard subcompact, standard rental, $131–132: Ansa, Budget
Minimum cost rental, $124: Kemwel
Four-passenger car rental, $220–225: Ansa, Avis

**Norway**

Lowest cost and competitive suppliers:

Standard subcompact, standard rental, $188: Auto Europe
Minimum cost rental, $151–164: Auto Europe, Kemwel
Four-passenger car rental, $276–284: Avis, Hertz

**Portugal**

Lowest cost and competitive suppliers:

Standard subcompact, standard rental, $101: Ansa
Minimum cost rental, $90: Ansa
Four-passenger car rental, $266–270: Ansa, Europe by Car

**Spain**

Lowest cost and competitive suppliers:

Standard subcompact, standard rental, $132–144: Ansa, Avis, Foremost
Minimum cost rental, $117–127: Ansa, Auto Europe, Europe by Car, Foremost
Four-passenger car rental, $225: Budget

**Sweden**

Lowest cost and competitive suppliers:

Standard subcompact, standard rental, $204–209: Avis, Budget
Minimum cost rental, $155: Kemwel
Four-passenger car rental, $285–290: Avis, Budget

**Switzerland**

Lowest cost and competitive suppliers:

Standard subcompact, standard rental, $134: Foremost
Minimum cost rental, $99: Foremost
Four-passenger car rental, $196–198: Budget, Foremost

**United Kingdom**

Lowest cost and competitive suppliers:

Standard subcompact, standard rental, $123: Europe by Car
Minimum cost rental, $99: Kemwel
Four-passenger car rental, $193: Ansa

**Yugoslavia**

Lowest cost and competitive suppliers:

Standard subcompact, standard rental, $169: Auto Europe
Minimum cost rental, $125–133: Auto Europe, Europe by Car, Kemwel
Four-passenger car rental, $224: Europcar

**Continental One-Way**

Lowest cost and competitive suppliers:

Standard subcompact, standard rental, $143–159 a week on a three-week basis: Auto Europe, interRent
Minimum cost rental, $143–154 a week on a three-week basis: Europe by Car, interRent
Four-passenger car rental, $230 a week on a three-week basis: interRent

*Comments:* Rates are based on one-third of three-week rental—not available for one week, and more expensive for two. Also note that other approaches based on the rental rates of the originating country, with no drop-off charge, may be better than this specific one-way plan.

## Arranging Your Rental or Lease

With no firm 1987 rates available at press time, you should verify current rental-cost information from several of the lowest-cost suppliers when you're ready to reserve. When you get the brochures, be sure to note which rates are officially established in dollars and which are in local currency. Then recalculate all rates based on local currencies to dollar figures with the latest exchange rates and make your comparisons.

Also, check with the airline you're planning to use—or any others that serve the route you're going to take—to see if any are offering subsidized rentals in the areas you plan to visit. If you decide to rent your own car (no airline tie-in), you can arrange your rentals either through your travel agent or directly. If you want one of the purchase-repurchase leases, contact one of the European auto specialists—the major international chains generally don't handle the leases. French and Belgian purchase-repurchase leases may also be offered by one of your local European car dealers.

Major Car Rental Companies Serving Europe

Ansa International (American International Rent-a-Car): 800-527-0202; 800-442-5757 (TX); 800-527-0160 (AK and HI)
Auto Europe: 800-223-5555; 800-942-1309 (NY); 800-268-8810 (Canada)
Avis Rent-a-Car: 800-331-2112; 800-272-3299 (CA)
Budget Rent-a-Car: 800-527-0700
The Cortell Group: 800-223-6626; 800-442-4481 (NY)
Europe by Car: 800-223-1516; 212-581-3040 (NY)
Foremost Euro-Cars: 800-423-3111; 800-272-3299 (CA)
Hertz Rent-a-Car: 800-654-3001
interRent Car Rental System (Dollar): 800-421-6878; 800-421-6868 (Canada)
The Kemwel Group: 800-468-0468; local numbers in thirty major U.S. cities
National Car Rental System: 800-328-4399; 800-227-7368 (Canada)

# 15

# Flying Around Europe

*For Long Distances,
or if You Have Lots of Money*

Most official European air fares are high in comparison with domestic U.S. fares for comparable distances. The contrast in fares is highlighted even more since the deregulation of the U.S. airline industry. The officially sanctioned airline cartel agreements in Europe place travel consumers' interests well behind the profitability of the national airlines and of the governments' desires to minimize competition from other countries—including the United States.

Until recently, the collaboration between scheduled IATA airlines and European governments maintained a very rigid official air-travel market. Bucket shop travel agents that sold discounted airline tickets were considered shady, at best, and often operated mainly within ethnic communities.

But that picture has changed radically in the last few years. With increased publicity, various forms of discounted tickets have become more and more popular, for both vacation and business travel. Publications such as *Holiday Which?* and *Business Traveller* in the United Kingdom and *Consumer Reports Travel Letter* in the United States have turned the light of open disclosure on ticket-discounting practices. American experience with deregulation has not been lost, either. European travelers now know that the old IATA cartel arrangement is not the only way an air-transport system can be run. As a result, ticket discounting has become common practice in most European countries, with respectable travel agencies, corporate travelers, and individual vacationers all benefiting.

Flying is the only viable alternative for some types of trips. As discussed in chapter 12, the fastest surface transportation may be impractical if you want to visit two or three spots in opposite corners of Europe on a single short trip. To travel from London to Athens by train (and channel boat), for example, means leaving on a Monday evening to arrive Thursday afternoon. The somewhat more prosaic train trip from Paris to Naples takes twenty-one hours; from London to Venice takes thirty-two hours. And even such short trips as London to Paris or Copenhagen to Stockholm can use up a full day of travel time, largely because of the necessary train-boat-train connections required to get across various channels and straits. If your trip involves one or more intra-Europe links like these, you should think about flying as a timesaving mode of travel that may justify its higher cost in the usable touring time you gain over train or car.

Fortunately, you're not always stuck with the official fares. European travelers don't like high air fares any better than we do, and there are some ways that Europeans use to avoid them that American travelers should use, too.

### Official Air Fares

How high are regular European air fares? For a sample trip like Frankfurt-Munich-Zurich-Paris-Frankfurt, the lowest available air fare would be about $460 a person. That's about 47¢ a mile. At that rate, you'd pay $181 from San Francisco to Los Angeles, compared with the lowest unrestricted fare of $59; or $359 from Chicago to New York, compared with the actual $99. There-and-back round-trip excursions are somewhat less expensive—but also less useful for Americans who want to see a fair bit of Europe.

As in the United States and across the Atlantic, the airlines within Europe offer the restricted excursion as their best deal for cost-conscious vacation travelers. On some routes, a spectrum of excursion fares is offered, with (typically) comparatively few seats allocated to the very lowest-price tickets.

Most of the lowest official fares have a minimum-stay requirement—usually one Saturday night or one week. Some have other restrictions such as advance-purchase requirements (APEX), or they are offered only on selected (usually off-peak) flights (Super APEX, Super PEX). All these fares are intended for round trips, although you may be able to book open-jaw itineraries for some low fares, providing that both the arrival and departure cities are within one country—for example, fly from London to Nice and return to London from Bordeaux. You can also get Standby fares on flights from London to Athens and Tel Aviv and on some domestic British services, but not on most other European routes.

If you want a one-way ticket, you will pay dearly for it. The lowest official one-way fare is the fairly expensive Eurobudget fare. In practice it may be cheaper to buy a round-trip discount or charter ticket and not use the return half.

The recent important exception to Europe's normal arrangements for setting fares of international flights has already been noted. In late 1984, the British and Dutch governments negotiated a new "country-of-origin" system that requires the approval of only one government for a new air-fare proposal rather than the traditional requirement for both country-of-origin and country-of-destination approvals. If, for example, a British airline wants to introduce a new low fare to Amsterdam, it now needs only the consent of the British government, not of the Dutch as well.

Did it work? Reasonably well. British Airways and KLM jointly introduced a $61 late-booking round-trip fare between Heathrow and Amsterdam; British Caledonian (from London Gatwick) and Air UK (from London Stansted) both offered a $61 fare, valid only on specified flights. This $61 fare for these trips was exceptionally low by the standards of European scheduled services, and at the 1986 level of $79 remains a good buy.

There are some halting moves afoot to liberalize the entire airline system within the European Economic Community (EEC). In 1979 the European Commission—the EEC bureaucracy—produced some very cautious proposals for introducing more competition between airlines. After five more years of consultation and amendment it came up with a new (and even more cautious) set of proposals in 1984.

It's still open to question whether these proposals will produce any more improvement than the last lot. They certainly won't do you any good in 1987. Nor is it likely that the cartel arrangements that exist at the moment will be disbanded at any foreseeable point. At best, liberalization will allow competition among those who want to compete and will sanction those who don't want competition to carry on pretty much as they have thus far.

It's more likely that the milestone British-Dutch agreement will trigger some comparable agreements between other individual countries. Watch for one or two more continental governments to cut similar deals with the British sometime this year.

Meanwhile, if you prefer air travel within Europe as the best alternative for your trip, there is one more option to check: full-fare Economy-Class tickets to Europe. While full-fare Economy is a poor buy for point-to-point travel, it allows stopovers at no extra charge within specified generous mileage limitations. Thus you may book a flight from your home city to the most distant city you want to visit in Europe that will provide stopovers at the other cities you want to visit at no additional cost. Your transatlantic airline or travel agent can give you the specific costs for the itinerary you may be planning.

The foregoing comments apply to international fares within Europe—that is, traveling from country to country. But some of the European countries are big enough that you may be interested in domestic service as well. All European countries of any size have well-established domestic air services, in most cases operated by the national airline. In a few countries, the fares are subsidized at low levels. For example, in Greece a one-way fully flexible Economy fare from Athens to Rhodes (264 miles) costs just $31 at current exchange rates. But in most, fares are at the same high levels as the international fares.

Air Inter, the French domestic air carrier, introduced an unlimited air travel pass valid from April to December 1987. It is priced at approximately $225 (1400 FF), offering unlimited travel on any seven days over a thirty-day period. It also provided for a 50 percent discount on specified car rentals and up to a 40 percent discount on selected hotels. Air Inter flies to thirty cities within France, and may prove to be a possible alternative to the unlimited rail pass—France Railpass—discussed in chapter 13.

Braathens Safe, the domestic air carrier of Norway, offers three special fares during the peak summer season: (1) "Minifare"—a special round-trip fare between all major cities within Norway; (2) "Summer Fare"—a flat rate fare of NOR 340 for one-way travel in southern Norway; and (3) "Visit Norway Pass"—fixed fares for tickets with either four ($195) or eight ($295) flight coupons.

British Airways has instituted a "Highland Rover" in Scotland on eight separate flights that can be taken on the ticket in a fourteen-day period on the Highlands Division network of British Airways, which stretches from the Shetland Isles in the far north to the Hebridean Islands off the west coast, across to Aberdeen in the northeast and Glasgow in the south. The ticket can also be used to fly to the Orkney Islands and Inverness. The ticket must be bought and paid for not less than fourteen days before the first flight. It can only be used on one return trip between any two points. The cost is £149 ($216). But, unfortunately, in most cases, fares are at the same high levels as the international fares.

One final note on the scheduled airlines. If high fares are not bad enough, intra-European airline comfort levels are well below those in the United States. Seat pitch routinely is as low as 29 inches, allowing substantially less front-to-rear room than even the lowest quality U.S. airlines. And, on the very popular A300 Airbus planes—the main workhorse of the heavy-traffic routes—some airlines stuff nine seats in each row, compared with the eight seats that are normal for U.S. operators of the same equipment.

Charter and Inclusive Tour Flights

One of the big differences between civil aviation in the United States and Europe is the tremendous importance of the charter in Europe. About a third of all air passengers leaving Britain, Germany, and Scandinavia each year travel on charter flights. These are mainly holiday-makers flying off to Southern Europe. But there are also some specialized charter flights on routes linking major cities.

In general, these charter flights provide the cheapest way to fly within Europe. Although the "minimal accommodation" requirements (explained below) may sound rather suspicious, this kind of arrangement is available from all the largest and most respectable tour operators as well as a multitude of small companies.

International regulations require that, within Europe, charter seats can be retailed only as part of an "inclusive tour" holiday that includes some "land-package" arrangement such as a hotel room or rental car. But most European tour operators sell at least some of their charter seats with only the barest minimum accommodation to satisfy the letter if not the spirit of the regulation—a bed in a dormitory or accommodations in a hostel. The traveler therefore pays only slightly more than the price of the air ticket, and this price is often well below the cheapest fare on the scheduled flights.

The prices of seats on charter flights are not government controlled, and the market works very much according to supply and demand. Prices rise steeply at peak periods on the "sunshine" routes to the Mediterranean. They may also be cut dramatically if a tour operator is left with unsold seats shortly before flight date.

The European charter business is so big that the major airlines regularly sell blocks of seats on their scheduled flights to tour operators. Once again, regulations state that these seats can only be sold as part of a package holiday that includes accommodations. But these rules are widely ignored by tour operators with the full knowledge of the airlines. These fares are known as "inclusive tour" fares or consolidations. Tour operators who specialize in selling this type of "package" are generally known as "consolidators."

Charter flights do have some disadvantages. They are generally even less comfortable than scheduled flights—with less legroom and fairly basic in-flight catering. Tickets are normally available only for round-trip travel. One-way fares are occasionally offered but these are usually 70 to 80 percent of the round-trip fare. The other major disadvantage is that many routes are served by only one flight each way, each week.

However, on a few main routes there are charter operators with daily or almost daily flights that allow you to choose any length of stay. From London, Pegasus Skybus and Pilgrim Air offer this kind of quasi-scheduled service to Italy; GTF Tours offers it to Austria, Germany, and Switzerland; and Swiss Airtours provides services to Switzerland. Falcon and Slade also offer quasi-scheduled services to a wide selection of European destinations.

For a wider choice of flight dates at slightly higher prices, it is worth looking at the inclusive tour deals on scheduled flights—sold on the same minimal accommodation basis as the charters. They are also available only as round trips (no open-jaw travel); most require that you stay a Saturday night at your destination. However, they do not have any advance booking restrictions, so they are particularly useful on routes like those from London to Scandinavia or Italy, where the lowest official fares on scheduled flights are APEX-type fares that must be booked three or four weeks in advance. The two best-known companies selling such tickets from London to many European destinations are Falcon and Slade. There are also companies that specialize in selling tickets for one area: Citalia for Italy, or Scantours and Nordic Fare Deals for Scandinavia, for example.

### Discount Fares

Just about any discussion of European airfares ultimately turns to bucket shops and discount tickets. Unfortunately, if you are planning flights only within Europe, they won't help you much. They are rarely available for intra-European services. Discount tickets are more frequently available on long-haul routes to the Middle East, Africa, Asia, Australasia, and South America. However, several Asian, African, and Middle Eastern airlines operate flights that stop at more than one point in Western Europe to add traffic, and some of them discount these intra-European segments.

Discounting comes about because most airlines have more seats than they can sell at the officially agreed high prices. So they sell them off unofficially at much reduced rates. Discounting is against the rules of IATA, but it is certainly not illegal for customers to buy such tickets. Several European governments—notably the British and Dutch—believe that many of the official fares are much too high and have consistently turned a blind eye to discounting. The Germans, on the other hand, sporadically attempt to "clean up" the airline ticket marketplace to no ultimate avail—but to the short-term consternation of airlines and travel agents alike.

### Buying Your Tickets

If you're interested mainly in excursion tickets on the scheduled airlines, you can buy them from your regular travel agent, at home, at the same price as you would pay in Europe. As a result of attorney Don Pevsner's 1978 action, airlines can no longer prevent U.S. travel agents from selling even the lowest price intra-European tickets. The price you pay is simply the going price in the country where the trip originates, as expressed in local currency, converted to U.S. dollars on the day you buy the ticket. Of course, you can wait until you get to Europe to buy, but you don't have to, or you may not be able to, depending on restrictions that may apply to the fare you are prepared to pay.

You do have to wait to get to Europe to buy charter and discount tickets. Until quite recently, these tickets were sold mainly by bucket shops. These agencies, usually in inner-city areas, were partially outside the system and not fully accredited by the organizations that accredit European travel agencies. But recently more and more respectable, fully accredited travel agents have started selling discount tickets quite openly. The large travel agency chains now sell discount tickets in all their retail shops. The small bucket shops are still very much in business, though. They operate primarily by placing small advertisements in the classified columns of newspapers and magazines.

It's often suggested—especially by IATA apologists—that buying discount tickets is courting disaster: the agent will disappear with your money or the airline won't honor the ticket or some other catastrophe will occur. *Holiday Which?*—the British consumer travel magazine—suggests that these fears are much exaggerated. A survey carried out during the summer of 1984 indicated that while the incidence of minor problems is quite high—particularly ticket delivery later than expected—major problems were not common. However, anyone planning to buy a discount ticket should take some commonsense precautions:

- Get full details of takeoff and landing times, plane changes, and so on. For scheduled flights you can check the details with the airline itself.
- Get full details about your tickets: are there minimum- and maximum-stay requirements? Can you alter your flight dates after booking? What refund can you expect if you cancel?
- Find out if the travel agent is fully accredited. If not, be wary of paying more than a small deposit before tickets are delivered.

If you're interested in buying from a bucket shop, you may well find that you don't have enough time after your arrival in Europe to make the necessary arrangements. Bucket-shop ticket purchases are seldom as quick as purchases from an airline or conventional travel agent. The only easy answer to this problem is to have friends or acquaintances who live in Europe buy the tickets for you. However, that suggestion doesn't help the vast majority of Americans who do not have such European friends or relatives. A few U.S. agents that sell discounted transatlantic tickets may be able to obtain intra-European tickets given sufficient lead time. It's worth asking, if you're dealing with a discount-ticket agent here. And, of course, Americans can write to British or Dutch agents that advertise in publications available here. But frankly, none of the alternatives measures up to the standards of convenience and reliability that would warrant an endorsement in this guidebook.

Don't try to buy unofficial tickets at an airline office—even on that particular airline. An airline will offer you only the officially approved fares; it will not tell you about any cheap package deals (even on its own flights) or any other forms of discount travel.

Air-Fare Examples

Here is a sampling of intra-European air fares—official, charter, and discount. These are high season (summer) fares at the levels in effect as of late 1986. Off-season fares—especially the various discount types—can be much lower.

The lowest available one-way tickets are typically Eurobudget fares. They have no advance-purchase restrictions, but the number of Eurobudget seats allocated to each flight may be small.

The lowest cost scheduled airline excursion fares available (APEX and PEX) typically have restrictions, including advance purchase and/or a required minimum stay over a weekend. The number of seats allocated is also usually small.

The discount tickets typically have fewer or no restrictions, other than a round-trip purchase, but many of them are available only on connecting flights or flights that make one or more stops. For example, the lowest available fare from Amsterdam to Athens is offered only by Interflug (the East German airline) on a connection through East Berlin.

All air fares for trips originating in London were provided in pounds sterling by British Airways (unless otherwise noted) in 1986, and converted to U.S. dollars at the then-prevailing rate. Many of the excursion or special-discount fares have restrictions, including purchase in Britain. All fares are for peak summer 1986 travel (June, July, and August).

**London-Amsterdam**

Official airline fares

> Lowest-cost unrestricted Economy (one way): $117
> Lowest-cost excursion (round trip): $100

Special 1986 discount fare

> Round trip: $79 (quoted by KLM)

**London-Frankfurt**

Official airline fares

> Lowest-cost unrestricted Economy (one way): $160
> Lowest-cost excursion (round trip): $113

Typical 1986 charter/discount fare

> Round trip: $100

**London-Paris**

Official airline fares

> Lowest-cost unrestricted Economy (one way): $103
> Lowest-cost excursion (round trip): $113

Typical 1986 charter/discount fare

> Round trip: $75

**London-Rome**

Official airline fares

> Lowest-cost unrestricted Economy (one way): $308
> Lowest-cost excursion (round trip): $212

Typical 1986 charter/discount fare

Round trip: $175

**London-Athens**

Official airline fares

Lowest-cost unrestricted Economy (one way): $405
Lowest-cost excursion (round trip): $230

Typical 1986 discount fare

Round trip: $220

**London–Tel Aviv**

Official airline fares

Lowest-cost unrestricted Economy (one way): $668
Lowest-cost excursion (round trip): $711

Typical 1986 charter/discount fare

Round trip: $270 ($125 on a last-minute basis)

**London-Cairo**

Official airline fares

Lowest-cost unrestricted Economy (one way): $490
Lowest-cost excursion (round trip): $805

Typical 1986 charter/discount fare

Round trip: $250

All fares for trips originating in Amsterdam were provided by KLM–Royal Dutch Airlines in 1986. All fares were quoted in Dutch guilders and converted to U.S. dollars at the then-prevailing rate. All of the excursion fares are either APEX or PEX, requiring advance purchase and a stayover of one Saturday night at destination.

**Amsterdam-Rome**

Official airline fares

Lowest-cost unrestricted Economy (one way): $300
Lowest-cost excursion (round trip): $273

Typical 1986 charter/discount fare

Round trip: $123

**Amsterdam-Madrid**

Official airline fares

Lowest-cost unrestricted Economy (one way): $302
Lowest-cost excursion (round trip): $345

Typical 1986 charter/discount fare

Round trip: $134

**Amsterdam-Stockholm**

Official airline fares

Lowest-cost unrestricted Economy (one way): $307
Lowest-cost excursion (round trip): $325

Typical 1986 charter/discount fare

Round trip: $163

**Amsterdam-Athens**

Official airline fares

Lowest-cost unrestricted Economy (one way): $435
Lowest-cost excursion (round trip): $301

Typical 1986 charter/discount fare

Round trip: $163

**Amsterdam–Tel Aviv**

Official airline fares

Lowest-cost unrestricted Economy (one way): $633
Lowest-cost excursion (round trip): $407

Typical 1986 charter/discount fare

Round trip: $235

This sampling should illustrate some of the important points about flying within Europe:

- There is no real consistency in the relationships among the lowest unrestricted one-way fares, the lowest excursion fares on scheduled airlines, and the lowest-cost discount ticket.
- In many instances, the least expensive scheduled airline excursion is less than half the cost of going one way, so you can save on one-way travel by buying an excursion even if you do not use the return.

Finally, those lowest available Eurobudget (one-way) and excursion (round-trip) fares on the scheduled airlines sell out very quickly during peak travel periods. If you think you're interested, make sure that you reserve as early as possible, preferably at the time you reserve your transatlantic flights. Waiting until you get to Europe could mean you'll have to pay a much higher fare.

To obtain information on the services described in this chapter, please contact the companies below.

### Discount London Agencies

**Citalia**
CIT, Ltd.
50/51 Conduit Street
London W1R 9FB
Cable: ITALCIT
Telex: 263962

**Falcon Leisure Group**
190 Campden Hill Road
London W8 7TH
Cable: None
Telex: None

**GTF Tours, Ltd.**
(German Tourist Facilities)
184 Kensington Church Street
Notting Hill Gate, London W8 4DP
Cable: FLYGERMANY
Telex: 263696

**Pegasus (Skybus) Holidays**
24A Earls Court Garden
London SW5 OTA
Cable: None
Telex: 8952011

**Scantours**
(Scanbreak/Escape Holidays)
8 Spring Gardens
London SW1A 2BG
Cable: SCANTOURS
Telex: 919008

**Slade** Travel, Ltd.
15 Vivian Avenue
London NW4 3UT
Cable: SLADE
Telex: 23425

**Swiss Airtours**
(Britalia Travel, Ltd.)
63 Neal Street
London WC2H 9PJ
Cable: None
Telex: None

**Pilgrim Air**
44 Goodge Street
London W1P 1FP
Cable: None
Telex: 267752

**Nordic Fare Deals**
Norwegian State Railways Travel
Norway House
21/24 Cockspur Street
London SW1Y 5DA
Cable: NORSTARYS
Telex: 28380

# 16

# Buses and Ferries

*Rounding Out the Picture*

The European railroad system is probably the finest in the world—an economical, comfortable, convenient, and reliable way to travel. The European countries regard railroads as the primary means of surface transportation for passengers and freight and have invested accordingly. Thus, while bus systems operate in each of the countries covered in this book, the intercity buses in Europe are generally regarded and run as a supplement to the rail system rather than as an alternative to it. They are intended mainly to serve localized transport needs in areas too sparsely populated to support rail service. In a few countries, bus systems are also operated to provide a minimum-cost alternative to rail travel.

Still, it's worth reviewing bus service for American travelers. Some will use buses to keep travel costs to an absolute minimum, others to reach remote corners beyond the reach of the rails.

The European countries covered in this book are separated by several channels and seas. An extensive system of ferry boats has been developed to cross these water barriers, closely linked with the railroads and highways. This system, too, is worth reviewing.

Much of the information and research here was originally compiled by *Holiday Which?*, the travel magazine published by the Consumers' Association of Great Britain. Especially with the ferries, the research shows that discerning choices can make the difference between a ferry crossing that is truly enjoyable and one that is barely tolerable. The ferry section has been expanded somewhat from previous editions, and we are now able to comment on many European countries not previously included.

Bus Services

As in the United States, buses are still the cheapest form of intercity transportation in Europe. And buses are the only mode of transportation to many smaller communities and areas of the countryside. When you consider a bus trip, remember that buses are usually slower, less comfortable, and more prone to delays than trains. Still there are plenty of circumstances when bus travel may make sense for a portion of your European trip, especially if there's no train service to the town or village that you've been dying to see.

**Austria**

Most buses are run by the post office; even small villages have a reasonable service. The system covers most of the country, including several areas not served by rail. Fares are similar to train fares. See railway listings in chapter 13 under **Austria**; unlimited mileage tickets can be used on the government post buses as well as the trains.

**Belgium**

The comprehensive and integrated bus and rail network covers the whole country with interchangeable special tickets and passes. There is no long-distance bus service. Everyone takes trains between cities. See the railway listing in chapter 13 under **Belgium** and the local transportation listing in chapter 17 under **Brussels** for a discussion of these special tickets.

**Denmark**

Buses connect most towns, but the flat terrain makes bus trips monotonous. Buses and ferries are integrated into the rail network operated by DSB (Danish State Railways) and private companies. Buses usually operate on low-traffic routes—connecting with trains or cutting across railway lines to join small towns. Fares are about half those of the railway for comparable distances. Often you can avoid a circuitous rail journey by cutting across the country by bus. Bus and ferry tickets for connections with trains can be bought at the railway station at the beginning of the trip; bus tickets are also usually available on the buses themselves. Bicycling is common in Denmark and many facilities are provided in the bigger towns and cities to make travel safer and more convenient for cyclists. Bicycles can be hired for between DKr 20–50 (approximately $2.60–$6.60) a day or DKr 100–200 ($13.15–$26.30) a week (add 30 to 50 percent for tandems). A valid passport is required, and a deposit of DKr 500 ($66) or the full rental charge must be paid in advance. Tourist offices can usually help with the rental of a bicycle. Bicycles can usually be rented in advance.

### France

Long-distance coach services are operated by Europabus and other companies. There is also a wide network of local services operated by SCETA (Services de Tourisme S.N.C.F. and Europabus) in conjunction with the French National Railroads. At present, there are ninety-five operators offering uncoordinated services. We do not recommend taking the bus in France as a primary mode of transportation. The train is a much better alternative.

### Germany

Buses are run by the subsidiaries of the German Federal Railway (GermanRail) with fares roughly equivalent to Second-Class rail fares. Most buses cover short routes that begin and end at railway stations. Rail passes are valid on those buses operated by the railway, including the buses that travel the "Romantic Road" through Bavaria between March and November. Reservations are required three days in advance, and there is a DM2 (approximately $1.00) charge for each piece of luggage carried. See the listing in chapter 13 on **West Germany** for a discussion of GermanRail.

### Greece

An extensive and frequent bus service is available—with air conditioning—on many intercity routes. Local routes can be less comfortable and very crowded. Sample approximate fares from Athens are about Dr730 ($5.10) to Patras, Dr890 ($6.50) to Delphi, and Dr2,100 ($15.00) to Thessaloniki. Bus fares in Greece are expected to rise 10 percent in 1987.

### Iceland

Local transportation within Iceland is by an integrated bus, air taxi (four- to six-seat planes), and ferry network. Services radiate from Reykjavik, Isafjordur, Akureyri, and Egilsstadir to most outlying districts. There are two special bus passes available. See **Reykjavik** local transportation section in chapter 17 for details.

### Ireland

A comprehensive intercity network (C.I.E.) links most main cities, with the frequency of service stepped up during the summer months. Sample fares from Dublin are Ir£12.30 ($16.60) to Galway and Ir£14.60 ($19.70) to Cork. Children pay half fare on all routes. In addition, Rambler passes are available offering unlimited bus and rail travel—eight days for $72, fifteen days for $104.

### Italy

Italy operates a comprehensive regional and national network of buses. In some remote areas—particularly in the mountains—buses are usually a more reliable method of transport than trains. However, longer-distance travel is frequently cheaper by rail than by bus. There are also several private long-distance bus services operated by Europabus and other companies.

### Luxembourg

The train and bus network of the Luxembourg National Railways covers 870 miles. Practically every locality has bus connections.

### Netherlands

The Netherlands operates an integrated bus-rail system, with buses covering the areas not served by trains. Bus terminals are located at or near main railway stations. Special tickets can be purchased that allow travel on both systems interchangeably. See chapter 13 under **Netherlands** for details.

### Norway

The system is comprehensive and efficient despite difficult terrain, which can make bus journeys a special problem in winter. Most of the 80,000 kilometers of roads in Norway are served by buses, which also serve ferry points, airports, and railway stations. In particular, buses operate in the mountains to link the railway network of east Norway with the boat and ferry services of the west. In the North, buses connect the end of the railway at Fauske to Kirkenes (past the North Cape). Children four to sixteen years old pay half fare, and children under four travel free if not occupying a seat.

### Portugal

Portugal enjoys a fairly comprehensive system. Normally there are at least two buses per day to all major cities. Bus information in Lisbon can be obtained by calling 725832.

### Spain

Spain has an extensive network of long-distance coaches, but fares can be more expensive than those for rail. With few high-quality highways, road travel in Spain can be arduous. Traveling time for a given distance may be considerably more than it would be in other countries. The average cost for travel by bus in Spain is around 2¢ per mile (3 pesetas per kilometer). Sample fares are Madrid-Córdoba, Pts1385 ($10.20); Madrid-Seville, Pts1621 ($11.90); Madrid-San Sebastián, Pts860 ($6.30); Madrid-Toledo, Pts228 ($1.70); Madrid-Valencia, Pts1000 ($7.40).

### Sweden

A comprehensive bus system provides cheap and efficient travel, augmenting the railway system. Services are limited, however, on long-distance routes. A sample Stockholm-Gothenburg fare is about $9, compared with about $21 by train, but the bus only operates on weekends. The Swedish Tourist Board recommends trains over buses.

**Switzerland**

Switzerland operates a completely integrated bus-rail system. All special rail tickets include bus service. See the listing for **Switzerland** in chapter 13 for details. The Swiss Holiday Card is valid on 160 postbuses and all boats/ferries on Swiss lakes. The Postbus Holiday Season Ticket, which costs SFr 50 (approximately $29.50), allows half-fare travel on all scheduled government post bus routes for one month, with unlimited free travel on any three selected days.

**United Kingdom**

State-owned companies—National Express in England, Scottish Bus Group in Scotland, and Ulsterbus in Northern Ireland—cover all of the United Kingdom. Additionally, private companies operate on some routes. Coach travel usually takes longer than train travel, but prices are lower. Sample fares, round trip from London, are £19.00, about $27.20 (Economy Return), to £20.00, about $29.00 (Period Return), to Edinburgh; and £17.00, about $24.50 (Economy Return), to £19.00, $27.20 (Period Return), to Manchester. A Period Return applies to an outward journey that begins on any Friday throughout the year, and on a Saturday in July and August. Economy Return fares are available Sunday through Thursday all year. Information on coach services can be obtained at the Central Enquiry Bureau, Victoria Coach Station in London, 01-730-0202.

National Express (NE) is a nationwide network of express-bus service using specially built long-distance buses on all the major routes throughout England and Wales and, in conjunction with Scottish Citylink Coaches, into Scotland. The faster, non-stop services, known as Rapide, cover more than 200 destinations. Rapide coaches feature toilet facilities, video tapes, and light refreshments.

*Britexpress Card*
Tourists can take advantage of a considerable discount by purchasing the Britexpress Card. This provides a discount of up

to one-third off the standard fare for any number of journeys taken in thirty consecutive days on all National Express services in England and Wales, selected services to and within Scotland, and on some other services of associated companies, including Flightline services from London Heathrow and between airports to central London. It also includes a discount on "London Crusader" sightseeing tours in London, a one-third discount on Culture Bus in London, and a London Pride sightseeing tour. The Britexpress Cards can be purchased in advance in the United States from any travel agency through The Kemwel Group in Harrison, NY, or Worldwide Marketing Assoc. in Chicago, IL, for $10. Cards can also be purchased in the United Kingdom upon presentation of your passport at London's Victoria Coach Station, London Heathrow Airport Central Bus Station, London Gatwick Airport Green Line/National Desk or Arrivals Concourse, Glasgow Bus Station, and Edinburgh Bus Station.

*Tourist Trail Tickets*
The British Bus Tourist Trail Ticket was introduced in 1986, providing the visitor with unlimited travel along three Tourist Trail routes for fifteen days:

- London–Oxford–Stratford-upon-Avon–Chester–Windermere–Edinburgh
- London-Cambridge-Lincoln-York-Durham-Edinburgh
- London–Oxford–Stratford-upon-Avon–Lincoln–York

Travel may start at any of these towns and cities and any combination of them can be selected. The ticket is good for travel between June 1 and October 25 and can only be purchased from Britexpress outlets. Price: £75.00 ($109) per person or £62.00 ($90) per person, if you hold a Britexpress Card.

Regional bus tickets are available in many other parts of Britain, including Scotland, Wales, Northern Ireland, and the Isle of Man.

*Other Discounts*
Persons aged sixty or over, and children ages five to sixteen (five to fifteen in Scotland) automatically qualify for one-third discount on the majority of express bus services without needing a Britexpress Card.

## Yugoslavia

Regular services operate along the coasts and within the coastal resort areas, but the buses are often very crowded. Buses are used primarily to fill the gaps in the rail system. Ticket reservations are recommended.

### Ferry Services

The English Channel is surely the best-known European ferry crossing among American travelers. Although most Americans think in terms of the Dover-to-Calais passage, there are actually more than a dozen individual Channel-crossing routes. In addition, there are scores of other important ferry links crisscrossing the waterways of Europe.

The following listings are meant to be representative of the services and fares available for passengers without cars on several of the more heavily traveled Channel routes. Passage across the Channel from England to France, Belgium, or the Netherlands is available as an extra-cost option on the Britrail Pass program, as is passage across the Irish Sea to Cork, Rosslare, and Dublin/Dun Laoghaire (Tables 7–9). Channel and Irish Sea crossings are not available through the Eurailpass program. Britain's Seapass program has been discontinued.

We have included Scandinavian services (Table 10) to Norway, Finland, Sweden, Denmark and Germany. Travel on many of these routes is included in Eurailpass. Finally, a listing of ferry services out of Lisbon to various points in Spain and Portugal is featured in Table 11.

**Table 7   Ferry Services: England to France, Holland, Belgium, and the Channel Islands**

| Route | Company | Time | Distance (miles) | Fare (in U.S. dollars) One way | Cabin |
|---|---|---|---|---|---|
| Cork–Le Havre | IC | 22 hr | — | $57* | 57 |
| Dover-Calais | HS | 30 min | 25 | 21–25 | N/A |
| Dover-Calais | S | 1 hr 30 | 25 | 21–25 | N/A |
| Dover-Calais | TT | 1 hr 15 | 25 | 22 | N/A |

| | | | | | |
|---|---|---|---|---|---|
| Dover-Boulogne | HS | 45 min | 30 | 21–25 | N/A |
| Dover-Boulogne | TT | 1 hr 40 | 30 | 22 | N/A |
| Dover-Boulogne | S | 1 hr 45 | 30 | 21–25 | N/A |
| Folkestone-Boulogne | S | 1 hr 45 | 31 | 21–25 | N/A |
| Folkestone-Calais | S | 1 hr 45 | 30 | 21–25 | N/A |
| Dover-Dunkirk | S | 2 hr 15 | 45 | 25 | N/A |
| Weymouth-Cherbourg | S | 4 hr 15 | 68 | 33 | INC |
| Portsmouth-Cherbourg | S | 4 hr 45 | 87 | 36 | INC |
| Folkestone-Oostende | S | 3 hr 45 | 71 | 25 | N/A |
| Newhaven-Dieppe | S | 4 hr | 74 | 32 | +15 |
| Heysham-Douglas | S | 3 hr 45 | 58 | 27 | +15 |
| Harwich–Hoek van Holland | S | 6 hr 45 | 121 | 28–40 | +6–28 |
| Dover-Oostende | S | 3 hr 30 | 71 | 25 | N/A |
| Dover-Oostende | TT | 3 hr 45 | 71 | 24 | N/A |
| Dover-Zeebrugge | TT | 4 hr | 82 | 22 | N/A |
| Felixstowe-Zeebrugge | TT | 5 hr | 110 | 26 | +32–56 |
| Portsmouth-Cherbourg | TT | 5 hr 45 | 87 | 36 | +16 |
| Portsmouth–Le Havre | TT | 5 hr 45 | 106 | 36 | +16 |
| Sheerness-Vlissingen | OL | 7 hr | 132 | 37 | +5–76 |
| Portsmouth–St. Malo | B | 9 hr | 169 | 38 | +18 |
| Portsmouth-Caen | B | 9 hr | 170 | 38 | +18 |
| Hull-Zeebrugge | NSF | 15 hr | 235 | 49–90 | INC |
| Hull-Rotterdam | NSF | 14 hr | 243 | 49–90 | INC |
| Plymouth-Roscoff | B | 6 hr | 111 | 38 | +18 |
| Plymouth-Santander | B | 24 hr | 487 | 63 | +28 |
| Poole-Cherbourg | B | 4 hr 30 | 100 | 40 | N/A |
| Portsmouth-Jersey | S | 8 hr 45 | 135 | 49 | +7–9 |
| Portsmouth-Jersey | CH | 8 hr | 135 | 43–54** | +26–60 |
| Portsmouth-Guernsey | CH | 8 hr | 135 | 43–54** | +26–60 |
| Portsmouth-Guernsey | S | 10 hr 45 | 135 | 49 | +7–9 |
| Rosslare-Cherbourg | IC | 18 hr | — | 55 | 55 |
| Rosslare–Le Havre | IC | 22 hr | — | 57 | 57 |
| St. Malo–Jersey | VA | 1 hr 35 | 20 | 25 | N/A |
| St. Malo–Guernsey | VA | 2 hr 10 | 35 | 25 | N/A |

Company abbreviations: HS—Hoverspeed; S—SeaLink; TT—Townsend Thorsen; NSF—North Sea Ferries; OL—Olau Line; B—Brittany; CH—Channel Island Ferries; VA—Vedettes Armoricaines; IC—Irish Continental

N/A—Not applicable
INC—Included
*Eurailpass may be used on this route.
**There is a $3 surcharge for a reclining chair.

NOTE: All cabin fares are add-ons to one-way fares. All fares shown above may increase by about 10 percent in 1987.

### Table 8  Ferry Services: England to Germany and Scandinavia

| Route | Company | Time | Distance (miles) | Fare (in U.S. dollars) One way | Cabin |
|---|---|---|---|---|---|
| Harwich-Hamburg | DFDS | 21 hr 30 | 417 | $ 56–72 | $ 9–57 |
| Harwich–Hoek van Holland | DFDS | 6 hr 45 | 121 | 27–39 | 6–28 |
| Newcastle-Esberg | DFDS | 19 hr | 394 | 96–105 | 15–70 |
| Newcastle-Bergen | NL | 25 hr | 456 | 70–108 | 30–85 |
| Newcastle-Stavanger | NL | 18 hr 30 | 400 | 100–152 | INC |
| Harwich-Kristiansand | FO | 23 hr | 527 | 99 | 0–66 |
| Newcastle-Gothenburg | DFDS | 26 hr | 554 | 123–128 | 15–75 |
| Harwich-Gothenburg | DFDS | 23 hr | 605 | 110–128 | 7–67 |
| Harwich-Gothenburg | FO | 23 hr | 605 | 110–128 | 7–67 |

Company abbreviations:   DFDS—Danish Ferry Services; FO—Fred Olsen Lines; NL—Norway Line

INC—Included

NOTE: All fares are for peak summer season. Cabin fares are add-ons to the normal one-way fare and include a single berth in a four-berth cabin. Harwich-Kristiansand runs mid-June to mid-August 1987 only. All fares shown above may increase by about 10 percent in 1987.

### Table 9  Ferry Services: England to Ireland

| Route | Company | Time | Distance (miles) | Fare (in U.S. dollars) One way | Cabin |
|---|---|---|---|---|---|
| Fishguard-Rosslare | S | 3 hr 30 | 60 | $37 | $ 8 |
| Holyhead–Dun Laoghaire | S | 3 hr 30 | 60 | 37 | 8 |
| Stranraer-Larne | S | 2 hr 15 | 40 | 31 | N/A |
| Cairnryan-Larne | TT | 2 hr | 37 | 18 | N/A |
| Liverpool-Belfast | BC | 9 hr | 135 | 45 | — |
| Liverpool-Dublin | BI | 8 hr 45 | 156 | 47–51 | 3–21 |
| Holyhead-Dublin | BI | 3 hr 30 | 64 | 33 | 6–28 |
| Cork-Roscoff | B | 14 hr | 240 | 57 | 36–70 |

Company abbreviations:   S—SeaLink; TT—Townsend Thorsen; B—Brittany Ferries; BC—Belfast Car Ferries; BI—B & I Lines

N/A—Not applicable

NOTE: All fares shown above may increase by about 10 percent in 1987.

**Table 10  Ferry Services: Scandinavian Routes—Norway, Finland, Sweden, Denmark, Faroe Islands and Germany**

| Route | Company | Time | Fare (in U.S. dollars) One way | Cabin |
|---|---|---|---|---|
| Stockholm-Helsinki | SI | 15 hr | $40 | $30–74 |
| Stockholm-Turku | SI | 11 hr 15 | 26 | 20–63 |
| Mariehamn-Turku | SI | 5 hr 10 | 15 | 6–34 |
| Stockholm-Mariehamn | SI | 5 hr 30 | 11 | 9–34 |
| Copenhagen-Oslo | DFDS | 10 hr 15 | 42–50 | 0–47 |
| Esbjerg-Torshavn | DFDS | 21 hr | 105–116 | 10–83 |
| Copenhagen-Malmö | HS | 2 hr | 7 | N/A |
| Frederikshavn-Oslo | DNO | 11 hr 30 | 31–117 | INC |
| Frederikshavn-Oslo | ST | 13 hr | 22–34 | 7–65 |
| Frederikshavn-Moss | ST | 7 hr | 22 | 12–25 |
| Frederikshavn-Göteborg | ST | 3 hr 15 | 14 | N/A |
| Frederikshavn-Frederikstad | DNO | 6 hr 45 | 15–22 | 8–38 |
| Frederikstad-Larvik | LL | 6 hr | 14–31 | 4–44 |
| Hirtshols-Kristiansand | FO | 5 hr 15 | 6–14 | 14–22 |
| Hanstholm-Egersand | FO | 8 hr 30 | 6–22 | INC |
| Hirtshols-Stavanger | FO | 9 hr 45 | 20 | 10–20 |
| Hirtshols-Bergen | FO | 25 hr | 248 | 10–20 |
| Oslo-Kiel | JL | 19 hr | 55 | 15–64 |
| Göteborg-Kiel | ST | 14 hr | 50 | 12–80 |
| Gedser-Travemunde | GT | 45 min | 8 | N/A |
| Helsingborg-Helsingor | GT | 55 min | 8 | N/A |
| Dragor-Limhamn | GT | 1 hr | 8 | N/A |

Company abbreviations:  DFDS—Danish Ferry Service; DNO—Da-No Linjen; FO—Fred Olsen Line; GT—GT Line; JL—Jahre Line; LL—Larvik Line; SI—Silje Line; ST—Stena Line; HS—Hoverspeed

N/A—Not applicable
INC—Included

NOTE: All fares shown above may increase by about 10 percent in 1987.

## Denmark

Buses and ferries are thoroughly integrated into the rail system operated by the DSB (Danish State Railway). Ferry tickets can be purchased at rail stations for connections with trains.

## Table 11  Ferry Services: Lisbon Routes

| Route | Company | Time | Fare (in escudos) One way | Cabin |
|---|---|---|---|---|
| Lisbon-Cacilhas | TT | 10 min | 50 | N/A |
| Lisbon–Porto Brandão | TT | 15 min | 50 | N/A |
| Lisbon-Trafaria | TT | 15 min | 50 | N/A |
| Lisbon-Seixal | TT | 20 min | 105 | N/A |
| Lisbon-Montijo | TT | 30 min | 135 | N/A |
| Lisbon-Alcocheta | CP | 40 min | 145 | N/A |
| Lisbon-Barreiro | TM | 25 min | 100 | N/A |
| Setubal-Troia | TS | 20 min | 45 | N/A |
| V. Real Sto. Antonio–Ayamonte | TR | 15 min | 47.50 | N/A |

Company abbreviations: CP—Caminhas de Ferro Portugueses; TM—Troiamar; TR—Transportes do Rio Guadiana; TS—Transado-Transportes Fluviair do Sado; TT—Trans Tejo

N/A—Not applicable

NOTE: Tickets may be purchased in books of four to twenty at a time. All fares shown above may increase by about 10 percent in 1987.

**West Germany**

River steamers operate extensively up and down the Rhine daily, and a few traverse the Moselle. Trips can be broken as desired with many pickup and drop-off points along the way. Sample fares: one way, Mainz-Cologne, DM151.80 ($75.50); round trip, Koblenz-Ruedesheim, DM67.00 ($33.30); round trip, Bonn-Koblenz, DM57.40 ($28.50). Most rail tickets can be used with a small surcharge on steamers. These supplemented tickets must be purchased at the offices of the German Rhine Line (KD), not at the railway stations.

**Great Britain**

"Island Hopscotch" tickets are available for multiroute journeys on Hebridean and Clyde ferry services. Routes vary, tickets are valid for three months without restrictions, and they are available from Caledonian MacBraye, Ltd., in Gourock, Strathclyde.

## Greece

A comprehensive ferry service operates to the Greek Islands. Timetables change every three months, and travelers are well advised to check schedules and availability a few days in advance of sailing.

## Ireland

See Table 9 for a breakdown of routes and fares. Ferries scheduled to the Aran Islands from Galway City depend on the tides; prospective passengers should check times just prior to travel. There are a variety of ferries, including one that allows a day-stop on Aran Island. Others call at each island in turn. Visitors who choose to stay on any island must spend the night to catch the next day's ferry. Fares range from $10 to $15.

## Italy

Italy enjoys an extensive ferry service—both coastal and inter-island. There is also frequent service between Brindisi, Italy, and Patras, Greece, on which the Eurailpass can be used with an $8 surcharge.

## Norway

Fast coastal boats are becoming more prevalent. Generally, it's necessary to book in advance as ferries sell out quickly. Smaller vessels that carry significant tourist traffic also operate on the lakes and inland waterways.

## Spain

Travelers planning to visit the Spanish islands may depart from the mainland using the Compañía Trasmediterránea. This national carrier has good connections from Barcelona, Valencia,

Almería, and Cádiz to the Balearic Islands and from Cádiz to the Canary Islands. The same company offers interisland services from Almería and Málaga to Melilla and from Algeciras to Ceuta and Tangiers in North Africa. Trasmediterránea also offers interisland services in the Canaries.

**Sweden**

The coastal ferries are operated by the regional transport authorities.

**Switzerland**

Regularly scheduled boats provide extensive local services among the communities that line the shores of Lake Geneva and Lake Zurich. Schedules are seasonal; fares based on distance traveled. These boats are a great way to combine local transportation and sightseeing.

**Rates and Fares**

Ferry prices provided are for foot passengers during the peak 1986 summer season. It is worth noting that foot-passenger fares differ from those charged for passengers with cars. When available, we have also included cabin rates. The rates shown are a range from lowest (one berth in four-berth cabin) to highest (deluxe cabin). Cabin rates are add-on fares to the one-way foot-passenger fares listed. If you plan on using a cabin during a ferry crossing, we suggest that you make reservations early as space sells out quickly during the peak summer season. Assessments of the various ferry lines were developed in a survey conducted by *Holiday Which?* a few years ago.

*B & I Lines* (BI)—Passenger and car ferry services from Liverpool, Pembroke, and Holyhead, England, to Rosslare and Dublin, Ireland.

*Belfast Car Ferries* (BC)—Passenger and car ferry service between Liverpool and Northern Ireland.

*Brittany Ferries* (B)—French-owned service operating several comfortable ships.

*Channel Island Ferries* (CH)—This line operates between Portsmouth and Jersey/Guernsey, Channel Islands.

*Danish Ferry Service* (DFDS)—Generally high standards on the North Sea routes.

*Da-No Linjen* (DNO)—This line operates two ships serving Oslo, Frederikshavn, and Frederikstad.

*Fred Olsen Lines* (FO)—Limited high-season service only.

*Hoverspeed* (HS)—The only Hovercraft service across the Channel. It is the fastest crossing, but more susceptible to weather problems than conventional ferries.

*Jahre Line* (JL)—This Norwegian line operates two large modern vessels.

*Larvik Line* (LL)—This line operates one large ship capable of carrying 2,000 passengers.

*North Sea Ferries* (NSF)—This line operates four ships on the long North Sea crossing. Rates include meals and berths or reclining seats. NSF will add two additional large ships in 1986.

*Norway Lines* (NL)—This line operates vessels between England and Norway.

*Olau Line* (OL)—German-owned line with two large ships providing very high levels of comfort.

*Sally Line* (SA)—New standards of service on the short crossings.

*Sealink* (S)—Joint operations involving French, Belgian, Dutch, and British. Reservations can be made through Britrail. However, services have been found to be inconsistent.

*Silja Line* (SI)—This line operates three ships between Norway and Sweden.

*Stena Line* (SL)—A Scandinavian line serving Göteborg, Frederikshavn, Oslo, and Kiel.

*Townsend Thorsen* (TT)—Overall, the best and most consistent operation of the big fleets, with reliable and efficient services on all routes.

Ferry/Waterways Representatives

To obtain information on the ferry/waterways services described in this chapter, please contact the companies below. General information on ferry services and routes may also be obtained through the various governmental tourist offices (addresses and telephone numbers are listed at the end of chapter 17).

**Bergen Lines**
505 Fifth Avenue
New York, NY 10017
212-986-2711
For DFDS Seaways, Silgi Lines, Norway Line, TOR, and Cornwall Lines

**Britrail**
630 Third Avenue
New York, NY 10019
212-682-5153
For SeaLink, Hoverspeed

**Extra Value Travel**
437 Madison Avenue, 26th Floor
New York, NY 10017
212-750-8800; 800-223-1980
For Olau Line, Adriatic Line, and Tirrenia Line

**Lynott Tours**
350 Fifth Avenue
New York, NY 10118
212-760-0101; 800-537-7575 NY state; 800-221-2474 continental U.S.
For B & I Line

**Townsend Thorsen Ferries**
P. O. Box A
Saltillo, PA 17253
800-458-3606 (except PA and AK); 814-448-3945/6
For Townsend Thorensen Ferries, Brittany Ferries, North Sea Ferries, Channel Island Ferries, GT Line, Vedettes Amoricaines, Stena Line, Karageorgis Line, Minoan Lines, and Sol Lines

# 17

# Urban Transportation

*Getting Around Town in the
Major Cities*

Your final transportation question may seem the simplest, but it may well determine—from day to day—how well you spend your time in Europe. Whether you plan to visit just one city or hope to visit a different one every day, the question remains: What's the best way to get between hotel, restaurants, and the sights you want to see? The answers naturally lead to a review of buses, streetcars, subways, and taxis in Europe's major cities.

Of course, one way to get around is to rely on organized sightseeing tours. They virtually guarantee that you'll see at least those attractions that conventional wisdom decrees you should see, without any real mental or physical effort on your part. The price you pay for this security is partly money—sightseeing excursions are among the most expensive ways of touring a city—and partly the loss of flexibility and independence. Nevertheless, tours are a viable option, especially the lower-cost tours run by the local public transit system in many major cities. If nothing else, such tours are a good way to familiarize yourself with a new city that you can later explore on your own.

The other end of the transportation spectrum is walking. Don't sell it short. Americans are so used to jumping into cars to go only a block or two that we sometimes forget how easy it is to see a place by walking through it. Most European city streets were laid out long before anyone ever thought of automobiles, and despite some heroic engineering accomplishments in roads and parking, an automobile can be more of a liability than a convenience in the historic city centers. Even if

> A detailed city map is perhaps the best single investment you can make for each city you visit. While guidebooks often contain highly stylized and simplified maps, there's no substitute for a really detailed map that shows *all* the streets, *all* the transit stops, and many of the most important buildings and sites. Good city maps will rarely cost more than a few dollars and are available at almost any newsstand, bookstore, or information bureau. You might also pick up a current transit map—usually free at transit stations—that will highlight the routes and stations better than a detailed street map.

you're touring by rented car, you may find it easier and cheaper to leave your car parked and get around the city on foot.

If you want to see as much as you can in a limited time, consider a do-it-yourself taxi tour. Find a driver with reasonably good English (if you don't speak the country's language) and tell him or her what you want to see. Taxis in most of Europe are considerably less expensive than American taxis. In fact, two people usually see more in less time, and at less cost, by sharing a taxi than by buying two tickets on a commercial tour bus.

But neither walking, on the one hand, nor tour buses and taxi tours, on the other, are really a complete intracity transportation solution for most travelers. Many of the things you want to see are too far to walk, and the cost of all-day taxis and tours can add up to more than many want to pay. So you'll get around the city the way most Europeans do: on their generally excellent local and regional transit systems.

The following information was developed primarily through contacts at various local tourist offices within each city covered or with the national tourist bureaus based in New York City and London. It provides a general overview of the public transportation systems—and costs—in Europe's major cities, plus a few comments based on first-hand observation and use of these systems by foreign visitors. The information here should be used for trip planning and budgeting. No guidebook of this type can substitute for the detailed fare data, schedule information, and system maps that travelers should acquire as soon as they arrive in each new city. For example, although only regular adult transit fares and special tickets designed for tourists are cited here, many of the systems offer special reductions for children and seniors. These and other details should be checked on arrival.

Unlike the rest of this book, public transportation charges are quoted in local currency only. Regardless of what happens to exchange rates, these fares and ticket costs will remain reasonably stable in local value. Besides, if you're going to be riding around with the locals, you might as well start thinking in terms of the local money. While no general increase in transportation prices is forecast, rates could still rise about 10 percent in 1987.

**Amsterdam**
**Bus/Streetcar/Metro/Taxi**

Streetcars are the backbone of Amsterdam's transit system; most routes begin and end at the Amsterdam Central Station. The city has a zone-fare system, with tickets in strip form called *strippenkarte*. The *strippenkarte* is valid on the entire municipal transport system (buses, streetcars, and metro).

The best value is the fifteen-strip card, available for purchase *only* at the Central Railway Station and other GVB (public transport) outlets. The six-strip tickets can be purchased on the buses and trams or in the metro stations. The ten- and fifteen-strip tickets can be stamped at time of purchase for immediate use. The fifteen-strip tickets can also be overstamped to provide for unlimited one day's use.

Unlimited-use passes—called Rover tickets—can be purchased for periods of one, three, and seven days. Special multiperson Rover tickets are also available. Tickets must be validated, usually by a *stampel* machine, and a DFl26 fine is assessed for those who ignore the regulation.

Streetcar service ends at midnight, when a night bus service takes over. A map of all systems is available from the Transit Office, opposite the Railroad Station, for DFl2.50. English-language public-transport information can be obtained by calling 272727.

The Schiphol Line, which is an intercity train line, operates between Schiphol Airport and the city. There is also service to The Hague and Central Station from the airport.

Boats are good for initial sightseeing tours of the canals, but are generally not recommended for getting around the city.

Taxis are normally hailed at cabstands. Taxis are also dispatched from 777777.

Costs in Dutch guilders ($1 is about 2.30 guilders):

*Strippenkarte*: ten-strip, 8.40; adult fifteen-strip, 8.45; child fifteen-strip, 4.05

Day in Amsterdam Ticket (one-day pass good on all modes of public transit): 8.40

Rover Ticket (covers bus, streetcar, and metro journeys): First Class one-day, about 7.20; three-day, about 15.75; seven-day, about 20.90

Taxi: per kilometer, 2.17 (in city); 2.38 (to points outside city and night rate); pickup charge, 3.60; maximum of four persons per taxi; no charge for luggage

From downtown Amsterdam to airport:

Taxi: 40–45

KLM bus: 8

Regular bus (routes #143, #144, #145): 7.50

Intercity train (Schiphol Line): 2.60

*Comment*: The Netherlands Board of Tourism is offering two new cards designed for tourists: the Holland Leisure Card and the Holland Culture Card. Both are available from the Netherlands Board of Tourism offices.

The Holland Leisure Card costs $7.50 and is valid for one year. It comes with a voucher book that includes a 55 percent discount on a first-class Day Pass for unlimited travel by rail, bus, streetcar, and metro throughout the country; a 30 percent discount on domestic air flights on NLM CityHopper planes; a 25 percent discount on car rentals; a 25 percent discount on 12 sightseeing excursions by motorcoach and/or boat; 20 to 50 percent discounts on admission tickets to 18 tourist attractions in the Netherlands; a 10 percent discount on the National Museum Card, which gives free entry to 250 museums; a 10 percent reduction on purchases at department stores and at the Amsterdam Diamond Center; free admission to Holland's four casinos; a free drink at any of the 30 Romantic Restaurants throughout the country; and no reservation fee when booking for theater, opera, or ballet performances through the VVV (tourist offices).

The Holland Culture Card is an upgraded version of the

Leisure Card, costs $15.00, and is valid for one year. Besides including all of the discounts of the Leisure Card, it also gives free access to all the museums and galleries at which the National Museum Card is honored.

### Athens
### Bus/Metro/Taxi

Athens Urban Lines operates forty bus routes. Buses run twenty hours a day between 5:00 AM and 1:00 AM. Buses are very crowded during the four daily rush hours, normally between 7:00 AM and 9:00 AM, 1:00 PM and 2:00 PM, 5:00 PM and 6:00 PM, and 9:00 PM and 10:00 PM. The fare is 30 drachma. There are also fourteen yellow trolley-bus routes operating between 5:00 AM and midnight.

There is only one metro line, linking the port of Piraeus with the suburb of Kifissia, and running through the center of the city. It operates from 5:30 AM to midnight.

Taxis are relatively cheap in relation to other cities in Europe, but increases are expected for the summer of 1987.

Costs in Greek drachma ($1 is about 140 drachma):
Bus: fare, 30
Metro: maximum fare in either direction for city center, 30
Taxi: per kilometer, 20; pickup charge, 25
From downtown Athens to airport:
Taxi: 500–750
Bus: 60

### Barcelona
### Bus/Metro/Taxi

The metro operates between 5:00 AM and 11:00 PM Monday through Friday. On Saturdays, Sundays, and holidays it runs till 1:00 AM. Bus service begins about 5:30 AM daily. Buses begin their last runs at approximately 10:30 PM, although a few lines operate until 1:00 AM. Check the schedules posted at individual bus stops. Special tickets may be purchased that are valid on both the bus and metro.

Taxis circulate at all hours. Extras are charged for luggage, pets, trips to the bullfights, or night service. The color of the

taxi is different from those of Madrid. Vacant taxis have a *Libre* (or "free") sign or an illuminated green light, or both.
Costs in pesetas ($1 is about 136 pesetas):
Bus: 45 (flat fare); ten-ride book, 350
Metro: 50 (flat fare)
Taxi: per kilometer, 27; pickup charge, 60
From downtown Barcelona to airport:
Taxi: per kilometer, 25; pickup charge, 60
Bus: 45 (flat fare)

**Berlin**
**Metro/Bus/Taxi**

Berlin has one of the world's most efficient metro systems, which is operated by the BVG (Berlin Metropolitan Transport). The *U-Bahn* now has nine branch lines. Tickets are valid from one end of the city to the other and provide free transfers on the *U-Bahn*, on three *S-Bahn* routes (the suburban metro services), and any of the eighty-one bus routes. The *U-Bahn* and *S-Bahn* are closed between 1:00 AM and 4:00 AM Monday through Friday, and from 2:00 AM to 4:00 AM Saturday.

Tourist tickets provide unlimited use of bus and metro services. They are available for either two- or four-day periods. The Unlimited use tickets can be purchased at the BVG offices at either Kleistpark metro station or the Zoo. Rover tickets good for twenty-four hours can be bought, but note that they are validated by date rather than time of purchase. Buy them in the morning, if possible, for maximum value.

The *U-Bahn* also operates in East Berlin on somewhat limited routes; the trains are not quite up to the standards of West Berlin. The cost of entry into East Berlin is 5DM plus a compulsory exchange of at least 25DM for East German marks, which will not be reexchanged upon leaving. All travel into East Germany must be cleared in advance through the Travel Agency of East Germany at DER-Zeisbura Direktion Berlin Augsburger Str. 27 1000, Berlin 30; tel.: 240121.

Tourists on one-day visas are not allowed to leave the city limits and must return to the West before midnight by the same checkpoint by which they entered.

Taxis may be hailed in the streets or found at cabstands. Taxi travel into East Berlin is possible on special request basis. To have a taxi dispatched, call 2458085 or 261026.

Costs in Deutschmarks ($1 is about DM2.00):
Bus and metro: 2.20 (city-center trip)
24-hour Rover ticket: 9.00
Tourist ticket: two-day, 15.00; four-day, 30; children under fourteen: two-day, 16; four-day, 20
Taxi: per kilometer, 1.58 (6:00 AM to midnight); pickup charge, 3.40; 1.69 (midnight to 6:00 AM); to East Berlin (special request), 40–50, depending on arrangement with the driver
From downtown West Berlin to airport:
Taxi: 15–20
Bus: 2.20

**Brussels**
**Bus/Streetcar/Metro/Taxi**

This Belgian capital is a crossroads for visiting Bruges, Antwerp, Ghent, and Tournai.

The majority of public transport is handled by the S.T.I.B. (Société des Transports Intercommunaux Bruxellois). It consists of a network of 20 kilometers of metro lines that connect the east and west quarters of the city and is augmented by three pre-metro lines (tramways and tunnels). The metro offers clean and efficient service, costing about 15 percent of an equivalent taxi ride.

Trams and buses are yellow and stop at red-and-white or blue-and-white signs. At stops marked *sur demande*, raise your hand for the bus to stop.

The S.T.I.B. system operates from 6:00 AM to midnight. Maps of the system are available from the Tourist Information Office (T.I.B.) at rue Marché aux Herbes/Grasmarkt 61 (tel.: 02-512-30-30); or in Part B of the Brussels Yellow Pages. Transfers are free if requested when the ticket is purchased. A tourist ticket called the Twenty-four-hour Ticket gives the user unlimited travel on all modes of S.T.I.B. transportation in and around Brussels, including the orange buses of the S.N.C.V. (Société Nationale des Chemins de Fer).

Local train service is handled by the S.N.C.B. (Société Nationale des Chemins de Fer Belges), which operates five large train stations in greater Brussels. These trains serve the airport with frequent service throughout the day from the Gare Centrale and the Gare du Nord stations. Information can be obtained by calling 219-26-50.

Taxis are plentiful, but relatively expensive. They must be hired from any designated taxi rank. The tip is included in the fare.

Costs in Belgian francs ($1 is about 42 Belgian francs):

S.T.I.B.: single ticket (called "direct"), 30; card for five journeys, 130; card for ten journeys, 200
24-hour ticket: 140
Taxi: per kilometer, 26.50 in town, 54 out of town; pickup charge, 55
From downtown Brussels to the airport:
Taxi: 700–800
Train: 95 (first class); 65 (second class)
Bus: (route #358): 37

**Copenhagen**
**Bus/Train/Taxi**

The Central Station is the terminus for intercity rail lines, and suburban electric S-trains link it with local stations within the metropolitan area. Sightseeing is easy on foot.

Bus is the main means of transport within the city. All routes go through the city center; fares are cheap. Local buses and S-trains start at 5:00 AM (6:00 AM on Sundays), and last services are around 1:00 AM. Buses and railways are run on a collective fare system. All tickets and discount cards are good for a full hour of travel within defined zones. Prepayment is not obligatory, but tickets should be stamped once on board. Tourist tickets can account for big savings. English-language information is available at the Transport Agency on tel.: 1-141701 or 1-951701, twenty-four hours a day, and at the Tourist Information Office, tel.: 1-111325.

Taxis are fast and efficient. Prices are less than major U.S. and European cities. Tips are included in the meter price. A taxi to the airport is about six times the price of the official airport bus (operated by SAS). In normal traffic, the taxi trip to the airport takes about fifteen minutes. Taxis can be telephoned at 1-353535.

The airport bus operates from Copenhagen Central Station at twenty-minute intervals. Late at night, the bus meets arriving and departing aircraft only. The trip takes thirty minutes.

Costs in Danish Krone ($1 is about 7.6 Krone):

Tourist ticket, known as the Copenhagen Card: one-day, 60; two-day, 110; three-day, 150
Bus: minimum fare, 6 (with one-hour time limit; also applies to S-train); maximum fare, 18 (with 2.5-hour time limit)
Taxi: per kilometer, 7.15; pickup charge, 12
From downtown Copenhagen to airport:
Taxi to airport: 80
SAS bus to airport: 18

### Dublin
**Bus/Train/Taxi**

Most Dublin bus routes pass through the city center. City buses are double-deckers, in contrast with single-height long-distance buses. Fares are payable once you're seated; exact fares are not required. Fare structures are based on stages (a measure of distance along the route). Information may be obtained by telephone at 787777 from C.I.E. Tours, which operates all public transport in Dublin. Bus and rail timetables are available at newsstands.

Daily, weekly, and monthly Rover passes for unlimited travel on the city's bus and rail network are available from C.I.E. on O'Connell Street. A photograph is required for the weekly and monthly pass to be issued. C.I.E. also operates the airport buses, which leave from the central bus station and make a circuit of the larger hotels in Dublin.

There are many taxi stands, especially near major hotels. Taxis hired at stands, hotels, and the airport will charge for pickup. Taxis may also be hailed in the street, in which case there is no pickup charge.

Costs in Irish punts ($1 is about .74 punts):
Bus: 1–3 stages, 0.45; 4–7 stages, 0.55; 8–12 stages, 0.65; 12 or more stages, 0.80; one-day pass, adult 2.70, child (under sixteen) 1.35, family (two adults with up to four children) 3.75

Weekly passes: adult 9, family 17; monthly passes: adult 35

Taxi: per kilometer, 0.75; pickup charge, 1.05 (at taxi stands or airport only); extras: 0.40 per kilometer for each additional adult or for two children under ten; 0.40 added for evening rates between 8:00 PM and 8:00 AM; minimum fare: 1.80

From downtown Dublin to the airport:
Taxi: 10–12 (two persons plus luggage), plus 1.85 pickup charge

C.I.E. airport bus: adult 2.50, child 1.50
Regular bus (route #41, from Quay with stops): adult .80, child .45

**Edinburgh
Bus/Taxi**

This city is probably best explored on foot because most sights are in the immediate vicinity of the main artery—Princes Street.

Most bus routes include Princes Street stops. All require exact fare and issue tickets upon boarding. Bus fares as stated are for services on the Lothian Regional Transport (LRT), which operates within the old City of Edinburgh boundaries. Services to adjoining towns (within the new Greater Edinburgh environs, e.g. Musselburgh) are operated by the Scottish Bus Group.

The Touristcard incorporates three discount vouchers for use on sightseeing tours, unlimited travel on city bus services for two to thirteen days, and special discounts at tourist attractions and restaurants.

The Edinburgh Freedom Ticket is valid for one-day's unlimited travel within the old city on LRT buses. Other special fares are also available. Touristcards, Freedom Tickets, or Ridacards can be purchased at the Ticket Centre on Waverly Bridge (tel. 031-226-5087) or the LRT office at 14 Queen Street.

Taxis can be taken from cabstands at St. Andrews Square Bus Station and the Waverly Street Station.

Taxi and tourist information is available from the Edinburgh Tourist Office at tel. 557-2727. For bus information call LRT at tel. 554-4494.

Costs in UK pounds ($1 is about .70 pounds):

Bus: minimum, .15; maximum, .50 (limited-stop bus has flat fare of .40)

Touristcard: adult, two-day, 8.60; three-day, 9.70; four-day, 10.80; five-day, 11.90; six-day, 13.00; seven-day, 14.10; thirteen-day, 20.70; child, two-day, 5.55; three-day, 6.10; four-day, 6.65; five-day, 7.20; six-day, 7.75; seven-day, 8.30; thirteen-day, 11.60

Freedom Ticket, valid for calendar day: adult, 1.25; child, .65

Ridacard tickets, valid Sunday to Saturday: two-week ticket, 9.40; four-week ticket, 16
Taxi: per kilometer, .40; pickup charge, .70; evening hours, .30 additional
From downtown Edinburgh to airport:
Taxi: 10
Bus: 1.65

### Florence
**Bus/Taxi**

It's possible to see all the major sights in Florence on foot, although traffic noise and congestion can make this less than a pleasant choice at times. Bus fares are cheap, and tickets can be purchased at newsstands, tobacconists, and bars. Tickets should be purchased in advance, and you should be sure to validate your ticket onboard the bus with the automatic punch machine. Severe fines can be imposed for nonvalidation. Bus service is complicated by one-way streets—outbound and return trips often take different routes.

Taxis may be hailed, but there are taxi stands in the main piazzas. There are extra charges for night service, Sundays, public holidays, luggage, and journeys outside the city. Fares are normally rounded off to the nearest 500 lire by a tip.

Costs in lire ($1 is about 1,300 to 1,500 lire):
Bus: single ticket, 600; four tickets, 1,450; eight tickets, 2,900.
City tour (on route #7 bus): 800.
Taxi: per kilometer, not available.

### Frankfurt
**Bus/Metro/Streetcar/Taxi/Train**

Metropolitan transport in Frankfurt is operated by the FVV *(Frankfurter Verkehrs und Tarifverbund)*. Metros, commuter trains, buses, and streetcars are operated by regions or zones with uniform tariffs that include transfers. Tickets are sold in blue automats (ticket machines), which take only coins. No tickets are sold on board the trains and streetcars. Bus drivers do, however, sell tickets. Downtown Frankfurt is within Zone 1 (yellow). There is a slight increase in ticket prices during rush hours (6:30 AM–8:30 AM; 4:00 PM–6:30 PM). FVV information may be obtained at Mannheimer Strasse 15-19, tel: 269462 or 269463. Tourist information is available at tel.: 2128849.

Buses and streetcars *(stadtbus* and *strassenbahn)* are cheap, and they travel to all parts of the city and most of the suburbs. The metro *(S-bahn* and *U-bahn)* Eurailpasses are valid on the *S-bahn*, which is operated by the national railway, but not on the *U-bahn*, which is operated by the metropolitan transit. Eurailpass travelers should be sure to take trains on which their passes are valid whenever possible.

*S-bahn* and GermanRail intercity trains operate frequently from a station in the lower level of the Frankfurt airport to downtown Frankfurt, Mainz, Wiesbaden, Cologne, Bonn, Dusseldorf, and via connections to all major German cites in the Federal Republic.

Taxis can also be hailed in the street, and most telephone booths have radio taxi call numbers posted (tel.: 230001, 250001, 230033, or 545011). Taxis operate twenty-four hours a day with the same rates throughout. The price on the meter is the inclusive price, regardless of how many passengers are in the cab or how many pieces of luggage are transported.

Costs in Deutschmarks ($1 is about DM2.00):
Bus and metro: Zone 1, 1.50 (2.10 in rush hours); children (four–fifteen years old): Zone 1, .80 (1.10 in rush hours); twenty-four-hour pass: Zone 1, 7.00; children, 3.50
Taxi: per kilometer, 1.60; pickup charge, 3.60
From downtown Frankfurt to airport:
Taxi: 30
Bus (route #61): 3.10; 4.20 (rush hours)
Train (S14, S15): 3.10; 4.20 (rush hours)

**Geneva**
**Bus/Streetcar/Taxi**

Geneva has an efficient system of public transport run by the TPG (Geneva Transport), with stations at the Cornavin Main Railway Station and Place Bel Air. Buses and streetcars run throughout the city into the outlying villages. Tickets for buses and streetcars should be purchased before entry from the automatic vending machines that are situated at boarding points. It is not necessary to show your ticket unless asked to do so. However, it is illegal and subject to fine to board a bus or tram without a ticket. Bus and streetcar service ends at midnight daily.

There are basically two types of tickets available in Geneva—City Network and Country Network. City Network tickets are available from ordinary vending machines and are good for journeys within the city. These tickets are also sold by about 175 agents throughout the city, usually tobacconists. Country Network tickets are sold by conductors for trips to the outskirts of Geneva. Prices depend on the distance traveled.

Taxis in Geneva, as in Zurich, are among the more expensive in Europe. Taxis may be hailed in the streets if they are more than 50 meters from a cabstand. Or, you may call for a taxi at tel.: 141-TAXIPHONE. When taxis are cruising for hire, they show two lights if available for hire and charging the city rate, or one light if available and charging the country rate (outside city).

Costs in Swiss francs ($1 is about SFr1.70):

Bus and streetcar:

City Network ticket, three stops (no change of vehicle); one-hour, 1.20 (change of vehicle or route allowed); two-hour, 2.40; ten-day unlimited travel, 30; twenty-day unlimited travel, 45

Multijourney discount tickets are available at rail stations and range in price from 4.50 to 6.50

Country Network ticket, one-day, 5.00; one-day, child, 2.50; ten-day unlimited travel, 38; twenty-day unlimited travel, 57

Taxi: per kilometer, 2 (city rate); 3.50 (country rate); pickup charge, 5; holiday/evening rates, 2.50

From downtown Geneva to airport:
Taxi: 20
Bus (from rail station): 5
City bus (route #10): 1.20

**Helsinki**
**Streetcar/Bus/Metro/Taxi**

Helsinki features a special streetcar (route #3T) specifically designated for sightseeing. It can be boarded anywhere on its route and provides an extensive tour of the business and residential areas of the city. It features a taped commentary in English about the sights of the city.

Helsinki has just opened a brand-new subway system. Tickets are interchangeable on all modes of transportation.

Special transport offers include a ten-strip ticket and the Helsinki Card, which provides unlimited transportation plus free admission to some museums, free desserts at some restaurants, and gifts at some department stores.

Costs in Finnish marks ($1 is about 4.90 Finnmarks):

Bus and streetcar: minimum fare in city center, 6; ten-ride strip, 45

Helsinki Card: one-day, 55 (includes free sightseeing tour by bus); two-day, 75; three-day, 90

Children's Helsinki Card (ages four–twelve): one-day, 30; two-day, 35; three-day, 45

Taxi: per kilometer, not available; pickup charges: 9.60 (Helsinki central); 8.60 (metropolitan area Helsinki); evening rates: 4 extra

From downtown Helsinki to airport:

Taxi: 100

Airport bus: 11 (from/to the Hotel InterContinental)

Bus (route #614): 8.50 (from platform #45 at Coach Station)

Streetcar: 8.50

## Lisbon
**Bus/Streetcar/Funicular/Metro/Taxi/Train**

Information on municipal transport fares and schedules may be obtained from the Transit Information Office next to the Santa Justa Elevator (inclined railway) near Rua do Carmo (tel. 327944). For English-language tourist information call tel. 367031.

Bus and streetcar fares depend on the number of zones crossed. Tickets for buses and streetcars can be purchased either on board or in advance *(Modulus)*, at a slight discount. Books of ten and twenty tickets are offered. A tourist ticket good for either four or seven days allows travel on all municipal transport. These tourist passes can be bought at booths marked *Carris* in transit stations between 8:00 AM and 8:00 PM.

Lisbon's subway (metro) is clean and fast. Rossio and Restauradores are the main stations on the line. The streetcars are not the fastest mode of transportation, but they offer some good sightseeing routes into the hills out of the city center. Trains are your best choice for travel to outlying areas and the coastal resorts.

Taxis, which can be hailed or picked up at a stand, are metered and inexpensive in the city. But for trips outside the city, you must pay a set rate per kilometer going to your destination plus the price of the return journey, whether or not you actually make it.

Costs in escudos ($1 is about 150 escudos):

Bus: one zone, 27.50; two to four zones, 55; five or more zones, 85; express bus (limited stops), 85; ten-ticket book, 375 (all three zones); twenty-ticket book, 375.

Bus *Modulus:* one zone, 18.75; two to four zones, 37.50; five or more zones, 56.25

Streetcar: one zone, 27.50; two or more zones, 55; ticket purchased from driver, 67.50; ten-ticket book, 375; twenty-ticket book, 750

Streetcar *Modulus:* one zone, 18.75; two or more zones, 37.50

Subway: one ticket, 35 (if purchased at selling machine, 32.50); ten-ticket book, 272.50

Santa Justa Elevator and Funicular cars: 17 per ride

Tourist ticket (unlimited travel on *all* modes of municipal transport): four-day, 740; seven-day, 1,025

Taxi: per kilometer, 29; pickup charge *(bandeirada)*, 66; evening fares, add 20 percent; 50 percent surcharge for luggage to airport

From downtown Lisbon to the airport:

Taxi: 500

Green Line *(Linha Verde)* bus: 170 (preferred)

Regular Bus (route #44 and 45): 85.00

Comment: Since very few buses or streetcars have conductors, it's advisable to buy your ticket in advance.

**London**
**Bus/Underground/Taxi**

London enjoys a reasonably efficient municipal transport system, although it is not as integrated as in other cities. This is now changing as the London Regional Transport (LRT) takes over from the Greater London Authority with the goal of fully integrating the transport system. At present, there is integration with Britrail.

The Greater London area is divided into zones. The cheapest bus fare in the central zone (which encompasses most of the sights) is 30 pence (for journeys of up to three-quarters of a mile). Besides the central zone, there are the inner zone and three concentric outer zones.

Most regular bus routes end operations at midnight when a less extensive night bus service comes on duty. Methods of payment vary on buses; some require exact fare. Tickets should always be retained for inspection.

A similar zone system works on the Underground, with the minimum fare of 50 pence. The Underground covers almost all of the Greater London area except the southeast, which is served by Britrail.

Bus tickets and Underground tickets are not interchangeable, although London Explorer and Travelcards are valid for both.

The London Explorer ticket—available at all Underground stations and at Travel Information centers throughout London—is an unlimited pass good within the London area. Besides unlimited travel on both London Regional Transport red buses and the Underground, it also offers discounts on some sightseeing and includes the fare on the Airbus to any of the three international airports serving London. The usual price of a one-day Explorer is £3.50, but the cost decreases to £2 if you buy it after 10 AM. London Explorer cards can also be purchased for three, four, and seven days. In addition to unlimited travel, the visitor receives a miniguide to London's best known attractions plus a selection of discounts off tours and admissions to places of interest. In the United States, the London Explorer card can be purchased from Britrail.

For tourists staying in London more than a few days, Travelcards are a good value. They are zonal and can be used at any time. A current photo is required. A seven-day all-zones Travelcard is cheaper than the Explorer for the same period, but does not include the Airbus. Travelcards can be bought at any Underground station and are available in various time increments: seven days, one month, three months, and one year. Off-peak Travelcards, which are valid after morning rush hour (9:30 AM), are good for one-day travel on the bus and Underground.

The Capitalcard is a variant on the Travelcard. This pass also includes travel on Britrail, which may be worth having if you plan to do any sightseeing or traveling south of the River

Thames. There, the Underground service is minimal and Britrail service is extensive. The Capitalcard also allows use of the North London Link circumferential railway from Richmond to the East End. The Capitalcard can be purchased at any Underground station or British Railroad ticket office.

Other discount tickets include a one-day bus pass good for unlimited travel on buses outside central London; the Golden Rover Ticket, which is valid on all Green Line coaches and London Country buses after 9:00 AM Monday through Friday and anytime on weekends for one day. The Golden Rover ticket is not valid on the Green Line Jet Link; a seven-day Golden Rover Ticket is also available.

Another way to get around to the attractions in London is the London Pride Culture Bus. It passes close by all the major tourist sights in the downtown area, and ticket holders can get on and off the bus at will at more than twenty points along its route. Tickets are sold for one- and three-day periods. For information, in the United States telephone: 800-458-3606, or in London: 01-629-4999.

Taxi rates are higher after 8:00 PM and on holidays, weekends, and public holidays. All regular London cabs (painted black) are metered, and a 10 percent tip is normal. Fares are based on the combination of time plus distance. Taxis can be hailed in the street, at a cabstand, or by telephone (Radio Call) at 272-3030, 272-0272, and 286-0286. London cab drivers are trained and experienced in using the shortest, cheapest routes. They should know every street and building in the London area. Vacant taxis display an illuminated "Taxi" light on the front. Always check that the cab is a licensed "Hackney Carriage" with a number on the back, as unscrupulous drivers may try to pick you up at the airports or railway stations and grossly overcharge you for a trip.

A new type of taxi was introduced in 1986. These new cabs are maroon and look much like Land-Rovers. They are able to accommodate persons in wheelchairs.

Costs in U.K. pounds sterling and pence ($1 is about .70 pounds sterling):

Bus: minimum central fare, 30 pence; Red Arrow limited-stop bus, 40 pence (operates on a few city-center routes); one-day bus pass, 60 pence (for inner or outer zones); £1.20 (for both zones)

Underground: minimum central-zone fare, 50 pence

London Explorer ticket (includes both bus and Underground): one-day, adult £3.50, child £1.30; three-day, adult £9, child £3; four-day, adult £11.50, child £3.50; seven-day, adult £16, child £4

Travelcards (seven days): £4.80 (central zone); £5.60 (two-zones); £8.40 (three zones); £11.20 (four zones), £14 (all five zones); children (ages six–fifteen): £1.50 (two zones), £2.20 (three zones), £3 for four zones, off-peak Travelcards (one-day): £2 (five zones), £1.70 (four zones)

Capitalcards (seven days): £6.50 (any two adjoining zones); £16 (all zones)

One-day bus pass: 60 pence (travel in either inner or outer zone), £1.20 (travel in both inner and outer zone)

Golden Rover ticket: one-day, adult £3.75, child £1.88

London Pride Culture Bus: one-day, adult £3.50, child £2 (ages five–fifteen); three-day, adult £8 and child £5. Hours of operation: 9:20 AM–6:00 PM.

Taxi: for first 976.58 meters (1,068 yards), 80 pence; 20 pence for each additional 488.29 meters (534 yards) or for each 1 minute 48 seconds until the fare exceeds 4.40; 20 pence thereafter for each 325.53 meters (356 yards) or 1 minute, 12 seconds.

From central London to Heathrow (15 miles):
Taxi: £20–22
Airbus (London Regional Transit): £3
    Route #A1 serves Victoria Station (SW central)
    Route #A2 serves Paddington Station (NW central)
MiniBus (Airliner): £6; Tel.: 01-759-4741
Underground: £1.50
From central London to Gatwick (29 miles):
Taxi: £35
MiniBus (Airliner): £8; tel.: 01-759-4741
Bus (Green Line route #777): £2.25
From central London to Stansted (34 miles):
Taxi: £26
Train: £3.70 (second class)
Bus (Green Line route #799): £2.25

**Luxembourg**
**Bus/Taxi**

The National Tourism Office is located at B.P. 1001, 1010 Luxembourg; tel. 48-79-99.

Cost in Luxembourg francs ($1 is about 42.00 Luxembourg francs):
Bus: 25
Taxi: per kilometer, 19; waiting time, 6.25; evening fares, add 10 percent
From downtown Luxembourg to airport (6 kilometers):
Taxi: 400
Luxair bus: 100; children under twelve free
Bus: 50 (including one piece of luggage)

**Madrid**
**Bus/Metro/Taxi**

Madrid has an excellent, inexpensive bus system. Routes are marked at each bus stop. Microbuses, which operate in addition to regular buses over the same routes, are slightly more expensive but are more comfortable. Special tickets include a ten-ride and a morning ticket, which if purchased before 9:00 AM is valid for a free return journey anytime on the same day on the same route.

The subway system has ten lines all clearly marked on color-coded metro maps posted in the stations. Tickets may be purchased from booths or machines and are inserted into automatic turnstyles as the rider enters the system. Do not discard your ticket until the end of your trip! Special tickets include a three-day and five-day pass that includes unlimited travel.

Taxis are no longer the bargain that they once were. Fares are based on time and distance. There are also four different surcharges that may be added to the meter reading (for trips to the stations or bullring, luggage, and holidays). Few city rides exceed 700 pesetas. Metered taxis in Madrid are white with a red diagonal line (in other cities in Spain the taxi color varies). Vacant taxis have a *libre* (or "free") sign, or an illuminated green light, or both.

Besides taxis, there are also public service cars known as *gran tourismos*. Rates are higher than regular taxis, and these cars have no meters; negotiate with the driver prior to your journey.

Costs in pesetas ($1 is about 136 pesetas):
Bus: 45 (flat fare); ten-ride book, 350
Subway: 50 (flat fare); twenty-ride book, 550; three-day ticket, 350; five-day ticket, 550
Taxi: per kilometer, 27 (pickup charge, 60)

From downtown Madrid to airport:
Taxi: 1,000–1,200
Bus: 150 (special airport bus does not accept tourist tickets)

**Milan**
**Bus/Streetcar/Subway/Taxi**

Bus and streetcar service connects most parts of a spread-out city. Tickets are sold at newsstands, tobacconists, and special kiosks. Purchase your ticket in advance, and take care to have the ticket validated on board. There are severe fines for non-validated tickets. Tickets are good for a maximum seventy-five-minute ride.

The subway, called *Metropolitana Milanese*, is cheap, fast, and generally clean. The Duomo Station is the main central stop. Bus and subway tickets are not interchangeable.

Taxis can either be hailed or met at cabstands. A 400 lire surcharge per kilometer is added at night, and a 500 lire surcharge is collected on Sundays and public holidays. There are also extra charges for luggage and for journeys outside the city.

Costs in lire ($1 is about 1,300 to 1,500 lire):
Bus, streetcar, or subway: 600 (unlimited travel for seventy-five minutes) for a single ticket
Taxi: per kilometer, 450; pickup charge, 1,500
From downtown Milan to Linate Airport (domestic travel):
Taxi: 20,000
Bus: 1,700
From downtown Milan to Malpensa International Airport:
Taxi: 30,000
Bus: 6,000

**Munich**
**Bus/Streetcar/Metro/Train/Taxi**

Munich has an integrated public transport system that operates the buses, streetcars, *U-* and *S-bahns*. Tickets can be obtained from blue dispensers (automats) at stations and streetcar stops, and from those vehicles marked with a white-and-green *K* sign. Only a canceled ticket is valid for travel. Automatic canceling machines are identified by a large *E* on a yellow background.

The tariff is calculated by a system of circular zones. Fares are based on the number of zones passed through to reach your destination. Fare structures can be complicated. There are three main regions indicated throughout the system by colors—dark blue (city center), light blue (downtown fringe), and green (outer Munich); and within these larger regions are smaller zones. On buses and streetcars, a succession of single-fare tickets can become quite expensive, so it's a better idea to use a blue-strip ticket (*streifenkarte,* or tourist ticket). Two strips must be canceled for each ride (minimum fare), which will take the user anywhere inside the extended city area. For short rides within the city-center area (dark blue on transit maps), use a short-trip card—*kurzstreckenkarte.* It is also valid for travel between fare stages. A twenty-four-hour ticket is also available and is valid for unlimited travel on the *S-bahn, U-bahn,* and all public transportation. It must be signed before it is used, and the user must carry his or her passport. There are two types—one for use in the blue zones and one for use in the blue and green zones. GermanRail and Eurailpasses can be used on the *S-bahn.*

The subway, or *U-bahn,* covers an extensive area throughout the city. Lines extend to all outlying districts. Its major crossing points are Marienplatz, the main connecting station for the surface suburban railway—*S-bahn*—that runs east and west, and Hauptbahnhof, the station from which the airport buses depart. These buses operate from 5:00 AM to 9:00 PM daily, with departures every fifteen minutes. Later buses operate on demand. The ride takes twenty minutes.

Taxis are expensive.

Costs in Deutschmarks ($1 is about DM2):

Bus and streetcar: single ride in city center, 2.30; short trip in city center, 1.60; twenty-four-hour ticket, 6.50; three-strip ticket, 5; seven-strip ticket, 6.50; thirteen-strip ticket, 12

Taxi: per kilometer, 1.70; pickup charge, 2.90; luggage (per piece), 0.50

From downtown Munich to airport:
Taxi: 25
Bus: 5

## Oslo
**Bus/Streetcar/Taxi/Train**

The area of the National Theatre gives easy access to all forms of public transportation—most routes on most systems pass it at some point. The central spine of the city is the pedestrian mall, Karl Johans Gate, which runs from the Central Station to the Royal Palace. However, many of the sights of Oslo are outside the city center, requiring use of public transport. A Tourist Information Center is located at the City Hall building.

The purchase of single tickets can be an expensive way to travel around the city. The twenty-four-hour pass, ten-trip ticket, Universal Card, and the Oslo Card are better values.

The tourist card, known as the Oslo Card, features unlimited travel on the *Oslo Sporveier* and *Norges Statsbaners* commuter trains. Included in the ticket price are discounts at restaurants, car and bicycle rentals, sightseeing, and free admission to various museums. The Oslo Card may be purchased at the Tourist Information Center.

Taxis may be summoned by dialing 38-80-90, or they may be found at taxi stands. They may also be hailed on the street, but not within 100 meters (328 feet) of a cabstand. Taxis for a prearranged pickup should be contacted an hour before required.

Costs in Norwegian kroner ($1 is about 7.6 kroner):

Bus, streetcar, subway, suburban/commuter train, ferries: single ticket, 9 (not transferable); *Miniflerreisekort* (four coupons and the right to change), 30; *Flerreisekort* (twelve coupons and the right to change), 90; twenty-four-hour ticket, 30; ten-trip ticket, 60; Universal Card, 140 (valid for two weeks, purchased on the first or fifteenth of the month), 270 (valid for one month)

Oslo Card: one day, adult, 60, child, 30; two days, adult, 90, child, 45; three days, adult, 120, child, 60

Taxi: per kilometer 3.10; pickup charge, 12.60; evening rates, 15 percent additional; luggage (per piece), 1

From downtown Oslo to airport:
Taxi: 73.6; 15 to 20 percent higher at night
Special bus: 20

**Paris**
**Bus/Metro/Taxi**

The difficulties of driving and parking in Paris make public transportation the preferred mode of getting around for Parisians as well as tourists and visitors. Fortunately for all, the system generally works well.

The Urban Metro (or subway) is the most popular part of the system. Stations in the downtown area are very close together, so that no location is more than a few blocks from a Metro entrance. However, because these stations are clustered together, service can be slow. Lines are identified by a number designation and by the names of their terminal stations. Each line has two names (one for each end of the line). At the entrance to each station look for a map of Paris with all the Metro lines identified. Tickets are checked at all entrance and exit turnstiles. Keep your ticket for inspection! If you have to change lines, follow the signs marked *correspondances* and watch for the name of your endpoint-terminal. Be wary of anyone selling single tickets on the concourse. This is illegal. Another caution: pickpockets are reportedly at work on the Metro—so be careful! The Metro is open from 5:30 AM to 1:15 AM.

There is also a Regional Express Metro Line (RER), which operates to the surrounding areas of Paris. It is a zone-fare system, which runs four suburban lines. Lines are designated alphabetically, A, B, C, and D, and by final destination.

Buses operated by the Paris Transportation Authority (RATP) are cheap and a good way to sightsee. Stops are marked by yellow disks, which bear a route number and a list of principal stopping places, and schedules are posted at all bus stops. Despite extensive bus lines, service is generally slow. Buses run from 7:00 AM to 9:30 PM with a few services operating until 12:30 AM. There is some limited service through the night. For information call the Central Inquiry Office at tel. 43-46-14-14.

A Tourist Ticket is available for two, four, or seven days. It provides unlimited travel on first-class Metro carriages (urban and regional express network) and bus services operated by RATP. Presentation of your passport is required to purchase this ticket.

There is also a special season ticket. It is good for travel over six consecutive days totaling twelve journeys (two round trips per day), and costs 22.50 francs. The pass called *Carte Orange* is available as either a weekly or monthly ticket, and the user is charged by zones in either first or second class. Both weekly and monthly passes are valid for unlimited travel on Urban Metro, Regional Express Metro, suburban routes of the SNCF (French National Railroads), bus routes of RATP, and some private coach lines operating in Paris.

Unlimited bus and metro travel may also be included in the France Railpass used on the French National Railroads. See the listing for **France** in chapter 13 for a complete explanation. For English-language train information in Paris call 43-80-50-50.

Taxis can be found at taxi stands on street corners, at main intersections, at railway stations, and on the street. On radio calls, the meter starts running at the time the cab is dispatched. Rates are increased at night. There are also extra charges for airport or railway pickup and baggage. Tips range from 10 to 15 percent. Taxis take a maximum of three persons. The average ride within Paris runs between 20 and 60 francs.

Costs in French francs ($1 is about 6.6 francs):

**Bus and Metro**

|  | 1st Class | 2nd Class |
|---|---|---|
| 1 Ticket | 6.80 | 4.60 |
| *Carnet* of 5 Tickets | 21.00 | 14.20 |
| *Carnet* of 10 Tickets | 42.00 | 27.50 |

Children will receive a 50 percent reduction in fare on all *carnets* of 5 or 10 tickets.

Carte Orange *(weekly)*

|  | 1st Class | 2nd Class |
|---|---|---|
| 2 zones | 82.00 | 43.00 |
| 3 zones | 106.00 | 56.00 |
| 4 zones | 142.00 | 76.00 |
| 5 zones | 161.00 | 91.00 |

Carte Orange *(monthly)*

|  | 1st Class | 2nd Class |
|---|---|---|
| 2 zones | 290.00 | 152.00 |
| 3 zones | 366.00 | 195.00 |
| 4 zones | 496.00 | 266.00 |
| 5 zones | 564.00 | 320.00 |

Tourist Ticket: two-day, 53; four-day, 80; seven-day, 133
Taxi, per kilometer, 2.39 (pickup charge, 8.50)
From downtown Paris to Roissy Charles de Gaulle Airport–CDG (23 kilometers):

Taxi: 150–250
RATP bus (Routes #350, #351): six tickets
Train (Roissy-Rail): 23; 27.60 (with urban Metro)
Autobus-RER: 15 (first class), 10 (second class)
From downtown Paris to Orly Airport—ORY (14 kilometers):
Taxi: 150
RATP Bus (Routes #215, #285, #183A): three tickets
Train (Orly-Rail): 15:30; 19.90 (with urban Metro)
From downtown Paris to Le Bourget Airport—LBG (13 kilometers):
Taxi: 80–100
RATP bus (Routes #152, #350): two tickets
Train: none
Air France buses: Orly to Invalides, 27; Roissy Charles de Gaulle to Etoile via Portemillo, 34; Orly to Roissy shuttle, 58

**Reykjavik**
**Bus/Taxi**

The Reykjavik Public Transit *(Straetisvaginar Reykjavikur, S.V.R.)* operates sixteen bus routes in the city. There are two main terminals—Laekjargata (downtown) and Hlemmur (east of city center). The sign *SVR* denotes a bus stop. Transfers are free but must be used within forty-five minutes. Daytime buses operate every fifteen to thirty minutes. Evening and weekend buses operate every thirty to sixty minutes.

A tourist ticket called the Reykjavik Card is available for unlimited bus travel in Reykjavik from one to three days. It also entitles the user to admission to two museums, an art gallery, and use of all public swimming pools in the city.

Bus travel is also the main mode of transportation throughout Iceland. There are two special bus passes available to tourists that are valid between June 1 and September 15. One is the Full-Circle Passport, which goes along Highway #1 utilizing three different bus lines. The other is the Omnibus Passport, which is available for unlimited travel throughout the system for one to four weeks. Information on these passes can be obtained from the Iceland Bus Routes Union in Reykjavik at tel. 91-2-23-00.

More than 600 taxis serve the downtown area of Reykjavik. The charge on the meter is all-inclusive; tipping is not expected. Taxis display the sign *Laus* in the lower lefthand

corner of their windshields when they are available for hire.
Costs in Icelandic Kronur ($1 is about 41 Kronur):
  Bus: one ticket, 25 (exact fare); four-ticket book, 100; twenty-six-ticket book (available at bus terminals only), 500
  Reykjavik Card: one-day, 157; two-day, 235; three-day, 275
  Full-Circle Passport: 3,330; children four to eight, 1,665; children nine to eleven, 2,500
  Omnibus Passport: one-week, 4,115; two-week, 4,900; three-week, 6,270; four-week, 7,055
  Taxi: per kilometer, 9.65
  From downtown Reykjavik to airport (35 miles):
  Taxi: 1,960
  Limo: 588 per person
  Airport bus: 117

### Rome
Bus/Streetcar/Subway/Taxi

Termini (the main railroad station) is the central point for all transportation in the city. There are fifty-eight bus and streetcar lines; the city Yellow Pages provides maps of the various routes. Buses in Rome are among the cheapest in Europe. Many central routes, however, are extremely crowded.

The recently completed subway system—Metropolitana—has two lines, which intersect at Termini. Bus and subway tickets are not interchangeable.

Tickets can be purchased in advance from newsstands, tobacconists, and special kiosks. Be sure to have your ticket validated on board. There are severe fines for failing to do so.

Rome now has weekly and monthly unlimited bus passes available to both tourists and residents.

Taxis may be hailed or met at numerous stands. After 10:00 PM an extra 2,500 lire night fare is added to the meter reading. There are also extra charges for Sundays, public holidays, luggage, and journeys outside the city. Fares to Fiumicino Airport are those shown on the meter plus 5,500 lire; the airport shuttle bus is a better value.

Costs in lire ($1 is about 1,300 to 1,500 lire):
  Bus, streetcar, and Metro: 700 (unlimited travel for seventy-five minutes on a single ticket, not interchangeable among modes)

Weekly Tourist Pass: 10,000
Monthly One-Route Pass: 15,000
Monthly Unlimited Bus: 22,000
Taxi: per kilometer, 450; pickup charge, 2,800; 200 for each 60 seconds or 300 meters; night surcharge, 2,500
From downtown Rome to the airport:
Taxi: on meter plus 5,500
Bus: 5,000

**Stockholm**
**Subway/Bus/Taxi**

An excellent system operates on a zone-fare basis, in which the central zone covers the whole of downtown Stockholm.

One of the best special passes is the Key to Stockholm, also called the Stockholm Card—*Stockholmskortet*, which entitles the traveler to unlimited free use of buses, subways, ferries, and suburban railway services throughout Stockholm (except the airport buses). The card gives the user a free excursion by boat to Drottningholm Palace, plus sightseeing. It also provides free admission to fifty of Stockholm's main attractions, including the Royal Palace, the Wasa Museum, and Gripsholm Castle. It is available at the Tourist Center in Sweden House, Kungstradgarden, and at the *Hotelcentralen* on the lower level of the Central Railway Station. Similar discount cards are available for two other major Swedish cities—Gothenburg and Malmo.

A Tourist Card is also available that provides unlimited travel on bus, subway, and ferry services operated by Djurgarden Ferry Company. It is available in either twenty-four- or seventy-two-hour variants. The seventy-two-hour version includes free entrance to two museums and one amusement park. Both are valid for either the Central Zone or the whole city. If you are just traveling around the center of the city and are not interested in the admissions to various cultural attractions covered by the Stockholm Card, you're probably better off with the Tourist Card.

Transit tickets can be bought at newsstands marked *Pressbyra*. Bus routes 54 and 63 conduct circular tours of the downtown area for tourists. All parts of the city are linked by bus service, but the system tends to slow down during rush hours. Another caution: stringent drunk-driving laws keep drinkers on the public transport system rather than on the roads, especially at night.

Taxis are plentiful except during rush hours and inclement weather. Taxi rates vary according to the time of day and the number of passengers.

Costs in Swedish kroner ($1 is about 7 kroner):

Bus and subway: minimum fare, 8; ten-trip ticket, 40; Tourist Card (twenty-four-hour pass for central Stockholm), 19; Tourist Card (twenty-four-hour pass including suburbs), 33; Tourist Card (seventy-two hours), 65

Stockholm Card: one-day, 66; two-day, 110; three-day, 165; four-day, 220; children between six and twelve years of age pay half price

Taxi: per kilometer, 3 (day); 5 (evening)
From downtown Stockholm to airport:
Taxi: 200
SAS Limo: 150
Bus: 28

*Comment:* Public transport fares may increase by 10 percent in 1987.


**Venice**
**Bus/Boat**

There is no car traffic in the center of Venice. People walk or move about on water. The only road-based public transport is the bus from the airport to the Piazzale Roma, which costs 3,500 lire. Within Venice proper, there are three water-based alternatives to walking: waterbuses, watertaxis, and gondolas.

Costs in lire ($1 is about 1,300 to 1,500 lire):

1. Waterbuses: An excellent and entertaining form of transport known as *vaporetti* (canal steamers) chug slowly up and down the canals. These charge a flat rate of 200 lire for most destinations within the city, with gradual increases for longer distances. For travelers in more of a hurry, the *motoscafi* (motorboats) make fewer stops on similar routes. Interesting routes include No. 1, which stops at every landing stage on the Grand Canal; and No. 5, which runs a circular route around the city. Tickets cost about 4,000–5,000 lire and can be bought at land-

ing stages or at some newsstands and tobacco shops. Paying on board costs an extra 300 lire. An 8,000-lire ticket gives the user one-day's unlimited travel. Information is available in a free booklet, *Un Ospite di Venezia*, at the Tourist Office. Books of 10 or 20 tickets are available, but at no savings.
2. Watertaxis: Prices are controlled, but it is important to establish the fare with the driver before boarding. Fares will vary according to the distance covered. Tariffs are posted in *Un Ospite di Venezia*. Sample fares: Piazzale Roma–San Marco, 26,000 lire; Piazzale Roma–Lido, 43,500 lire; Santa Lucia Railway Station–San Marco, 30,000 lire; Santa Lucia Railway Station–Lido, 43,500; Airport–San Marco, 55,500 lire; Airport-Lido, 58,000 lire. Supplements: for radio dispatch, 5,500 lire (within the city); 7,500 (outside the city); night charge, 5,500 lire; luggage (each item), 2,000 lire; waiting time (per 10 minutes), 5,500.
3. Gondolas: Often some bargaining is advisable. The average rate is 50,000 lire per 50 minutes for up to five people, and then 22,500 lire for every 25 minutes thereafter. Evening rates (9:00 PM–8:00 AM) are 60,000 lire initially. Special hire may be agreed upon for at least 50,000 lire per hour. The only gondola bargains are the *traghetti*—regular gondolas that traverse the Grand Canal for 400 lire.

### Vienna
### Metro/Streetcar/Bus/Train/Taxi

Vienna has a comprehensive but complicated municipal transport system. Visitors are well advised to buy a map that covers all the modes of travel in Vienna and Lower Austria operated by the Transport Association (VOR) from the Vienna Public Transport office near the Opera underpass.

A three-day pass, called the 3-day Vienna Ticket, is available for travel on the *U-Bahn* (Metro), *Schnellbahn* (Rapid Transit), *Strassenbahn* (Tramway) or *Regionalbahn* (Commuter train). It may not be the best value if you only want to travel within the city, which is one zone. Other regions of Lower Austria near Vienna, e.g., Baden, are in different zones.

Interchangeable tickets are available at Vienna Public Transport information points, advance sales offices, tobacconists, and official tourist information offices. There is a slight reduction in ticket price for advance purchase, which is recommended. Conductors and automats sell only single tickets. Tickets must be stamped or validated by machine *(Entwerter)* at the beginning of each journey. Otherwise, a stiff fine may be levied. If you buy a book of tickets (called Important Ticket), there is a reduction as well.

The Vienna Public Transport closes down shortly after midnight. Downtown buses operate only until 8:00 PM on weekdays, and 2:00 PM on Saturdays. The new subway is the best development in the system. Children under fifteen ride free on Sundays, holidays, and school vacations. A valid passport with a current photo is required for children to obtain free travel.

Costs in Austrian schillings ($1 is about 14.2 schillings):

Bus, streetcar, metro: single ticket, 19; children's single ticket, 6; Advance-Purchase Tickets (book of 5), 65; multiple-strip tickets (4 short-distance journeys), 26
3-Day Vienna Ticket, 92
Season tickets: Weekly (Monday–Sunday), 106; Monthly, 380
Taxi: per kilometer, 10
From downtown Vienna to airport (10 miles):
Taxi: 400
Bus: 50
Train: 24

## Zurich
### Streetcar/Bus/Taxi

Zurich enjoys an exceptionally efficient system of public streetcars and buses. The Swiss consider it to be the most modern in Europe. The dense network extends not only to the remotest corners of the city, but also to the most popular starting points for walks just outside its gates.

Automatic machines at every bus or streetcar stop issue tickets for exact change. Payment on board is not permitted (as there are no longer conductors), and there are hefty fines (as in Geneva) for traveling without tickets. Rates vary according to distance traveled (measured in stops). Bahnhofplatz is the main terminus for both bus and streetcar routes. Information booths marked *VBZ* can be found throughout the city at which multilingual brochures giving details of routes and rates can be obtained. Bus and streetcar service ends at midnight daily. The twenty-four-hour ticket represents the best bargain for municipal transport in Zurich and provides unlimited travel throughout the city. Switzerland as a nation operates a totally integrated bus-rail system. Depending on your travel plans, it may be more cost-effective to purchase a Swiss Holiday Card or Regional Half-Fare Travel Card or Regional Holiday Season Ticket, which will cover local transport as well as travel from city to city. Consult the listing for **Switzerland** in chapter 13 for details. Tourist information in Zurich may be obtained from the Tourist Office at tel: 01-211-40-00.

Zurich taxis are among the most expensive in Europe.

Costs in Swiss francs ($1 is about 1.7 Swiss francs):

Streetcar and bus: one to five stops, stops over five, 1.60; twenty-four-hour ticket, 5; book of twelve tickets: one to five stops, 10; over five stops, 16

Taxi: per kilometer, 2.20; pickup charge, 5

From downtown Zurich to airport:

Taxi: 35–40

Train: 6.60 (First Class); 4.20 (Second Class)

Tourist Offices

To obtain additional information on the countries and cities described in this chapter, plus others, please contact the tourist offices listed below.

**Austrian National Tourist Office**
500 Fifth Avenue
New York, NY 10110
212-944-6880

500 North Michigan Avenue
Chicago, IL 60611
312-644-5556

**Belgian Tourist Office**
745 Fifth Avenue
New York, NY 10151
212-758-8130

**British Tourist Authority**
40 West Fifty-seventh Street
New York, NY 10019
212-599-5400

875 North Michigan Avenue
Chicago, IL 60611
312-787-0490

Ceder Maple Plaza
205 Ceder Springs
Dallas, TX. 75201-1814
214-720-4040

612 South Flower Street
Los Angeles, CA 90017
213-623-8196

**Danish Tourist Board**
655 Third Avenue
New York, NY 10017
212-949-2333

**Finnish Tourist Board**
655 Third Avenue
New York, NY 10017
212-949-2333

**French Government Tourist Office**
610 Fifth Avenue
New York, NY 10020
212-757-1125

645 North Michigan Avenue
Chicago, IL 60611
312-337-6301

9401 Wilshire Boulevard
Beverly Hills, CA 90212
213-272-2661

**German National Tourist Office**
747 Third Avenue
New York, NY 10017
212-308-3300

444 South Flower Street
Los Angeles, CA 90017
213-688-7332

**Greek National Tourist Organization**
645 Fifth Avenue
New York, NY 10022
212-421-5777

168 North Michigan Avenue
Chicago, IL 60601
312-782-1084

611 West Sixth Street
Los Angeles, CA 90017
213-626-6696

**Iceland Tourist Board**
655 Third Avenue
New York, NY 10017
212-949-2333

**Irish Tourist Board**
757 Third Avenue
New York, NY 10017
212-418-0800

**Italian Government Travel Office**
630 Fifth Avenue
New York, NY 10111
212-944-6880

500 North Michigan Avenue
Chicago, IL 60611
312-644-0990

360 Post Street
San Francisco, CA 94108
415-392-6206

**Luxembourg National Tourist Office**
801 Second Avenue
New York, NY 10017
212-370-9850

**Monaco Government Tourist Bureau**
845 Third Avenue
New York, NY 10022
212-557-2520

**National Tourist Office of Spain**
665 Fifth Avenue
New York, NY 10022
212-759-8822

845 North Michigan Avenue
Chicago, IL 60611
312-944-0215

8383 Wilshire Boulevard
Beverly Hills, CA 90211
213-658-7188

**Netherlands Board of Tourism**
355 Lexington Avenue
New York, NY 10017
212-370-7367

225 North Michigan Avenue
Chicago, IL 60601
312-819-0300

605 Market Street
San Francisco, CA 94102
415-543-6772

**Norwegian Tourist Board**
655 Third Avenue
New York, NY 10017
212-949-2333

**Portuguese National Tourist Office**
548 Fifth Avenue
New York, NY 10036
212-354-4403

**Swedish Tourist Board**
655 Third Avenue
New York, NY 10017
212-949-2333

**Swiss National Tourist Office**
608 Fifth Avenue
New York, NY 10020
212-757-5944

104 South Michigan Avenue
Chicago, IL 60603
312-641-0050

250 Stockton Street
San Francisco, CA 94108
415-362-2260

**Yugoslav National Tourist Office**
630 Fifth Avenue
New York, NY 10111
212-757-2801

# 18

# Hotels and Tour Packages

*It's Important to Know
What You're Buying*

In this updated edition of *Fly/Ride Europe, 1987*, we thought it worthwhile to provide some basic information on accommodations and the inclusive airfare–land packages commonly known as tours. Most Americans traveling to Europe will utilize some type of hotel accommodations, and the classification systems used by national governments, the various travel destination guidebooks, and the travel industry itself are not by any means consistent, as you will see. Knowing what to expect may save you both dollars and disappointment once you've checked into a hotel that you may have booked weeks or months in advance. The pictures and number of stars in the guidebooks or brochures don't always tell the story as accurately as one would like.

## How Hotels Are Classified

"The tour brochure said we'd have a first-class hotel, but the one we got was a dump." We've heard complaints like this from time to time from travelers who assume either that the tour brochure described the hotel inaccurately or that the tour operator substituted an inferior hotel for the promised first-class one. In fact, the hotel in question may well have been properly labeled "first class," but that designation does not always imply the standards you might expect.

If you haven't had personal experience with a hotel or a personal recommendation from someone you trust, you'll probably select a hotel on the basis of some sort of hotel-classification system. And if you don't know how these systems work, you can be seriously misled. It would be easy, for example, to assume that in hotel grading, as in the airline class system, first class represents the best available. Actually, in hotels, first class often represents something closer to the midpoint than to the top of the quality scale.

We examined the hotel class systems used by a sample of governments, guidebooks, industry references, and tour operators to help you understand what these classifications mean and how to use them.

### Governments

Many governments—national, provincial, state, and local—establish and maintain official hotel-classification procedures. Most of these government rating systems use four to six major gradations, expressed in terms of numbers of stars or classes:

**Table 12    Hotel Classes**

| Country | Number | Lowest | Highest |
|---|---|---|---|
| Austria | 5 | 1 star | 5 stars |
| Belgium | 4 | 1 star | 4 stars |
| France | 5 | 1 star | 4-star luxe |
| Greece | 6 | Class E | Deluxe |
| Ireland | 4 | Class C | Class A+ |
| Italy | 5 | Class IV | L (luxury) |
| Netherlands | 5 | 1 star | 5 stars |
| Spain | 5 | 1 star | 5 stars |
| Switzerland | 5 | 1 star | 5 stars |
| Yugoslavia | 5 | Class D | L (luxury) |

Where available, government classification systems are usually the most comprehensive and detailed. Hotel classes are determined by a combination of numerical data submitted by the hotels and on-site examinations. The personnel and financial resources of government agencies support extensive on-site examination and data collection. The law requires hotels to participate in the system, and the classifications are often used as one of the bases on which hotel room rates are regulated.

The French system, for example, takes twenty-four separate factors into account, including number of rooms, average room size, percentage of rooms with various bath facilities, elevators, telephone service, flooring materials, acoustic comfort, electrical outlets, and service personnel. Standards are updated to conform with changing tourist expectations: In 1971, the bath standards were upgraded to require that all rooms in 4-star deluxe hotels have bathrooms.

Several of Europe's most important tourist destinations do not officially classify hotels. Among them are Britain, Denmark, Finland, Germany, Norway, and Sweden.

We also examined the classification systems used in several of the most frequently used guides with extensive listings in Europe (the *AA Tour Guides* in Britain and the *Michelin Red Guides* in ten countries).

We examined hotel recommendations in typical travel guidebooks by testing four popular guidebook series: Birnbaum, Fisher, Fodor, and Frommer.

Travel-industry references were identified through discussions with travel agents; reference publishers were contacted to determine how they developed or compiled their classification data.

Tour operator practices were evaluated by reviewing the brochures of five large tour operators and by contacting them to determine their classification methodology.

**Guidebooks**

Tourist guidebooks can be divided into two main categories: those containing extensive hotel and restaurant listings, and those offering overall travel guidance including hotel and restaurant recommendations. Guides with extensive listings—such as the *Michelin Red Guide* series—try to provide basic information on large numbers of hotels, motels, and restaurants. They often contain very little narrative material.

**Table 13   Hotel Classes**

| Guide | Number | Lowest | Highest |
|---|---|---|---|
| AA Tour Guides | 5 | 1 star | 5 stars |
| Michelin Guides | 6 | Birdhouse | 5 hotels |

Some of these guides use classifications and research methods as systematic and elaborate as those used by government tourist offices. Michelin maintains an air of mystery about its system, but the industry speculates that Michelin maintains a staff of full-time inspectors and bases its classifications on the results of on-site inspections and data collection.

Quite often in countries that do not provide government classifications one of these guides becomes the de facto standard: Many hotels in the United Kingdom post their Automobile Association (AA) or Royal Automobile Club (RAC) class in much the same manner as hotels in other European countries post their government class plaques.

The British Consumers' Association travel magazine, *Holiday Which?*, uses a similar classification system, with numerical levels from 1 to 5, based on on-site inspection by *Holiday Which?* staff members. In some articles, however, *Holiday Which?* relies on the official government classifications—for example, in its survey of Paris hotels.

Unlike the guides with extensive hotel and restaurant listings, the overall travel guidebooks—such as the popular Birnbaum, Fisher, Fodor, and Frommer series—don't try to list or evaluate a large percentage of the hotels in the areas covered. Instead, they combine their authors' personal selections of certain hotels and restaurants with extensive information on sightseeing, shopping, and transportation. Some of these guidebooks designate hotels by specific classes while others do not.

- Birnbaum, for example, generally does not use specific quality categories, relying instead on commentary to convey the authors' impressions of quality and service.
- Fisher, on the other hand, adopts the frequently used 1- to 5-star system to indicate quality and comfort, based on independent on-site evaluations by the authors and editors. Fisher provides a separate classification by price.
- Fodor uses five standard classes, ranging from *inexpensive* to *super deluxe*, based primarily on price but also on subjective evaluations of comfort and service.
- Frommer lists hotels under four general categories, ranging from "the budget line-up" to "the top hotels"; the categorization is subjective.

Quite a few guidebooks of this type include the official government class in their hotel descriptions.

**Industry References**

Several hotel reference books are published for use by travel agents and corporate travel departments. One of the most comprehensive and widely used is the *Official Hotel and Resort Guide*, or *OHRG*, published in four editions: North America, Europe, Western Hemisphere (except the United States), and Other Areas. The *OHRG* uses nine quality categories (see *The OHRG Hotel Classification*).

Hotels are classified by *OHRG* staff members on the basis of materials provided from a variety of sources, including the hotels themselves, government travel offices, and convention and visitors bureaus. *OHRG* does not conduct any independent on-site investigations; the listings contain a specific disclaimer that hotels have not been inspected.

*Hotel & Travel Index (HTI)* is a different hotel directory published by the same company that publishes *OHRG*. Most travel agents use both directories. Besides offering the listings of hotels, *HTI* provides maps of most major cities pinpointing each hotel's location. The listings include rates, location, and telephone/telex number, representatives, manager's name, credit cards accepted, number of rooms, etc. *HTI* accepts advertising from the hotels and also includes a front section on hotel representatives and hotel/motel systems.

Another industry reference, the *OAG Travel Planner* series of guides, lists hotels in the world's most important tourist areas. European hotel listings are based on official government classifications, where available, or on "judgment" where hotels are not officially classified.

The *Star Service* is an independent publication providing highly detailed evaluations of more than 9,000 hotels worldwide, "each inspected and rated by a travel professional." There is no advertising and no payment for listing. It is the only industry reference we examined that included independently derived hotel data. Ask your travel agent to consult this reference when recommending hotels (The Star Service, Box 15610, Ft. Lauderdale, FL 33318; tel.: 305-472-8794).

## The OHRG Hotel Classification

The hotel-classification system used by the *Official Hotel and Resort Guide* may be the most frequently used of all systems. Chances are that this is the reference your travel agent uses to recommend a hotel for you. Here are the actual standards used by the *OHRG* (quoted verbatim from the publication):

- Superior Deluxe: An exclusive and expensive luxury hotel, often palatial, offering the highest standards of service, accommodations and facilities—Elegant and luxurious public rooms—A prestige address—Establishments in this category are among the world's top hotels.
- Deluxe: An outstanding property offering many of the same features as Superior Deluxe, except in some cases (mainly in Europe), a small number of minimum rated accommodations may be of inferior grade—May be less grand and offer more reasonable rates than the Superior Deluxe properties, yet in many instances may be just as satisfactory—Safe to recommend to most discriminating clients.
- Moderate Deluxe: Basically a Deluxe hotel, but with qualifications. In some cases the hotel may be a well-established famous name, depending heavily upon past reputation. In other cases some accommodations or public areas may not be up to Deluxe standards. If modern, the hotel may be heavily marketed to business clients, with fine accommodations and public rooms offering Deluxe standards in comfort, but lacking in atmosphere or personal service—May be overpriced—Recommend with caution to fussy clients expecting full Deluxe facilities or much pampering—Consulting OHRG description will be helpful.
- Superior First Class: An above average hotel—May be an exceptionally well-maintained older hotel, more often a superior modern hotel specifically designed for first class market, with some outstanding features—Accommodations and public areas are expected to be tastefully furnished and very comfortable—May be a good value, especially if it is a commercial hotel—May

be recommended to average clients and in most cases will satisfy the discriminating ones.
- First Class: An average, comfortable hotel—The majority of accommodations are good, although some may be below First Class standards—May have some Deluxe rooms or suites—Public areas are standard—Usually nothing special—May safely be recommended to average clients not expecting Deluxe facilities or special services—Should also be satisfactory for better groups.
- Moderate First Class: Basically a First Class establishment, slightly below average—Generally has comfortable, simple accommodations and public areas, though not always kept up to standards—May be lacking in some features (e.g., restaurant)—Some of the rooms or public areas may tend to be small and functional—Usually suitable for cost-conscious clients, but should not be recommended to the fussy or complaining ones unless the OHRG description implies otherwise.
- Superior Tourist Class: Primarily a budget property with mostly well-kept, functional accommodations, some up to First Class standards—Public rooms may be limited or non-existent—Often just a place to sleep, but may have some charming or intimate features—May be a good value. Will satisfy clients on a budget (sometimes even discriminating ones), groups or student groups.
- Tourist Class: Strictly a budget operation with some facilities or features of Superior Tourist Class, but usually no (or very few) First Class accommodations—Should under no circumstances be recommended to fussy or discriminating clients—Should generally be used with caution.
- Moderate Tourist Class: Low-budget operations, often quite old and may not be well-kept—Should only be used in a pinch if no others are available—Clients should always be cautioned what to expect.

Many other references are simply listings, without classifications. Some include only hotels that have paid for a listing; listings in others are confined to members of sponsoring tourist or trade organizations.

## Tour Operators

The tour brochures we examined generally conform to the industry references. American Express's hotel-class policy, clearly stated in its tour brochures, is typical: "Hotel grades generally conform to those established by the *Official Hotel and Resort Guide (OHRG)*. When the OHRG has not established a grade, Tourist Board ratings may be used. If neither source is available, grades will be based on American Express evaluation."

Some tour operators use terms that make hotels sound good at any price level. For example, the three hotel categories used by TWA Getaway tours—*First Class, Top Value,* and *Super Saver*—all evoke a prestige image.

### Guidelines for Choosing a Hotel

In general, we find we can rely on government hotel classifications, as well as the classifications in such widely used guides as *Michelin Red Guides*. These classifications are based on factual data and on-site inspections. While you (or we) might disagree in an individual case, as a rule:

- Classifications within a single country are generally quite consistent—a three-star hotel in one city will be quite similar to a three-star hotel in other cities in that particular country.
- Since most formalized systems use five or six similar grades, classifications are reasonably consistent among different countries with similar living standards.
- The middle classifications are generally suitable for cost conscious American tourists throughout the world.
- Whenever our own on-site evaluations have disagreed with official classifications, the difference was usually because most official systems emphasize the quantitative measures—number of rooms, room size, number and size of lobbies and public rooms, and the like—rather than the more subjective measures of charm, friendliness, and comfort.

Hotel evaluations in travel guidebooks are more a reflection of the authors' informed opinions than numerical measures.

- A few hotels recommended by guidebooks appeared unacceptable to us, probably reflecting changes that had occurred since the evaluation by the authors.
- Relatively similar descriptions and ratings were assigned to hotels with substantially differing levels of quality.
- Recommendations in some guidebook series tended to concentrate on the high-priced, "safe," well-known names. Travelers looking for inexpensive lodging should consult budget-travel guides.

Information about hotel quality in guidebooks intended for consumers is as good as, or better than, the reference information intended for travel agents or tour operators.

- Some travel-industry references used by agents (with the notable exception of the *Star Service*) contain information derived from the same official hotel-classification rating systems that are available to consumers from government tourist-office lists or in guidebooks. Because of the publishing cycles, the data in the travel-industry references may be up to a year behind the ratings in current official government publications and consumer guidebooks.
- If you depend on your travel agent for hotel recommendations, by all means ask if the recommendation is based on the agent's first-hand experience. If not, you may be better off consulting an up-to-date guidebook or two.

Evaluate carefully the hotel accommodations offered in package tours. While American tour operators almost never use hotels that aren't suitable for the mass American tourist market, they sometimes try to make the accommodations sound better than they really are. Many tour operators rely on classifications listed in the *OHRG*. As noted earlier, in the *OHRG* system, *first class* is the middle—not the top—of the quality range (see *The OHRG Hotel Classification*).

- Be especially careful when hotels are described as "tourist" or "moderate tourist" establishments. As with airfares, "tourist" is a code word for the lowest-quality service offered.
- If you're uncertain about the hotels to be used in a tour you're considering, check the hotels in one or two guide-

books. (Checking tour hotels in a guidebook is also useful when you calculate whether a tour is a good buy compared with independent travel.)

## Tours—Bundled versus Unbundled Travel and Accommodations

In earlier chapters, we discussed wholesale tour operators. Seemingly, they wear many hats. Basically, however, they are packagers. They put together, or bundle, various travel/accommodation/sightseeing components. Wholesale tour operators are the middlemen between the charter airlines, hotels, car-rental firms, sightseeing operators, motorcoach/ground transportation companies, and you—the traveler.

In turn, there are primarily four kinds of tour packages: independent tours, escorted (group) tours, independent charters, and escorted (group) charters.

**Independent Tours**

Independent tours are available in many different varieties. A fly/drive package is one of the most common. Hotel accommodations are often included in the tour price as well. In some tours, airfare may not be included. In such cases, the tour should entitle you to purchase an ITX/GIT fare that is usually the same as APEX. Wholesalers normally negotiate special deals with hotels, car-rental firms, and ground transportation operators for special "net" rates. These various rates are then bundled together to form the price that you pay, including the tour operator's mark-up and your travel agent's commission.

The "net" rates for hotels are normally much lower than a full-paying guest would pay because the wholesaler buys up large blocks of rooms, often guaranteeing the hotel that it will have 100 percent occupancy during a given period. Bearing the risk of booking all the rooms for a hotel entitles the wholesaler to greatly reduced rates.

Independent tours can be organized and sold by tour operators, airlines, large retail travel agencies, or any travel company that wants to put together the ingredients to make up a package.

The point is, beyond whatever components of travel and accommodations or sightseeing you may purchase in an independent tour, you're completely on your own to do what you wish, at your own pace.

**Escorted Tours**

A fully escorted tour provides, in a single bundled package, just about all of the travel services required for touring: hotel accommodations, local transportation within the area or region you're visiting, sightseeing guides, and some (but usually not all) of your meals and entertainment.

Fully escorted tours are the most comprehensive type of package tour: "Fully escorted" means that a tour guide accompanies the tour participants throughout their stay in a destination area and travels with the tour group to the various stops on the itinerary. Fully escorted tours normally include all necessary local transportation within the destination area and extensive sightseeing and entertainment. All breakfasts and all (or many) dinners are also usually included in the bundled price. On less expensive packages, "hosts" at key destination stops replace full-time guides.

Fully escorted tours are available just about anywhere that Americans may want to visit. In fact, escorted tours are sometimes the only way to visit some countries that do not permit independent tourist travel.

*The Experience*
Sightseeing is the key to escorted tours: the fully escorted tour is, first and foremost, a means to take you somewhere and show you something. While not quite as self-contained as a cruise, a fully escorted tour does provide many of the same features. Once you've selected the tour, the tour operator handles all the details, leaving you free to enjoy the experience. Someone else relieves you of the responsibility for deciding where to go and what to see, as well as arranging travel schedules, accommodations, and other trip details. Schedules are geared to the best times of the day to visit museums, churches, monuments, and natural attractions. This comprehensive tour planning virtually ensures that you actually get to see the attractions and participate in the activities for which each area or region is most famous. You're unlikely to miss any of the blockbusters.

For this reason, fully escorted tours are often suggested for a first trip to a foreign country. But many experienced travelers also prefer this type of travel; they simply enjoy the freedom from uncertainties and decision-making.

Preplanning is especially valuable for special-interest tours. On a golf tour of Scotland, for example, the tour operator obtains your starting time at each course (including those that normally exclude nonmembers) and organizes your foursome. You spend your time playing golf, not making arrangements.

*Accommodations*
Hotels and restaurants are (or at least should be) selected on the basis of demonstrated success in pleasing tourists. Thus most fully escorted tours—especially the more expensive ones—usually include accommodations at either top international chains or local hotels recommended by the major guidebooks. With a quality escorted tour, you'll seldom have any unpleasant surprises.

*Cautions*
The structure that provides the carefree certainty of fully escorted tours also leads to the main disadvantages. Although most fully escorted tours provide some time on your own, you have limited opportunity for any explorations off the beaten track or for repeat visits to places you particularly enjoyed during the group's initial fast pass. You have to put in your time at the Louvre, for example, whether or not you have any interest in art, before the tour proceeds to the Eiffel Tower. The pace is often wrong. Sometimes the length of the visit and the commentary seem geared to the most pedantic scholars; at other times, a world-famous monument rates no more than a slight slowdown of the tour bus as you drive past. And even when the tour-bus operator doesn't get a kickback, the inevitable stops at craft and souvenir shops often seem eternal.

The tour bus—almost universally the mode of transport for sightseeing excursions on escorted tours—epitomizes the problems with escorted tours. You're traveling with a group of other Americans in your own vehicle, insulated from most contacts with locals. You never have to try the local language. You're looking at a country, not experiencing its life. You seem to spend more time in lines and climbing in and out of buses than actually seeing and doing things. And with their steep stairs and narrow aisles, tour buses are poorly designed for frequent unloading and loading.

Some tours are dependent on weather—especially if the main focus is on outdoor sightseeing in such spectacular areas as the Swiss Alps. But a well-planned tour can provide more bad-weather alternatives than a cruise or resort. You can enjoy a famous art museum, a London play, or a thousand-year-old cathedral as much in a downpour as on a sunny day.

*Family Travel*
The escorted tour is probably the least suitable form of self-contained vacation for families with small children. Although a few tours are specially designed for family groups, children on most escorted tours are treated as adults—both in terms of activities and in terms of prices. If your children are mature enough to enjoy adult activities and mostly adult company, they'll do fine on a tour. But if they're not, neither they nor you will enjoy a family tour.

Package-Tour Advantages

Sometimes a package tour is the only way to assure a hotel room at a popular destination during peak seasons. Tour operators buy large inventories of airline seats and hotel rooms on a year-round basis, in effect sharply limiting the numbers of seats and rooms left for individual travelers.

With most package tours, you can reserve right up to the day before departure, if space is available. Indeed, some of the very best escorted tour prices can be found through the last-minute travel organizations. By contrast, the best airfares to many popular destinations require an advance-purchase period of up to thirty days, and airfares allowing last-minute travel can be astronomical.

But you can't depend on finding a package tour at the last minute. Package tours tend to sell out early during the most popular times, so you should reserve as far ahead as possible.

Although the package tour necessarily includes an extra profit margin for the tour operator that you don't pay on independent travel, the tour package almost always guarantees that you'll get the lowest possible airfare. Sometimes this lowest possible fare will also be available to independent travelers, but it often is not.

### Package-Tour Risks

Package-tour programs typically include a range of hotel options and other components from economy through deluxe. Some may include a minimum-price option as a loss leader. Typically, the accommodation will be a *minimum* room at one of the lowest-priced hotels. Moreover, only a few of these rooms may be available. We once reviewed a tour brochure that, in effect, conceded that travelers wouldn't really like one of these minimum rooms. As we discussed earlier, this type of tour is, in essence, a throwaway land package. It's fine to book this kind of tour if you can take advantage of a substantial savings on the airfare. But it's important to know what you're getting, and you should ask your travel agent specifically what kind of hotel room you can expect.

The main European tour operators do such a stable and consistent business that you really don't have to worry much about unpleasant surprises. You know when you reserve exactly which hotel you'll be using, and last-minute switches are rare.

But that isn't the case in all tour markets. You often see tour brochure fine print stating that the tour operator may *substitute alternative accommodations of equal value* for the hotels described. Of course, it's the tour operator, not the traveler, who decides what is or isn't *equal value*. Every year, you hear about a few totally unacceptable substitute hotels. Of course, you can usually get your money back, but a refund next month isn't usually a solution to tonight's hotel problem.

### Comparing Packages

A few phone calls to an airline or a short visit to your travel agent should provide all the data you need:

- Get the package prices for the tours you're considering. Make sure you get realistic figures for the hotels you really want on the dates you really want to travel. Don't use a loss-

leader figure for a tour that you probably can't get and might not want even if you could get it.
- Determine the costs of *the identical or the most similar* travel services when purchased independently. Be sure to use the lowest available airfare options, not the full-fare Coach or Economy fares the tour promoters often use to show what bargains their tours are.
- Compare the costs and the other advantages and disadvantages of package tour and independent travel. Then make your decision.

# 19

# Airport and Airline Security

*Today's Most
Troublesome Problem—
and No Easy Answers*

Does a traveler in Europe run higher risks from terrorism than a traveler in other parts of the world? Many Americans seemed to think so in 1986. It appears that substantial numbers decided to shun Europe in favor of other vacation venues last year, almost entirely because of fallout from the Rome and Vienna airport murders, the TWA and Egyptair airplane hijackings, and the *Achille Lauro* incident. Mail and phone calls to *Consumer Reports Travel Letter* clearly revealed that Americans are concerned about terrorism. And to those of us who act as professional travel advisers for consumers—whether we're travel agents or travel writers—the most frustrating aspect to the terrorism question is that there are simply no easy answers.

Can terrorism directed at air travelers be stopped? The best answer seems to be that terrorist attacks against airports and airplanes can be made more difficult, but not totally prevented. Virtually all of the world's major airports have announced a tightening of security measures: London's Heathrow airport looks like a military camp these days. And airlines are tightening their screening and baggage procedures.

But not even the tightest security measures can prevent all possible terrorist acts:

- The best airport screening procedures can be breached if (as is likely the case in the TWA hijacking at Athens) one or more airport security agents collaborate with the hijackers.
- Nothing short of 100 percent by-hand baggage inspection can deter a terrorist from checking a suitcase bomb on board an airplane—especially if the terrorist is sufficiently dedicated to check his own suitcase and board the sabotaged airplane himself.

Is Europe a riskier area than others—for example, the United States or Asia? Most of the recent terrorism against air travelers has taken place in Europe. It's easy for people to travel to Europe—and ship arms and explosives there—from the Middle East, where much of today's terrorism originates. Europe is also reasonably accessible to those countries—notably Libya and the Soviet Union—that appear to be abetting terrorism.

But other parts of the world aren't immune. The bomb that presumably destroyed the Air India 747 off the Irish coast was apparently put on board in Montreal—right in our own back yard. Remember that a terrorist bomb was set off at New York's LaGuardia airport a few years back. And perhaps it's been more a matter of luck than skill that the fanatical opponents of Narita Airport in Japan haven't succeeded in causing any death or destruction.

European airports are now scurrying to lock their security barn doors after several horses have been stolen. Terrorists may well select less wary targets for future attacks. Don't be surprised if a major U.S. airport is hit within the next year or two. And if that happens, will we then "stay away from the United States" to avoid risk?

Will your trip be affected by antiterrorist measures? To a degree. First, you'll notice a heavy presence of police and/or military around many European airports—all in all, a comforting rather than disquieting sight. You'll observe tighter security provisions—which invariably mean you should allow more time for check-in. You may also find somewhat more interest in your carry-on baggage than in prior years. Don't be surprised to experience a pat-down or two this year.

If you're making connections—especially with more than an hour or two between flights—you may have to claim your baggage from the first flight and personally recheck it onto the second. Airlines these days aren't happy to load any suitcase that has been sitting around on the ground for several hours without personal attention. Be sure to find out exactly how your baggage will be handled at any connecting airports this year. Ask specifically if you should claim and recheck it. If you don't take this precaution, you may find that your bag didn't make the connecting airplane—and that you'll have to wait a day or two for it to be delivered.

# Bon Voyage!

The objective of this book is to enhance your European travel experience. Depending on your personal situation, that may mean showing you how to save money on your airfare to Europe and your travel within Europe, by whatever modes, or it may mean pointing out some of the options that offer particularly good values—but not necessarily the absolute minimum price.

If we have one warning for inexperienced travelers, it's to be cautious about selecting any option that represents the absolute minimum level of price—and service. After all, you'll be investing a significant sum of money in even a budget trip. Chances are, it will cost somewhere between the absolute rock-bottom $500 a person for a short-stay trip originating on the East Coast to well over $2,000 a person for a more typical two- to four-week trip. A few extra dollars—for a more comfortable flight, a slightly larger rental car, a first-class railpass, some taxi rides rather than just the bus, for example—may make the difference between a relaxing, memorable trip and a grueling test of your physical and emotional endurance. If you're a knowledgeable traveler and dedicated to economy, and aware of the implications of minimum-budget travel, fine—use our data to find the least-cost options. But if you're unsure, before you try some of the very cheapest options, take the trouble to consult a reputable travel agent or, if you can, someone who may be more familiar with the travel service you're considering.

Also remember that many of the specific prices cited here will have changed by the time you make your final arrangements. Certainly, many of the air fares will have changed. Fares and charges keyed to local currencies will change with the changing fortunes of the U.S. dollar, and many will be climbing with local inflation. (Most of Europe is still faced with substantially greater inflation than we've had recently.) While the fares and charges we have reported should remain accurate *relative to one another,* amounts will certainly change. Most of the countries will have approximately a 10 percent increase in local transportation costs in 1987.

Transportation will probably be a big part of your expense, but, for many, it will be less than half the total. You should look with equal care at the other major components of your trip as well: hotels, restaurants, sightseeing tours, and shopping.

Finally, no book can make decisions for you. There are no substitutes for research, exploration, and comparison shopping. We've tried to give you the research tools and insights you'll need to do a good job. But only you can explore the specific questions that affect your individual itinerary. We've tried to show you what your options are, including—we hope—some new ideas you hadn't considered before. Armed with this information you can ask the right questions of travel professionals and ultimately make the decisions that are right for you.

Have a great trip!

# INDEX

*AA Tour Guides,* 267–68
Add-on travel services, 80
Adjacent-country car rental, 191–92
Advance-purchase requirements:
   for airline tickets, 12, 32, 33, 200, 207, 209
   for car rentals, 183
Aer Lingus, 31, 105–106
Air Charter, 60, 126
Aircraft seating, *see* Seating comfort, aircraft
Air fares:
   intra-European, 105–106, 140, 143–44, 147, 199–212
     for charter and inclusive tour flights, 203–205, 206
     discount, 199, 205, 206
     Eurobudget, 201, 207, 211
     examples of, 207–11
     official, 200–203
     one-way, 201, 204, 211
     restrictions on, 200–201, 204, 207, 208, 209
     Standby, 201
   transatlantic, 283
     APEX or Super APEX, 9–10, 11, 24, 32–35, 37–39, 97–98, 100–102, 104, 105, 106, 110
     bulk or net, 8, 10, 27, 52, 64–69
     Business Class, 10, 43, 44, 88
     charter, 10, 13, 27, 45, 46, 50, 52–53

     customs fee, 10, 110
     discount, 19, 28, 32, 79–89
     excursion, 13
     First Class, 10, 92–93
     First Class Charter, 10, 92
     "flexible schedule" travel, 71, 72
     full-fare Economy, 10, 44, 101, 202
     geographical variation within the U.S., 11
     group and tour, 40, 82, 278
     how to use this guide, 24–25, 283–84
     1987 outlook for, 34–35, 47, 52–53, 65, 84
     1987 projected, 109–33
     open-jaw route, 13, 106, 109, 144
     premium service, on low-fare airlines, 93
     promotional, 32
     restrictions on, 12–13, 33, 38, 66
     round-the-world excursion, 9, 42–43
     seasonal variations in 11–12, 52, 65, 84, 107
     Standby, 13, 40–41
     status fares, 13–14, 34, 41–42
     unconventional ticket sources, 9, 95–103
     *see also* Low-fare airlines; Major airlines; Transatlantic travel overview of

Air Florida, 46
Air France, 31, 37
Airhitch, 71, 72
Air India, 31
Air Inter, 202
Airline-regulation policies, government, 41, 43, 81, 86, 88, 201, 202, 205
Airlines, *see* Charter airlines; Low-fare airlines; Major airlines; *individual airlines*
Airline security, 280–82
Airline ticket offices, 26, 67–68, 103, 207
Airport security, 280–82
Air travel within Europe, 104–106, 107, 144–46, 199–212
  buying your tickets for, 205–207
  comfort of, 142–43, 203
  contingencies, 143
  convenience of, 140–42
  cost comparisons, 140, 143–44, 145–46, 147
  *see also* Air fares, intra-European
Air UK, 201
Alia, 31, 133
Alitalia, 31
Alternate gateways, flying to, 109–10, 192
American Airlines, 31, 96
American Airlines Senior Club, 41
American Express, 272
American International Rent-a-Car (Ansa), 189, 190, 193, 195, 196, 197, 198
Amsterdam, Netherlands, 65, 72, 106
  air fares to other European cities from, 209–10
  car rentals in, 191–92
  public transportation in, 232–34
  transatlantic air fares to, 65, 110–11
APEX or Super APEX fares, 9–10, 11, 24, 32–35, 39, 100–101, 105–106, 109, 110
  1987 outlook for, 34–35
Athens, Greece, 111–12, 234

Atlanta, Georgia, 106
Austria:
  bus service in, 214
  car rentals in, 193
  rail travel in, 139, 155–56
Auto Europe, 189, 198
Avis Rent-a-Car, 187, 189, 190, 198
Baggage:
  lost, 23, 38
  security measures, 280–82
  stolen, 143
Balair, 55, 60
Barcelona, Spain, 192, 234–35
Basic season air fares, 11, 65
Belfast Car Ferries, 227
Belgium, 43, 110
  bus service in, 214
  car rentals in, 193
  ferry service to, 220–21
  rail travel in, 156–57, 178
Belgrade, Yugoslavia, transatlantic air fares to, 112
Berlin, Germany, public transportation in, 235–36
Beverages on transatlantic flights, 22, 37, 91, 92, 93
Bicycling, 161, 215
Birnbaum guidebooks, 268
Boston airports, 104
Braathens Safe, 202–203
Braniff Airlines, 39
Britain, *see* United Kingdom
Britexpress Card, 218–19
British Airtours, 55, 60
British Airways, 31, 37, 81, 97, 106, 201, 203, 208
British Caledonian Airlines, 31, 37, 81, 85, 201
British Consumers' Association, 213, 268
Britrail Pass, 116, 149, 151, 175–76, 178, 220
Brittany Ferries, 227
Brussels, Belgium, 65, 72

Index  287

car rentals in, 191–92
public transportation in, 214, 236–37
transatlantic air fares to, 65, 113
"Bucket shops," 87–88, 106, 199, 205, 206–207
Budget Rent-a-Car, 188, 189, 190, 198
Bulkhead seats, 18
Bulk or net fares, 8, 10, 52, 64–69, 87
   buying tickets, 67–69
   comfort of, 66
   contingencies of, 67
   convenience of, 65–66
   explanation of, 64–65
   1987 fare outlook, 65
Business Class air service, 9, 43, 44, 54–55, 88, 91–92, 94, 97
   fares for, 10, 43, 44, 91–92
Business travelers:
   air fare restrictions and, 12–13
   frequent flier coupons, 28, 95, 97
   *see also* Business Class air service
*Business Traveller*, 105, 199
Bus services, 145, 213, 214–20
   city public transportation, 230–60
   comparisons by country, 214–20
   sightseeing by bus, 230, 231, 276–77
Buying your tickets:
   for intra-European air travel, 205–207
   for rail travel, 153–54
   for transatlantic travel, 25–27, 44, 49, 58, 63, 67–69, 77–78

Cabin comfort, 16–23
   load factors, 16, 18–21, 23
   seating, *see* Seating comfort, airline
Cairo, Egypt, transatlantic air fares to, 114
Cancellations by airlines, 23, 38, 48, 67
Cancellations by travelers, charges for, 27, 34
"Capacity control" restriction on APEX fares, 33–34
Capitol Airlines, 46
Car rentals and leases, 30, 74, 82, 110, 145–46, 180–98

adjacent-country, 191–92
airline rental programs, 80, 81, 188, 198
arranging, 198
comfort of, 142–43
contingencies, 143
convenience of, 140–42
cost comparisons, 137–39, 143–44, 145–48
credit card payment for, 189
driving tips, 182
exchange rates, 30, 190–91, 197
insurance for, 185
larger car models, 185–86
leases, 187–88, 197–98
lowest cost, in each country, 180–83, 192–97
one-way rentals, 181, 186, 197
rental companies serving Europe, 188–90, 198
restrictions on rental programs, 183
standard subcompacts, 183–85
tour packages, 274
Carefree David, 60
Channel Island Ferries, 227
Channel Islands, ferry service to, 220–21
Charters:
   for intra-European air travel, 203–205, 206
   transatlantic, 8, 27, 50–63,
      air fares, 10, 13, 27, 45, 50, 52–53, 92–93
      buying tickets for, 58, 63
      comfort of, 50, 54–55, 93
      connecting flights on, 15
      contingencies on, 50, 55–57, 58–63
      convenience of, 50, 53–54
      independent versus group, 276
      late-booking, 73
      myths about, 50
      tour operators' role, 51–52, 55, 56–57, 62, 67, 68
Children:
   air fares for, 13–14, 34

288  Index

Children *(cont'd)*
    on escorted tours, 277
    rail travel fares, 152
    *see also* Students; Youth fares
Citalia, 205, 211
Clergy, air fares for, 14
Clubs, *see* Travel clubs
Comfort:
    of intra-European travel methods, 142–43, 203, 204
    of transatlantic air travel, 9, 16–23, 24
    of bulk-fare travel, 66
    of charters, 50, 54–55, 91
    on low-fare airlines, 20–21, 48, 93
    on major airlines, 20–21, 36–37
    *see also* Load factors; Seating comfort, aircraft; Service quality, in-flight
Companion tickets, 76–77, 92
Computerized reservation systems, 26–27, 32, 44, 49, 63, 67, 86
Condor, 55, 60, 117, 124
Connecting flights, 15, 34–36, 54, 65, 86, 104–107
    missed connections, 23, 38, 67
    *see also* Stopovers
Consumers' Association of Great Britain, 213, 268
*Consumer Reports Travel Letter*, 199, 280
Comfort Index, 20–22, 36, 48, 55
Continental Airlines, vii–viii, 39, 96
"Continental one-way" car rentals, 181, 186, 197
*Continental Timetable*, Thomas Cook, 153
Contingencies, 9, 23, 24
    of bulk-fare travel, 67
    on charters, 55–57, 58–59
    ways to minimize, 60–62
    of discount and rebate travel, 85–86
    of intra-European travel methods, 143
    on low-fare airlines, 48–49
    on major airlines, 37–39
Convenience:
    of intra-European travel methods, 140–42

*see also* individual methods *of transatlantic travel*, 9, 14–16, 24, 35–36, 47, 50, 53–54, 65–66, 85, 106–107
Cook, Thomas, *Continental Timetable*, 153
Copenhagen, Denmark, 114–15, 237
Cortell Group, 189, 190
Council (formerly C.I.E.E.), 60
Country rovers (rail travel passes), 149, 151, 152
Coupons:
    frequent-travelers, *see* Frequent-traveler coupons
    promotional, 100
Credit cards, 87
    buying tickets with, 44
    car rental payment with, 190

Danish Ferry Service, 227
Da-No Linjen, 227
Delayed flights, 38, 48, 50, 56–57, 61–62
    *see also* Stranded, being
Delta Airlines, 30, 97
Denmark:
    bus service in, 214–15
    car rentals in, 193
    ferry services for, 223
    rail travel in, 139, 157–59
DER Tours, 60
"Direct" flights, 14–15, 35, 36,
Direct rebates, 80
Discount air fares, 9, 32, 79–90
    agency discounts, 83
    buying tickets, 86, 103
    convenience of, 85
    currency-conversion discounting, 89–90
    forms of, 79–83
    for intra-European air travel, 199, 205, 206
    legal questions about, 80, 86, 88–90
    1987 outlook for, 84
    risks and uncertainties of, 85–86
    seasonal variations in, 100

Index 289

travel agency, 83
travel-club, 83–84
Discounters:
  clearinghouses, 29
  consolidators, 28, 29, 79
  coupon brokers, 28, 29
  tour operators, 28, 29
Dollar, *see* Exchange rates
Drinks, *see* Beverages
Driving, *see* Car rentals and leases
DSB (Danish State Railway), 214, 223
Dublin, Ireland, 105, 115–16, 238–39
Dusseldorf, West Germany, car rentals in, 192

Eastern Airlines, 31, 97
Economy Class air service, 8, 9, 43, 44, 55, 88
*Economy Traveler*, 191
Edinburgh, Scotland, public transportation in, 239
Egyptair, 37
El Al, 30, 37
England, *see* United Kingdom
English Channel, crossing the, 144–45, 220–22
Entertainment on transatlantic flights, 22, 37,
Escorted tours, 275-77
Eurailpass, 145-46, 147, 150–53, 178, 220,
Eurobudget fare, 201, 207, 211
Europcar, 189, 190, 195
European Economic Community, vii, 201
European transportation, 72, 82, 105–106, 137–264
  avoiding frugality, 148
  being multimodal, 144–47
  the Channel crossing, 144–45, 220–22
  contingencies of, 143
  convenience factors, 140–42
  cost comparisons, 137–40, 143–44, 145–46
  options, 137–48

sample trips, 143–44
*see also individual forms of transportation, e.g.,* Air travel within Europe; Bus services; Car rental and leases
Europe by Car, 189, 190, 193, 194, 195, 196, 197, 198
Exchange rates, vii, 30, 208, 209
  car rental pricing, 190–91, 197
  purchasing tickets in foreign currencies, 101–103
Excursion fares, 13, 200, 211
  *see also* Round-trip purchase requirements

Falcon, 205, 211
Faroe Islands, ferry services for the, 223
Ferry services, 213–14
  by country, 220–26
  for English Channel crossing, 144–45, 220–22
  ferry/waterway representatives, 228–29
  major lines, 227
  rates and fares, 226
Finland, 193
First-Class air service, 9, 43, 88, 92–94
  fares for, 10, 92–94
  upgrading to, 76, 92–94, 95, 96–97
First-Class Charter air service, 9, 55, 92
  fares for, 10, 92
Fisher guidebooks, 268
Flexible-schedule travel, 70–78
  buying, 77–78
  companion tickets, 76–77
  explanation of, 70–71
  "generic" air travel, 71–73, 77
  last-minute travel clubs, 73–76, 77–78
  late-booking charters, 73
Florence, Italy, public transportation in, 240
Fly/Drives, *see* Car rentals and leases, airline rental programs
*Fly/Ride Europe 1987*, how to use, 24–25, 283–84

Fodor guidebooks, 268
Food:
    tour packages including, 275
    on transatlantic flights, 22, 91, 92, 93
    see also Beverages
Foreign-currency purchase of tickets, 101–103
Foremost Euro-Car, 190, 193, 194, 195, 196, 197, 198
France, 65
    air travel pass, 202
    bus service in, 215
    car rentals in, 192, 194
    ferry service to, 220–21
    rail travel in, 139, 159–60, 178
Frankfurt, West Germany, 72
    car rentals in, 191
    public transportation in, 240–41
    transatlantic air fares to, 116–17
    bulk-fare travel, 65
Fred Olsen Lines, 227
French National Railroads, 215
Frequent-traveler programs:
    broker, 28, 96–99
    companion tickets, 76–77, 78, 92
    coupons, 9, 28, 44, 92, 95–101
    restrictions, 96, 98–99
Frommer guidebooks, 267, 268
Full-fare Economy air fares, 10, 43, 44, 104, 202

Gasoline costs, 139
"Generic" air travel, 71-73, 77
Geneva, Switzerland, 72, 117–18, 241–42
Geographical variation in air fares, 11
    last-minute travel clubs and, 75–76
German Charters, 60
German Federal Railway (German-Rail), 162, 215
German Rhine Line (KD), 225
Germany, see West Germany
GIT (group-inclusive-tour) fares, 42, 82, 274
Gondolas, 257–58
Government hotel-classification systems, 266–67, 272
Greece, 202
    bus service in, 215–16
    car rentals in, 194
    ferry service in, 225
    rail travel in, 163
Group fares, 42, 82, 274
GTF Tours, 204, 211
Guidebooks, hotel-classification systems of, 265–67, 270, 271, 272
GWV Travel, 60

Headsets, see Entertainment
Helsinki, Finland, 118, 242–43
Hertz Rent-a-Car, 187, 189, 190, 198
*Holiday Which?*, 199, 206, 213, 226, 268
Holland, see Netherlands
Hotel accommodations, 74, 80, 81, 265–74
    guidelines for choosing, 272–74
    hotel-class systems, 265–71
        government, 266–67, 272
        guidebook, 267–69, 272, 273
        industry references, 267, 269, 273
        tour operator, 28, 267, 272, 273, 274
    through tour packages, 82, 274, 275, 276, 277–79
*Hotel & Travel Index*, 269
Hovercraft-rail service, 145
Hoverspeed, 227
Hydrofoil-rail service, 145

IATA (International Air Transport Association), 19, 31, 45, 89, 199, 205, 206
Iceland, bus service in, 216
Icelandair, 37, 45, 47, 48, 122
Illness, trip canceled or cut short by, 23, 38
Incentive fares, 42
"Inclusive tour" fares, see ITX (inclusive-tour) fares
Independent charters, see Charters
Indirect rebates, 80–81

Insurance:
  airline-failure, 61
  car rental, 185
  trip-interruption, 57, 61, 63
Interflug, 208
InterRent Car Rental System, 189, 190, 197, 198
Intra-European travel, see European transportation
Ireland, Republic of, 105
  bus service in, 216
  car rentals in, 194
  ferry service in, 225
  ferry service to, 222
  rail travel in, 162-65
Irish Sea crossings, 220
Israel, car rentals in, 190, 195
Italy, vii, 205
  bus service in, 216
  car rentals in 191, 192, 195
  ferry services in, 225
  rail travel in, 139, 165-66, 179
ITC (inclusive-tour) fares:
  within Europe, 203-205
  transatlantic, 42, 82, 274

Jahre Line, 227
Japan Air Lines, 97
JAT, 31, 37, 84
Jet Exchange, 58-59, 60, 61

Kemwel Group, 189, 193, 194, 195, 196, 197, 198
Kennedy Airport, 15, 106-107
KLM, 31, 37, 201, 209
Kuwait Airlines, 31, 84

Laker, Sir Freddie, 40, 46
"Last-minute" travel clubs, 73-76, 77-78
Larvik Line, 227
Layovers, 15
Leases, car, 186-88, 189, 197-98
  see also Car rentals and leases
Legality of discounting and rebates, 82, 86, 88-90

Length-of-stay requirements, 12, 33, 66, 200, 207, 209
Lisbon, Portugal:
  ferry services out of, 220, 224
  public transportation in, 243-44
  transatlantic air fares to, 119
Load factors, 16, 19, 21
London, England, 72, 105, 106, 107
  air fares to other European cities from, 208-209
  bulk-fare, travel to, 65, 120
  low-fare airlines flying to, 47, 120
  1987 projected air fares to, 120
  public transportation in, 244-47
  Standby fares to, 40
Loss of money paid for a flight, 57, 58, 59, 60-61, 87-88
Lost baggage, 23, 38
Low-fare airlines, 8, 10, 13, 44, 45-49, 52
  buying your tickets for, 49
  comfort on, 20-21, 48, 93
  competition from major airlines, 45-46, 81
  contingencies on, 48
  convenience of, 47
  1987 outlook for, 47
  origin of, 45
  premium service on, 93
  see also individual airlines
LTU, 55, 58-59, 60, 61, 117, 124
Lufthansa Airlines, 31, 33, 37
Luxembourg:
  bus service in 216
  car rentals in, 191, 192, 195
  public transportation in, 247
  rail travel in, 167
  transatlantic air fares to, 110, 121-22
Luxembourg National Railways, 216

Madrid, Spain, 72, 122, 248
Major airlines, 13, 31-44, 45-46
  APEX or Super APEX fares, 9-10, 11, 24, 32-35
  1987 outlook for, 34-35
  buying your tickets for, 44

Major airlines *(cont'd)*
  car rental tie-ins, 80, 81, 188, 198
  comfort on, 20–22, 36–37
  contingencies on, 37–39
  convenience of, 35–36
  full-fare Economy Class, 44
  group and tour status fares, 42
  listing of, 31
  round-the-world excursion fares, 42
  specials, 43
  Standby fares of, 40
  *see also individual airlines*
Maps, city, 231
Martinair, 55, 60, 111
Metro lines in European cities, 232–60
Miami International Airport, 93, 104
*Michelin Red Guides*, 267–68, 272
Milan, Italy, 123, 249
Military personnel, air fares for, 14
Minerve airline, 59
Miscellaneous Charge Order (MCO), 89–90
Missed connections or missed return flights, 23, 38
Monetary loss, 86
  by charter passengers, 58, 59, 60–61
Movies on transatlantic flights, 22, 37
Munich, West Germany, 72
  car rentals, in 192
  public transportation in, 249–50
  transatlantic air fares to, 124

National Car Rental System, 187, 189, 198
National Express (NE), 219
Net fares, *see* Bulk or net fares
Netherlands, 43, 111, 201, 202, 205, 207, 209–11
  bus service in, 216–17
  car rentals in, 191, 195
  ferry service to, 220–21
  rail travel in the, 168–69
Newark Airport, 104
*New York Times, The*, 99
Nice, France, transatlantic air fares to, 125

Nonstop flights, 14, 35, 38, 54, 65–66
  *see also* Connecting flights; Stopovers
Nordic Fare Deals, 205, 212
Northern Ireland, *see* United Kingdom
North Sea Ferries, 227
Northwest Orient Airlines, 30, 96
Norway:
  air travel pass, 202–203
  bus service in, 217
  car rentals in, 196
  ferry service for, 223, 225
  rail travel in, 169–70
Norway Lines, 227

*OAG Travel Planner*, 269
Objectives, clarifying your, 7–8, 9
*Official Hotel and Resort Guide (OHRG)*, 269, 270–71, 272, 273
O'Hare Airport, 15, 106
Olan Line, 227
Olympic Airlines, 31, 33
"One-way APEX" fares, 33
One-way intra-European air fares, 201, 204, 207–11
Open-jaw route, 13, 41, 52, 106, 109, 201
Operator failure, 58–59, 86
  being stranded due to, 24, 38–39, 55, 56, 57, 58–63
  money lost due to, 57, 59, 60–61
Orient Express, 152, 179
Oslo, Norway, 126, 250–51
Overbooking, 23, 38
"Overhead" costs, daily, 109, 191
"Override" commission, 28, 80, 83

Pakistan Airlines, 31, 84
Pan American Airways, 31, 51, 81, 85, 90, 97
  frequent-flyers program, 97
Paris, France, 72
  public transportation in, 251–54
  transatlantic air fares to, 127–28
Passes:
  airline, 202
  rail, *see* Rail travel

Passports, 154
Peak-season air fares, 11, 12, 34, 53, 66, 85
Pegasus, (Skybus) Holidays, 204, 211
People Express, vii
Pevsner, Don, 206
Pilgrim Air, 204, 211
Portugal:
   bus service in, 217
   car rentals in, 196
   rail travel in, 170–71
Premium service on low-fare airlines, 93
Promotional fares, 32
Public transportation, see Urban transportation

Qantas airlines, 97

Rail travel, 30, 145–46, 149–79, 213
   buying tickets for, 153
   city public transportation, 232–60
   comfort of, 142
   contingencies, 143
   convenience of, 140–42, 149
   cost comparisons, 139–40, 143–44, 145–46
   Hovercraft, 144
   individual tickets for 149, 151–53
   options by country, 155–79
   Orient Express trains, 152, 179
   passes, 30, 149, 155–76
      Britrail Pass, 116, 149, 151, 175–76, 178, 220
      country rover, 151, 153, 154
      Eurailpass, 145, 146, 147, 150–53, 178, 220
Rebates, direct and indirect, 80–81, 83–84, 86–87
Recreational vehicles, rental of, 186
Refunds, 86
   charter flights and, 56, 59, 60–61
   penalties, 27
Reyjkjavik, Iceland, public transportation in, 254–55
Restrictions:
   on car rentals, 183
   on intra-European air fares, 200–201, 204, 207
   on transatlantic air fares, 12–13, 32, 38, 66
Risk evaluation, see Contingencies
Rome, Italy, 72, 128, 255–56
Round-the-world excursion fares, 9, 42–43, 102
Round-trip purchase requirements, 12, 33, 200–201, 204, 207
Routes, convenience of, 14–15, 35, 36, 54, 65–66, 72

Sabena Airlines, 31
Sally Lines, 227
SAS, 31
Scandinavia, 65, 114–15, 126, 205
   ferry services, 222, 223
   rail travel in, 158, 172
   transatlantic air travel to, 65, 114–15, 126, 131
   see also individual cities and countries
Scantours, 250, 211
Schedule convenience, 15–16, 24, 35–36, 47, 53–54, 66, 106–107
SCETA (Services de Tourisme S.N.C.F. and Europabus), 215
Scotland, 176, 203, 276
   see also United Kingdom
Scottish Bus Group, 218
Scottish Citylink Coaches, 218
Sealink, 227
Seasonal variations in air fares, 11–12, 52, 65, 84, 100, 109
Seating comfort, aircraft, 17–21, 36–37, 48, 55, 91, 92, 93, 94, 203
Security, airline and airport, 280–82
Senior citizens, air fares for, 14, 41
Service quality, in-flight, 22, 37, 48, 85, 91
Shannon, Ireland, transatlantic air fares to, 106, 129
Shoulder season air fares, 11, 65
Silja Line, 227
Sightseeing, 230, 231, 274–76
Skytrain, 40, 46

Slade Travel Ltd., 204, 211
Spain, 170-72, 196, 217, 224-25
Spantax, 55, 60
Specials, 43
Standard subcompact, rental of, 183-84
Standby status, 40, 72, 102, 103, 201
*Star Service*, 269, 273
Status fares, 13-14, 33
Stena Line, 227
Stockholm, Sweden, 130, 256-57
Stopovers, 104-107
  versus nonstop flights, 14-15, 35-36, 38, 54, 65-66, 85, 202
  prohibitions on, 12, 33, 43, 104
  *see also* Connecting flights
Straight discount air fares, 79
Stranded, being, 24, 38-39, 50, 55, 56, 57, 58, 61-62
Students, 154
  air fares for, 14
  *see also* Children; Youth fares
Subcompacts, rental of, 183-84
Surveys, airline in-flight, 22-23
Sweden, 196, 217-18, 226
Swissair, 31, 37, 51, 93
Swiss Airtours, 204
Switzerland, 43, 48
  bus service in, 218
  car rentals in, 191, 196
  ferry service in, 226
  rail travel in, 173-74, 179

TAP-Air Portugal, 31
Taxi service:
  city public transportation, 232-60
  touring cities by taxi, 231
Tel Aviv, Israel, transatlantic air fares to, 131
Terrorism, vii, 280-82
Theft, 143
"Through" flights, 14-15, 35, 36
Throwaway packages, 82, 278
Total Air, 55
Tour fares, 40, 82, 277
Tour guides, 275
Tourist offices, national, 260-64

Tour operators, 82, 272, 278
  hotel-classifications systems of, 272, 273
  of "inclusive tour" holidays, 203-205
  *see also* Wholesale tour operators
Tour packages, 274-79
  advantages of, 277
  comparing, 278
  escorted tours, 275-77
  independent tours, 274
  risks of, 278
Tower Airlines, 45, 47, 93, 132
Townsend Thorsen, 228
Trains for public transportation in European cities, 232-60
  *see also* Rail travel
Transamerica, 46
Transatlantic air fares, *see* Air fares, transatlantic
Transatlantic air travel, overview of, 7-30
  clarifying your objectives, 7-8
  comfort factor, 16-23, 24
  contingencies factor, 23, 24
  convenience factor, 14-16, 24
  cost comparisons, 10-14, 23-24
  determining your personal benchmarks, 24
  exchange rates, vii, 30
  transportation options, 8-9
  travel agents, using and selecting, 25-30
  using this guide, 24-25
Travac, 60
Travel agents, 273, 283
  "bucket shop," 87, 106, 199, 205, 206-207
  buying tickets through, 25-27, 44, 63, 83, 86-87, 205-207
  car rental arrangements through, 198
  commissions, 27-28, 80, 83
  selecting, 28-30, 61, 87
Travel clubs:
  discounts on transatlantic air fares, 83
  "last-minute," 73-76, 77-78
*Travel Weekly*, 99
Trip-interruption insurance, 58, 61, 63

TWA, 31, 81, 85, 90, 97–98, 99, 100, 105

Ulsterbus, 218
United Airlines, 51, 97, 99
United European American Club, 84
United Kingdom, 43, 81, 201, 202, 205
    bus service in, 218–19
    car rentals in, 197
    driving in the, 182
    ferry service in, 224
    rail travel in the, 139, 149, 151, 175–77
Unitravel, 60
Urban transportation, 230–64
    maps, 231
    options by city, 232–60
    tourist offices, 260–64

Value Added Tax (VAT), 180–81
Value Vacations, 60
Venice, Italy, public transportation in, 257–58
Vienna, Austria:
    public transportation in, 258–59
    transatlantic air fares to, 132
Virgin Atlantic Airlines, 45, 47, 48, 81, 93, 111, 116, 117, 120

Wainwrights, 60
Wales, *see* United Kingdom
Walking, 230
*Wall Street Journal*, 38, 99
Washington, D.C. airports, 104
Waterbuses, 257
Watertaxis, 258
Weekend round-trip excursion fares, 42
West Germany, 43, 86, 110, 205
    bus service in, 215
    car rentals in, 191, 194
    ferry services, 222, 223, 224
    rail travel in, 139, 160–63
Wholesale tour operators, 51, 274
    bulk-fare travel through, 66–67, 68–69
    role in charter flights, 51-52, 57–58, 62, 67, 68, 73
    selecting, 60
    tour packages, 274–79
    *see also* Tour operators
World Airways, 46

Youth fares, 14, 41, 154
    *see also* Children; Students
Yugoslavia, 177, 190, 197, 220

Zurich, Switzerland, 72, 133, 259–60